MW00606362

LIBERTY JAIL AND THE LEGACY OF JOSEPH

Thomas D. Cottle and Patricia C. Cottle

Cover and Book Design by Bay Design and Illustration

Front Cover: Joseph Smith, Jr., courtesy of Reorganized Church of Jesus Christ of Latter-day Saints (RLDS Archives), Independence, Missouri. Liberty Jail courtesy of Clay County Archives and Historical Library, Liberty, Missouri.

Second Edition
Copyright© 1998, 1999 Thomas D. Cottle and Patricia C. Cottle
All Rights Reserved

ISBN 1-889063-04-5

Printed in the United States of America

Published by Insight
Portland, Oregon

FOR TWELVE CHILDREN

In Memory of
Mary Lou Olsen Cottle
1928-1993

CONTENTS

Acknowledgments ix

Introduction xi

Chapter 1: The Foundation of a Prophet 1

    Family Foundation 1

    Spiritual Foundation 4

    Scriptural Foundation 5

    Priesthood Foundation 6

Chapter 2: The Messengers of the Fullness 9

    The Messengers 10

    Messengers, Messages, and Assignments 14

Chapter 3: Joseph's Legacy of Scriptures 25

    The Most Correct Book on Earth 26

    The Plain and Precious Things 30

    Doctrines and Covenants of Our Dispensation 32

    Abraham's Knowledge of Heaven and Earth 33

    The Book of Life of a Living Church 34

Chapter 4: Jail Participants 35

    The Prisoners 35

    The Wives 45

    The Attorneys 52

    Sheriffs, Jailer, and Guards 63

Chapter 5: Liberty Jail 73

    The Dungeon Gaol (Jail) 73

    Prison Dialogue 75

    Notable Events 77

Chapter 6: Jail Breaks 87

    The Outside Break 89

    The Inside Break 91

Chapter 7: People and Spiritual Attributes 105

    Antagonistic Apostates 105

    Affidavits Signed by Thomas B. Marsh and Orson Hyde 105

    W. W. Phelps 107

    William Earl McLellin 109

    Alanson Ripley 111

    Emanuel Masters Murphy 113

    Heber C. Kimball and Theodore Turley 114

    The Saints 117

Chapter 8: Correspondence and the Gaol 119

    December 1838 Correspondence 119

    January 1839 Correspondence 121

    February 1839 Correspondence 121

    March 1839 Correspondence 122

    April 1839 Correspondence 133

Chapter 9: Revelation and Knowledge 141

Chapter 10: Doctrine to its Fullness 147

    "Nothing shall be Withheld" 147

    Development of Four Major Doctrines 149

Chapter 11: Living Oracles/Apostles of the Lord 175

Chapter 12: Passing the Mantle 183

Chapter 13: Prophecies 189

Chapter 14: Conclusion 197

Appendix A: Jail Calendar—128 Days 201

Appendix B: Visitors and Dates 209

Appendix C: Former Prisoners for Christ 213

Appendix D: Doctrinal Expansion 1839-44 215

Appendix E: Secular Knowledge After 1837 223

Notes 227

Bibliography 273

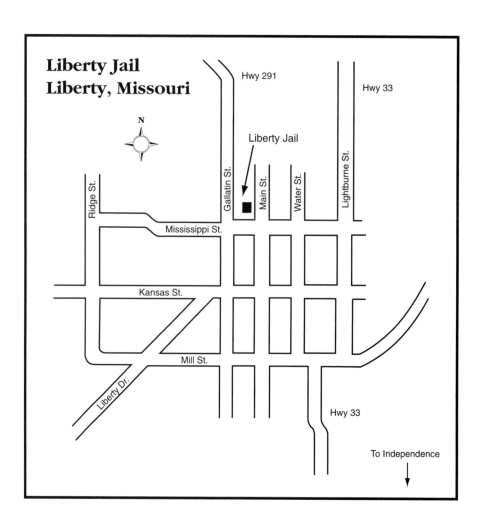

Liberty Jail
Liberty, Missouri

N

Hwy 291

Hwy 33

Liberty Jail

Ridge St.

Gallatin St.

Main St.

Water St.

Lightburne St.

Mississippi St.

Kansas St.

Mill St.

Liberty Dr.

Hwy 33

To Independence

ACKNOWLEDGMENTS

We acknowledge and thank those in Missouri who enriched our manuscript with their knowledge, personal pictures, and other treasures.

Richard Ware shared with us his immeasurable understanding of the doctrine and not only gave us encouragement but also shared his devoted time and expertise in the editing of the manuscript.

Ron Romig, archivist for the Reorganized Church of Jesus Christ of Latter-day Saints (RLDS) Library in Independence, and his staff were most helpful in bringing to our attention the rare photographs and various historical sources that were of great importance in the writing of *Liberty Jail and the Legacy of Joseph.*

We express special thanks to Henry Inouye, artist and curator, for permission to use his rendition of Joseph.

We thank several individuals who helped us with photographs. Evely Petty and Janie Lougkrey with the Clay County Archives and Historical Library in Liberty brought to our attention some valuable information that is not commonly known about the people of the book's time period. Bob Askrem, the photographic archivist, searched out original glass negatives taken in the early 1800s. The negatives had been found recently, and the images on some prints were greatly enhanced. Daniel J. Bortko and Ralph Brant of Liberty, Clay County, gave permission to use their one-of-a kind photographs that have not been previously published.

We express appreciation to Linda Adkins of the Daviess County Courthouse and the staff at the Clay County Courthouse for their help with original court documents.

We express our very sincere appreciation to Ben E. Rawlings, president of the Missouri Independence Mission (1994-97), whose interest and encouragement of our project, along with his patience, were much appreciated.

We express gratitude to Gary Cottle for his assistance in many hours of research.

We express much appreciation to Ted D. Stoddard, professor of Management Communication in the Marriott School of Management at Brigham Young University, for his work in the final editing of the manuscript before it was submitted to the publisher.

And finally, we express our grateful recognition to our sons, James Dean Cottle, who directed the last few months of the project from manuscript to publication with help from Thomas Jeffery Cottle and Michael Wade Cottle.

INTRODUCTION

In the first 165 years of the Church, knowledge of Missouri and specifically of Liberty Jail has taken a back seat to events associated with the Palmyra-New York, Kirtland-Ohio, and Nauvoo-Illinois periods because of the sacred beginnings of the Church and the two temples that were built in those areas. The First Vision, the Book of Mormon, the restoration of the priesthood, and Church organization all occurred in the New York-Pennsylvania area. Kirtland, Ohio, was the location of the first temple—the temple for the restoration of authority. Here, angelic messengers brought the supernal keys that established the mission of the Church. Through a prophet of God, these keys have formed the three dynamic goals of the Church.[1] Illinois is revered for the Nauvoo Temple where the ordinances of exaltation were received by the Saints, giving them the powers and blessings to build the foundation of the Church we have today.[2] Temple records show over five thousand saints were endowed at Nauvoo, fulfilling the golden thread of Joseph's magnificent tapestry.[3] These sacred places are certainly worthy of the accolades of honor, reverence, dedication, and eternal gratitude given to them.

The time will come, however, when Missouri with its three consecrated and holy locations—Independence, Far West, and Adam-ondi-Ahman—will surface to receive the recognition of the major roles they are destined to play. Their destinies become obvious with the first revelation given in Missouri and about Missouri—"the land which I appointed and consecrated for the gathering of the saints . . . the place for the city of Zion . . . the place which is now called Independence is the center place; and a spot for the temple is lying westward."[4] Sections 78, 107, 116, and 133 of the Doctrine and Covenants, of equal interest and importance, deal with Adam-ondi-Ahman, the city of Enoch, and the return of the Ten Tribes.

The area that is addressed in this book is the legacy of religious knowledge, as it correlates directly with Liberty Jail and pursuant years. To put in print the full legacy of Joseph Smith, Jr. would be an impossible task. His phenomena expanded through space, time, and matter. His mind was as wide as the cosmos and as deep as eternity. It touched every phase of the private, public, civic, military, education, and politics (administrative, legislative, and judicial)[5] arenas. Such an undertaking would be much like what was said about the Book of Mormon at the time of Christ: "And now there cannot be written in this book even a hundredth part of the things which Jesus did truly teach unto the people."[6] The same could be said of Joseph's work as the prophet, seer, and revelator for this dispensation.

Another obstacle in writing the full legacy in all its glorious aspects is Joseph himself. He said after Liberty Jail, "But I am learned, and know more than all the world put together. The Holy Ghost does, anyhow, and He is within me, and comprehends more than all the world: and I will associate myself with Him."[7] Joseph explained how this kind of learning could take place. A person would have to expose himself or herself to the other side of the veil. The enlightenment is there. "Every law, every commandment, every promise, every truth, and every point touching the destiny of man, from Genesis to Revelation, where the purity of the scriptures remain unsullied by the folly of men."[8] At another time, he said, "You don't know me; you never knew my heart. No man knows my history. I cannot tell it: I shall never undertake it. I don't blame anyone for not believing my history. If I had not experienced what I have, I could not have believed it myself."[9] And, finally, "Would to God, brethren, I could tell you who I am! Would to God I could tell you what I know! But you would call it blasphemy, and there are men upon this stand who would want to take my life."[10]

It is evident that Joseph was foreordained to bring about the restoration—"the times of restitution of all things."[11] He was destined to be the prophet to establish the foundation for a fullness, even everything of the highest theological order.

Liberty Jail seems to have been the pivotal period in Joseph Smith's tenure as prophet. The majority of information available on the events of Liberty Jail has been brief, fragmented, confusing, and sometimes inaccurate. Very little has been written about the jail itself and almost nothing about the events that transpired during the 128 days of the Prophet's confinement. In some cases, information was confused with the incarceration of the brethren at the Richmond

Jail. This confusion becomes evident from the earliest histories written about Joseph Smith by members of the Church of Jesus Christ of Latter-day Saints (LDS), the Reorganized Church of Jesus Christ of Latter-day Saints (RLDS), and other writers.[12] Thirteen of these books researched contain collectively 4,966 pages. Four of the books did not refer to Liberty Jail. The rest ranged from two sentences, a paragraph, or a few pages. These thirteen books combined contained about thirty-three pages on the subject of Liberty Jail and the events that transpired there.

One reason for this lack of information appears to be that Joseph did not keep a journal during this period of his life.[13] The void almost matches the period of confinements in Missouri from October 1838 to 16 April 1839. For early writers, events and facts during this interval had to be pieced together from other sources.

Even the narration given at the Liberty Jail Visitors' Center is slightly misleading. The audio states that "the prisoners had few visitors" and "the meager details they received concerning . . . members of the Church." Research shows that during the first three months, the prisoners had extensive visitors and therefore did know in detail about the hardships being faced by members of the Church. The prisoners had over sixty-seven visitors come to the jail, some multiple times, making a total of over ninety visits (see Appendix A). These visitors included the wives of the prisoners, relatives, attorneys, priesthood holders, members of the Quorum of the Twelve Apostles, and friends—both brethren and sisters. All the visitors, as well as the flow of information, were drastically reduced the last two weeks of February and the last twenty-three days of confinement. What few visitors came during this period brought the majority of correspondence received by the prisoners while at Liberty Jail. (See Appendix A and Chapter 8.) During Joseph's incarceration two men of Liberty were arrested on different charges, and each spent a short period of confinement in the jail with the brethren.

An intriguing thought on Joseph's situation leaves room for reflection. It has been said, that "only with his body captive could he truly liberate his mind."[14] This statement appears to be true of the Prophet during the Liberty incarceration, for doctrine was galvanized and solidified into a higher consciousness and understanding. He was told, "God shall give unto you knowledge by his Holy Spirit, yea, by the unspeakable gift of the Holy Ghost, that has not been revealed since the world was until now. . . . A time to come in the which nothing shall be withheld."[15] Revelations and visions came forth that have unique, intrinsic, and eternal value. These and the great discourses Joseph delivered his last six years are worthy of special consideration. They "draw aside the dark veil of futurity and penetrate into the invisible world, and contemplate the purposes of God as they shall roll forth in after ages in all their majesty and power and glory."[16] They speak of the designs and purposes of God that came forth and established Joseph's "legacy" of knowledge to us.

After leaving Liberty Jail, Hyrum said of his brother Joseph, "There were prophets before, but Joseph has the spirit and power of all the prophets."[17] Joseph's calling was to open a new dispensation—the last dispensation of the fullness of times—and to deliver the will of God to the world for our time. This prophet of all prophets has been an awesome messenger.

Chapter 1

THE FOUNDATION OF A PROPHET

I will gather together in one all things, both which are in heaven and which are on earth.[1]

Family Foundation

The beautiful and peaceful setting of Sharon Township, Windsor County, Vermont, was chosen to be the birthplace of the great prophet foreordained to establish the Lord's kingdom in the latter days. On 23 December 1805, Joseph Smith, Jr. was born to noble and goodly parents who would do much to prepare their son for his holy calling. Joseph Sr. and Lucy Mack Smith descended from generations of devout Christians who sought to live correct religious principles. Asael Smith, Joseph Jr.'s grandfather, predicted that a prophet would be raised up among his posterity. Years later, Joseph Jr.'s grandmother was convinced that Joseph Jr. fulfilled that prophecy.[2] This was the environment prepared to receive and nurture Joseph.

Hoping to improve their economic conditions, the Smith family moved several times before settling in Palmyra, New York. Here, a whole new era[3] had its beginning. Paul spoke of it in Ephesians 1:10: "That in the dispensation of the fullness of times he might gather together in one all things in Christ, both which are in heaven, and which are on earth; even in him."

The cohesiveness of the Smith family—father, mother, and children—to their God and to each other is not only admirable but also very remarkable. They followed the ageless pattern of stewardship established for an eternal family in the premortal world,[4] where all principles are based in agency, the freedom to choose, the very basis

1

of all existence.[5] The parents taught correct principles and gave counsel.[6] The children were obedient.[7] Brothers and sisters gave service.[8] The Smith family's entire incentive for life was based on these true Christian ethics. Indeed, they came close to perfection in the roles outlined for an eternal family.

Father Smith had implicit faith in his children. The trust he had in Joseph is evidenced in an account Joseph recorded in 1840. Referring to his father, Joseph said, "He was the first person who received my testimony after I had seen the angel, and exhorted me to be faithful and diligent to the message I had received."[9]

The love and respect of the Smith children for their parents are brought to light as we read some observations Father Smith gave in patriarchal blessings to his children. Joseph was told, "Thou hast been an obedient son: the commands of thy father and the reproofs of thy mother, thou hast respected and obeyed."[10] Hyrum was told in his blessing, "Thou has always stood by thy father, and reached forth the helping hand to lift him up when he was in afflictions."[11] To Samuel, "Thou hast been faithful in all thy days and ministered comfort to thy father's family."[12]

Love and service to each other established emotional support within the family. Their charity is truly worthy of mention. Mother Lucy Smith tells of caring for young Joseph during his serious leg infection and surgeries. She wrote:

> The anxiety of mind that I experienced, together with physical over-exertion, was too much for my constitution and my nature sank under it. Hyrum, who was rather remarkable for his tenderness and sympathy now desired that he might take my place. . . . Hyrum sat beside him, almost day and night for some considerable length of time, holding the affected part of his leg in his hands and pressing it between them, so that his afflicted brother might be enabled to endure the pain which was so excruciating that he was scarcely able to bear it.[13]

Hyrum, throughout his life, exhibited love and concern for his family, particularly toward Joseph.

Another example of pure charity happened at the time of the death of Joseph and Hyrum. Samuel was away when his brothers went to Carthage to give themselves up. Upon his return, he immediately obtained the fastest horse available and rode to Carthage in a desperate attempt to save his brothers. Samuel was one of the first to arrive at the scene of the martyrdom, but he was too late. The mob turned on Samuel, and he almost lost his life. The shock and devastation of the death of his brothers caused him to develop a serious fever. His health began to fail, and he died on 30 July 1844, just thirty-three days after his brothers were martyred.[14]

Many accounts are recorded of Joseph's giving away his own possessions to help someone in need. His uncle, John Smith, related an incident about Joseph and Bishop Knight coming to visit while John was very ill. "One thing is worthy of note and will never be forgotten by me, Joseph took the shoes from his feet and gave to me and rode home without any."[15]

That Joseph's work was foreordained is evident again in the patriarchal blessing given to him by his father on 9 December 1834. In reference to Joseph, who was the eleventh son of Jacob and who was sold into Egypt, Joseph Smith Sr. made this declaration:

> Behold, he [Joseph of Egypt] looked after his posterity in the last days, when they should be scattered and driven by the Gentiles, and wept before the Lord: he sought diligently to know from whence the son should come who should bring forth the word of the Lord, by which they might be enlightened, and brought back to the true fold, and his eyes beheld thee, my son."[16]

What a tremendous impression this statement must have made on the modern-day Joseph!

The dispensation Joseph opened, and in which we live, was from the very beginning a restoration of all things. Everything had to be reintroduced, disseminated, taught, learned, and internalized within the leadership of the fledgling kingdom of God upon the earth. All gloriously came to the prophet "called and prepared from the foundation of the world according to the foreknowledge of God."[17]

Shortly after Joseph and Oliver received the priesthood and its keys, they were shown in revelation "the precise day upon which, according to [God's] will and commandment, we should proceed to organize his church once again, here upon the earth."[18] A beautiful testimony is given by Oliver Cowdery during this period of Church history. "[B]ut one touch with the finger of his love, yes, one ray of glory from the upper world, or one word from the mouth of the Savior, from the bosom of eternity, strikes it [doubt] all into insignificance, and blots it forever from the mind."[19]

The organization of the Church of Christ took place on Tuesday, 6 April 1830, at the home of Peter Whitmer Sr. Approximately sixty people assembled to witness the fulfillment of this sacred commandment of the Lord. Joseph, twenty-four years old, designated five others—Oliver Cowdery, Hyrum Smith, Peter Whitmer Jr., Samuel H. Smith, and David Whitmer—to meet New York's legal requirements for incorporating a religious society. The organization of the Church was a never-to-be-forgotten occasion for those in attendance.

Spiritual Foundation

Early one morning in the spring of 1820, Joseph Smith, Jr. went into a grove of trees near his home. In keeping with the exhortation given in the scripture, he had read in James 1:5 that "If any of you lack wisdom, let him ask of God." Joseph humbly kneeled and began to express the desires of his heart. He wanted to know which church he should join. In response, a glorious vision opened to Joseph. God the Eternal Father and his Beloved Son stood before this young fourteen-year-old boy. "One of them spake unto me, . . . and said, pointing to the other—*This is My Beloved Son. Hear Him!*"[20]

Pure revelation with very little parallel in the history of mankind was imparted to the boy prophet. We can envision from Joseph's own words his feelings after having had such a marvelous manifestation. Years after it happened, he vividly remembered, "My soul was filled with love, and for many days I could rejoice with great joy, and the Lord was with me."[21]

Joseph was deeply affected by this experience. "For I had seen a vision; I knew it and I knew that God knew it and I could not deny it, neither dared I do it; at least I knew that by so doing I would offend God."[22] From that moment on, Joseph was a witness of the divinity and reality of the Father and the Son.

The eternal knowledge disseminated to him in the First Vision was an event that many would regard as the single most important incident in our dispensation. This one event changed the future of mankind. For the first time in eighteen hundred years, the "True and Living God" had been revealed!

Throughout his teen years, Joseph seemed to have an innate ability to know and understand the will of the Lord. The ideas of Joseph were not shaped by an environmental influence but were molded by the divine power of God himself. Joseph was prepared in a previous sphere of existence to assume the consequential role of restoring God's church to the earth. Speaking of his foreordination, Joseph said: "Every man who has a calling to minister to the inhabitants of the world was ordained to that very purpose in the Grand Council of heaven before the world was. I suppose that I was ordained to this very office in that Grand Council."[23]

Scriptural Foundation

Part of building the foundation of Joseph's legacy was the formative spiritual training to bring forth scriptures. This important phase began with a visit from an angelic being sent from the presence of God.

Joseph describes this monumental event:"After I had retired to my bed for the night, I betook myself to prayer and supplication to Almighty God for a forgiveness of all my sins. I had full confidence in obtaining a divine manifestation, as I previously had one."[24] In this guileless statement, an eternal truth is taught. Repentance is an on-going process of mortality. A person must be clean to have companionship with the Holy Ghost. Spiritual experiences with the Holy Ghost can then produce pure knowledge. Joseph wrote:

> While I was thus in the act of calling upon God, . . . a personage appeared at my bedside, standing in the air, for his feet did not touch the floor. He called me by name, and said unto me that he was a messenger sent from the presence of God to me, and that his name was Moroni; that God had a work for me to do; and that my name would be had for good and evil among all nations, kindreds, and tongues.[25]

This event stands as a divine testimony to the spirituality of the first eighteen years of Joseph's life. He had been tried, tested, and proven and could now be trusted with the sacred work ahead.

The scriptures recited by Moroni on his initial visit gave Joseph significant knowledge by weaving together a tapestry of prophecy from the past into future fulfillment.[26] The very first scripture quoted to Joseph for our dispensation depicted the heart and soul of the plan of salvation—root and branch, the sealing power of the priesthood and eternal families.[27] This, of course, is the very purpose of the creation, the fall, the Atonement, mortality, the priesthood, and temple ordinances wherein authority, power, and knowledge are given to man. Without it, "the whole earth would be utterly wasted."[28]

Moroni's appearance to Joseph that night turned out to be the first of many visits from this heavenly messenger. During the next six-year period, Moroni met with Joseph over twenty times.[29] The young, impressionable prophet, like Father Abraham, was certainly ready and eager to acquire knowledge. The tender bond that developed between Moroni and Joseph can only be surmised. Moroni gave Joseph instructions on many subjects of the plan of redemption, with emphasis on the covenants of the great latter-day restoration.[30] Except for the Savior, Joseph possibly could not have had a greater tutor than the Angel Moroni. Moroni's visits constantly impressed upon Joseph the necessity of faith, self-discipline, obedience, diligence, honesty, forthrightness, integrity, and virtue. Moroni knew only too well how these attributes would be needed in Joseph's prophetic calling. Joseph later received from Moroni additional gifts of divine power.[31]

Priesthood Foundation

The restoration of the holy priesthood of God with its keys commenced on 15 May 1829, as Joseph and Oliver went into the nearby woods along the Susquehanna River to pray. Oliver described this sacred occasion: "On a sudden, as from the midst of eternity, the voice of the Redeemer spake peace to us, while the veil was parted and the angel of God came down clothed with glory, and delivered the anxiously looked for message, and the keys of the gospel of repentance!—What joy! what wonder! what amazement!"[32] The angel was the resurrected John the Baptist who was acting under the direction of the Apostles Peter, James, and John. John the Baptist conferred upon Joseph and Oliver the Priesthood of Aaron, "which hold the keys of the ministering of angels, and of the gospel of repentance, and of baptism by immersion for the remission of sins."[33]

Approximately a month later, Peter, James, and John conferred upon Joseph and Oliver the Melchizedek Priesthood, which was the spiritual priesthood. The priesthood given them at this time authorized Joseph to organize the Church on earth and to ordain brethren to all the priesthood offices within the Church.

The year 1830 seemed to be a time of destiny in the history of the Kingdom of God on earth. This was a glorious period that previous prophets had envisioned. The Book of Mormon was published, the Church was officially organized, and missionaries were called to areas outside New England. Joseph received a number of profound revelations during this year.

In a revelation received on 6 April 1830, the Lord said Joseph was "through the will of God the Father, and the grace of your Lord Jesus Christ. . .to lay the foundation. . . [of the Church], and to build it up unto the most holy faith."[34] What an enormous directive! This revelation confirms that Joseph had all the power to formally organize and administer the kingdom of God on the earth. Liberty Jail appears to have been the layover station between "the foundation" and "the most holy faith."

In August 1830, the Lord compared Joseph's mission to that of Peter, James, and John. The Lord told Joseph:

> And also with Peter, and James and John [First Presidency of the Church for the dispensation of the Meridian of Time and last to hold the keys], by whom I have ordained you and confirmed you to be apostles and especial witnesses of my name, and bear the keys of your ministry and of the same things which I revealed unto them;
>
> Unto whom I have committed the keys of my kingdom, and a dispensation of the gospel for the last times; and for the fullness of times, in the which I will gather together in one all things, which are in heaven, and which are on earth.[35]

This event was profound and germane to the entire stewardship of Joseph and Oliver, for they now had the keys of the higher priesthood for the dispensation of the fullness of times with its powers, gifts, and attributes of the Holy Spirit.

In December 1830, more keys of knowledge were added:

> And I have sent forth the fullness of my gospel by the hand of my servant Joseph; and in weakness have I blessed him;
>
> And I have given unto him the keys of the mystery of those things which have been sealed, even things which were from the foundation of the world, and the things which shall come from this time until the time of my coming.[36]

In subsequent years, the concepts of Zion, the temple, and the law of consecration unfolded. The first temple site of this dispensation was dedicated in Independence with plans for a Zion city containing twenty-four temples. Much information followed concerning the Second Coming of our Lord. The keys for understanding ordinances through "a fullness of the Holy Ghost" were received. Joseph could now obtain "every needful thing."[37]

The Kirtland Temple period enlarged Joseph's spiritual base with power and knowledge. In April of 1836, at age thirty-one, Joseph again, but this time with Oliver Cowdery, saw the Savior for possibly the seventh time (see Chapter 2) and received "keys [power] of the gathering of Israel from the four parts of the earth and the leading of the 10 tribes from the Land of the north"[38] to bring them to the gospel of Abraham.[39] The ordinance would eventually be given to every worthy Saint.[40]

The unfolding of the Missouri expansion preceded Joseph's arrest in October of 1838 and his incarceration in Liberty Jail. During that imprisonment, we know from revelation that Joseph possessed all the "keys of this kingdom and ministry."[41] This moment appears to be one of his finest.

Joseph apparently received so much during the foundation period that only the Holy Spirit knows to what degree and how fast he comprehended and disseminated each doctrine. The following quotes may help us understand the magnitude of what he had been given. To his mother, "Mother, I can take my Bible, and go into the woods, and learn more in two hours, than you can learn at meeting in two years, if you should go all the time."[42] At another time, he said, "Could you gaze into heaven five minutes, you would know more than you would by reading all that ever was written on the subject."[43] After receiving the "Visions of Glory," Joseph made the following supernal comments: "Nothing would be more pleasing to the Saints upon the order of the Kingdom of the Lord, than the light which burst upon the world through the foregoing vision. . . . It came from God."[44]

Testimonies of the past foretold of the great prophet of the latter days. With the exception of the Lord, more prophetic verse was written about Joseph Smith, Jr. than any other.[45] Jacob, Joseph, Moses, and Isaiah of the Old Testament testified of this prophet. The Savior spoke of him during his early ministry, and prophets in the Book of Mormon wrote about him.

Those closest to the Prophet who knew him best spoke passionately of his spirituality. Brigham Young said of Joseph:

> The secret feeling of my heart was that I would be willing to crawl around the earth on my hands and knees, to see such a man as was Peter, Jeremiah, Moses, or any man that could tell me anything about God and Heaven. And then when I saw Joseph Smith, he took heaven figuratively, and brought it down to earth; and he took the earth, brought it up, and opened up, in plainness and simplicity, the things of God; and that is the beauty of his mission.[46]

> Wilford Woodruff said of Joseph, "His mind, like Enoch's, expands as eternity, and God alone can comprehend his soul." Also, "He seemed a fountain of knowledge from whose mouth streams of eternal wisdom flowed."[47]

Parley P. Pratt said of Joseph: "He could gaze into eternity, penetrate the heavens, and comprehend all worlds."[48]

Chapter 2

THE MESSENGERS OF
THE FULLNESS

But the Lord knoweth all things from the beginning; wherefore, he prepareth a way to accomplish all his works among the children of men; for behold, he hath all power unto the fulfilling of all his words. And thus it is. Amen.[1]

In the very beginning, God established a pattern for communicating with his prophets through messengers. The first to be instructed in this manner was Father Adam. Seeking direction from the Lord, Adam built an altar and offered sacrifices. In answer to his supplication for divine guidance, an angel of the Lord appeared to Adam and taught him the meaning of obedience and sacrifice. Messengers have been the medium for imparting knowledge and giving direction to holy prophets through the ages—to Adam, Enoch, Noah, Abraham, Moses, Isaiah, Ezekiel, Jeremiah, Lehi, Nephi, Alma, Joseph Smith, Jr., Brigham Young, Gordon B. Hinckley, etc.

We have assurance that this pattern of communicating will always be the case, for the Prophet Malachi closed the Old Testament with this great declaration: "The Lord's messenger shall prepare the way for the Second Coming."[2] We are told in the Book of Mormon how these messengers work. Nephi taught us that "angels speak by the power of the Holy Ghost."[3] Mormon advised us, "[T]he office of their ministry is to call men . . . to fulfill and to do the work of the covenants of the Father . . . by declaring the word of Christ unto the chosen vessels of the Lord."[4] These declarations were achieved during the Lord's ministry on earth with both the Israelites[5] and the Nephites[6] and is being fulfilled in this last dispensation.

The Messengers

A list of the emissaries, the times they appeared, and references may be helpful in identifying those who played significant roles with the genesis of this dispensation.

Eloheim,[7] The Father:

1820, Spring, First Vision
1832, 16 February, Doctrine & Covenants (D&C) 76:23
1835, A. H. Cannon Journal, 25 August, 1880
1836, 21 January, D&C 137:3

Jesus Christ, The Son:

1820, Spring, First Vision
1829, April, D&C 6:36-37
1830, 6 April, History of the Church (HC) 1:76, Voice of the Lord
1830, August, D&C 27, Voice of the Lord
1832, February, D&C 76:12, 14, 21, 23
1835, A. H. Cannon Journal, 25 August 1880
1836, 21 January, D&C 137:3
1836, 22 January, HC 2:383
1836, 3 April 3, D&C 110:2-4
1839, July, HC 3:388

Moroni:

Appeared over twenty times from 21 September 1823 into 1829.[8]

John the Baptist:

1829, 15 May, D&C 13

Peter, James, and John:

1829, June, HC 1:40-41 ftnt., D&C 27:12
1836, 21 January, HC 2:381
1836, 6 April (All three HC 2:435-36) and (Peter at Kirtland Temple, *BYU Studies* Vol. 15, No. 4 Summer 1975, 550-51.)

Adam and Abraham:

1834, December, HC 2:209-17 (Saw Adam-ondi-Ahman)
1836, 21 January, D&C 137:5
1839, July, HC 3:388, Journal of Discourses (JD) 21:94

Divers Angels:

1842, Joseph wrote it all down including divers angels, D&C 128:21. We know they brought keys, but concerning any other assignments, we know very little.

Moses, Elias (Noah-Gabriel), Elijah:
1836, 3 April, D&C 110:8-12

Joseph mentioned many other messengers. Subsequent prophets have told of others whom Joseph saw or who visited him. Dispensation heads, like Enoch, brought keys. The exact assignments or the purpose of visits of other messengers are not known:

Joseph, Jacob, and Isaac, (**1830**), D&C 27:10

Satan, (**1832**), D&C 76:25

Zelph the Lamanite, (**4 June 1834**), (Heber C. Kimball Journal same date)

Seth, Enos, Cainan, Mahalaleel, Jared, Enoch, and Methuselah, (**1835**), D&C 107:53; JD 21:94

Twelve Apostles, (**1836**), HC 2:381, possibly John, April 1829[9]

Paul, (**1841**), TPJS, 180, possibly January 1832, where Joseph received an explanation of 1 Corinthians 7:14

Raphael (see Raphael), (**1842**), D&C 128:21

Those **without a date** are Eve (Oliver B. Huntington Diary), Abel, and Lamech (JD 18:325)

Nephi and the twelve Nephite disciples, (JD 21:94)

Alma, (JD 13:47)

Angels:
Concerning angels, it is documented that besides the divers angels, on five other occasions, they were called *unnamed angel*, *Holy Angels* and *many angels.*

Undoubtedly, there were others whose visits may not have been recorded. Joseph gave additional information about certain disciples. Whether he saw or talked to them, we do not know. In April of 1829, he used the Urim and Thummim to learn about John the Beloved's physical and spiritual condition,[10] at which time we know Joseph saw the information in John's own handwriting. Then, again, in March of 1832, Joseph said, "I received the following explanation of the Revelation of St. John."[11] Could this be another time when he saw this beloved apostle? Could Joseph have had conversation with the Apostle Paul concerning 1 Corinthians 7:14? In January of 1832, just before conference, Joseph received an explanation on this subject.[12]

We perceive from the list of those he saw, or who visited him, that many were the "Fathers,"[13] with all the keys and glorious knowledge of their time—"the noble and great ones"[14] from previous dispensations.[15] Moroni would have discussed with Joseph the full concept of the fathers and turning one's heart to them. Further enlightenment on this subject may have come to Joseph while translating the Bible in which it was revealed that they (the fathers) were first given the priesthood keys while on earth and now hold them in heaven.[16] As the scroll unfolds, one soon realizes that the list would contain Adam, Enoch, Noah, Abraham, Isaac, Jacob, and Moses. Some promises of the fathers are the provisions of the Abrahamic covenant whereby the seed of the ancient patriarchs were entitled to receive the priesthood, the gospel, and eternal life (including celestial marriage). Understanding who "the Fathers" are is vital. Without it, there could be far-reaching consequences. The Lord informed us that if we do not turn our hearts to these fathers, "the whole earth would be utterly wasted at his coming."[17] The title page written by Mormon in the Book of Mormon makes it very plain. This record "is to show unto the remnant of the House of Israel what great things the Lord hath done for their fathers; and that they may know the covenants of the Lord, that they are not cast off forever."

The capstone to further understanding may very well be found in the Book of Abraham from the hand of this great tutor who started his record by expressing his desires for the blessings of the Fathers: "And finding there was greater happiness and peace and rest for me, I sought for the blessings of the fathers, and the right whereunto I should be ordained to administer the same."[18]

What would it be like to be visited by one of these messengers? Every person's imagination would portray a celestial being in a different way. It has been said by one who had this experience, "The light and glory of the messenger's countenance alone would be almost impossible to describe."[19] Certainly, the effect on any recipient would be similar. The message and the circumstances accompanying it would be a thrilling and overwhelming experience. As we read the touching account of the Lord's visit to the Nephites at Bountiful in 3 Nephi, we catch a mere glimpse of what it would be like to be in the presence of the Lord himself:

> And when he [the Savior] had said these words, he himself also knelt upon the earth; and behold he prayed unto the Father, and the things which he prayed cannot be written. . . .

And after this manner do they bear record: The eye hath never seen, neither hath the ear heard, before, so great and marvelous things as we saw and heard Jesus speak unto the Father.[20]

In our day, Oliver Cowdery, unable to contain the fullness of joy that came over him while he was in the presence of heavenly messengers, expressed these feelings:

And as we heard we rejoiced, while His love enkindled upon our souls, and we were wrapped in the vision of the Almighty! Where was room for doubt? Nowhere; uncertainty had fled, doubt had sunk no more to rise, . . . what joy filled our hearts, . . . but you will believe me when I say, that earth, nor men, with the eloquence of time, cannot begin to clothe language in as interesting and sublime a manner as this holy personage. No; nor has this earth power to give the joy, to bestow the peace, or comprehend the wisdom which was contained in each sentence.[21]

Joseph gave a vivid description of Moroni:

He had on a loose robe of most exquisite whiteness. It was a whiteness beyond anything earthly I had ever seen; nor do I believe that any earthly thing could be made to appear so exceedingly white and brilliant. His hands were naked, and his arms also, a little above the wrist; so, also, were his feet naked, as were his legs, a little above the ankles. His head and neck were also bare. I could discover that he had no other clothing on but this robe, as it was open, so that I could see into his bosom.

Not only was his robe exceedingly white, but his whole person was glorious beyond description, and his countenance truly like lightning. The room was exceedingly light, but not so very bright as immediately around his person. When I first looked upon him, I was afraid; but the fear soon left me.[22]

Joseph explained in the six lectures on theology (Lectures on Faith) that these angelic ministrants perform their assignments based on the foundation of faith. In the seventh and last lecture, Joseph culminated the powers of faith in item three, so that it "may be clearly comprehended." Joseph said, "[W]hen a man works by faith he works by mental exertion instead of physical force. It is by words, . . . which every being works when he works by faith."[23] Then, in item four:

this is the principle upon which all eternity has acted and will act; . . . it is by reason of this power that all the hosts of heaven perform their works of wonder, majesty, and glory. Angels move from place to place by virtue of this power; it is by reason of it that they are enabled to descend from heaven to earth; and were it not for the power of faith they never could be ministering spirits to them who should be heirs of salvation, neither could they act as heavenly messengers, for they would be destitute of the power necessary to enable them to do the will of God.[24]

The Lord told Joseph at Liberty Jail:

God shall give unto you knowledge . . . that has not been revealed since the world was until now;

Which our forefathers have awaited with anxious expectation to be revealed in the last times, which their minds were pointed to by the angels, as held in reserve for the fullness of their glory;

A time to come in the which nothing shall be withheld.[25]

It was all fulfilled, for these angelic ministrants brought from every previous dispensation all rights, keys, honor, majesty, glory, and the power of their priesthood to Joseph Smith, Jr., who was the designated Prophet of the Dispensation of the Fullness of Times.[26] This fulfillment answers the following questions: Who was Joseph Smith? How did an uneducated boy become so well schooled and astute as to the things of God? It was through the keys, gifts and power, signs and tokens delivered to him from the Lord Jesus Christ and the heavenly messengers he sent. It has been summarized this way: "The principles which he had placed him in communication with the Lord, and not only with the Lord, but with the ancient apostles and prophets. He seemed to be as familiar with these people as we are with one another."[27]

Messengers, Messages, and Assignments

In connection with the messengers of the fullness, following is a listing of the messengers and their messages and assignments.

1820, FATHER AND SON: The heavens were opened for the first time in over a millennium. On this sacred occasion, messengers were not sent to begin the great and glorious work of the restoration. It was God the Eternal Father himself who parted the veil and introduced his Son to Joseph Smith, Jr.

1823, MORONI: After imparting to Joseph knowledge about the plates buried in Cumorah, the former inhabitants of this continent, the Urim and Thummim, and other significant information, Moroni began quoting the prophecies of the Old Testament. In the scriptures Moroni quoted,[28] the plan of salvation was outlined. Oliver Cowdery related that while Moroni was speaking, a vision was also opened to

Joseph's mind, so that Joseph was permitted to see marvelous manifestations relative to what was being taught.[29] Moroni used "the keys of the record of the stick of Ephraim" to give Joseph all that Joseph needed.[30]

1824, 1825, 1826, MORONI: The enormous task of bringing forth the Book of Mormon required careful preparation. Joseph met with the angel annually on 22 September for the next four years. At these special meetings, Joseph received instructions regarding the sacred records of which Moroni held the keys. The Lord confirmed Moroni's authority when the Lord told Joseph, "Moroni, whom I have sent unto you to reveal the Book of Mormon, containing the fullness of my everlasting gospel, to whom I have committed the keys of the record of the stick of Ephraim."[31] During this time, other great Book of Mormon prophets played an integral part in Joseph's preparation. Nephi, Alma, the twelve Nephite apostles, and Mormon all instructed Joseph.[32]

1827, sometime before fall: Joseph received a severe chastisement from Moroni. He told his family that as he was passing by the Hill Cumorah, "The angel met me and said that I had not been engaged enough in the work of the Lord; that the time had come for the record to be brought forth; and that I must be up and doing and set myself about the things which God had commanded me to do."[33]

1827, 22 September, MORONI: Early in the morning, Joseph climbed the Hill Cumorah for his last annual meeting with Moroni. The angel gave to Joseph the plates, the Urim and Thummim, and the breastplate. He also warned him concerning his responsibilities by stressing that Joseph was now responsible for the sacred records and that if through carelessness they were lost, Joseph would be cut off. The promise was made, however, that if Joseph used every effort to preserve them, they would be protected.[34]

1828, between February and June, MORONI: Following the loss of the 116 pages of translation, Moroni appeared to Joseph and took from him the plates and the Urim and Thummim. The angel later returned the plates.[35] At this time, Joseph was instructed not to retranslate the same material but to translate the material found in the small plates of Nephi.

1829, April, JESUS CHRIST: The Lord told Joseph and Oliver to "Behold the wounds which pierced my side, and also the prints of the nails in my hands and feet" and charged them to "keep my commandments."[36]

1829, 15 May, JOHN THE BAPTIST: John the Baptist conferred upon Joseph and Oliver the keys of the priesthood of Aaron which holds the keys of the ministering of angels and of the gospel of repentance and of baptism by immersion for the remission of sins.

1829, June, MORONI: Moroni visited seven times during the month and paramount to these visits were the care of the plates[37] and the designation of the special witnesses. In his ancient capacity as recorder, Moroni was allowed to see this dispensation in vision and was permitted to write some instructions to the latter-day prophet who would translate the record. Moroni wrote of three sets of witnesses: eight witnesses who would be allowed to see the plates;[38] three witnesses who would be shown the plates "by the power of God";[39] and the Godhead who would be witnessed by the Father, the Son, and the Holy Ghost.[40] H. Donl Peterson, a great researcher on this subject, says, "Moroni displayed amazing patience. He was the author of the last portion of the Book of Mormon. He knew the language and the culture of the Nephite record keepers. He knew the Lord. But line upon line, here a little and there a little (Isaiah. 28:10), Moroni instructed Joseph how to perform his task, helping the young Prophet persevere in learning his role."[41]

1829, June,[42] PETER, JAMES, AND JOHN: The First Presidency of the Church in their day, Peter, James, and John, appeared to Joseph and Oliver on the banks of the Susquehanna River.[43] They conferred upon Joseph and Oliver the holy Melchizedek Priesthood, the keys of the apostleship,[44] and the keys of the dispensation of the fullness of times.[45]

1830, 6 April, JESUS CHRIST: Joseph Smith heard the voice of Jesus Christ during the time of the organization of the Church in which were laid out specific directions and commandments.[46]

1830, August, JESUS CHRIST: As Joseph set out to procure wine for the sacrament, he was met by a heavenly messenger who told him to listen to the voice of the Lord.[47] The Prophet was instructed and given beautiful, significant information concerning the sacrament. The messenger talked about an Elias[48] and other ancient messengers "unto whom I have committed the keys of my kingdom."[49] He concluded with, "And also with all those whom my Father hath given me out of the world."[50]

1832, February, FATHER AND SON: After the Prophet had translated John 5:29, he and Sidney Rigdon were permitted to see an extraordinary vision. By the power of the Spirit, their eyes were opened and their understanding enlightened. They saw the Son and conversed with him in heavenly vision. They beheld the glory of the Son on the right hand of the Father; and they heard a voice bearing record that he is the Only Begotten of the Father. They "saw holy angels and them who are sanctified before his throne, worshiping God, and the Lamb, who worship him forever and ever."[51]

1834, Father, Mother, and Son: Zededee Coltrin recorded this experience in his journal:

> One day the Prophet Joseph asked him and Sidney Rigdon to accompany him into the woods to pray. When they had reached a secluded spot Joseph laid down on his back and stretched out his arms. He told the brethren to lie one on each arm, and then shut their eyes. After they had prayed he told them to open their eyes. They did so and saw a brilliant light surrounding a pedestal which seemed to rest on the earth. They closed their eyes and again prayed. They then saw, on opening them, the Father seated upon a throne; they prayed again and on looking saw the Mother also; after praying and looking the fourth time they saw the Savior added to the group.[52]

1835, 28 March, Adam-ondi-Ahman: Joseph received a revelation about the events that took place at Adam-ondi-Ahman. It was not until four years later, however, that he put in writing an account of all he saw.[53]

1836, 21 January, FATHER AND HIS SON JESUS CHRIST, ADAM (see 1839, July, for Adam and his posterity) **AND ABRAHAM:** One of the most significant meetings held in the Kirtland Temple was recorded by the Prophet.

> I met with the presidency [in the evening] at the west school room, in the Temple, to attend to the ordinance of anointing our heads with holy oil. . . . We then laid our hands upon our aged Father Smith, and invoked the blessings of heaven. . . . The heavens were opened upon us, and I beheld the celestial kingdom of God, and the glory thereof. . . . I saw the transcendent beauty of the gate through which the heirs of that kingdom will enter, which was like unto circling flames of fire; Also the blazing throne of God, whereon was seated the Father and the Son. I saw the beautiful streets of that kingdom, which had the appearance of being paved with gold. I saw Father Adam and Abraham; and my father and my mother; my brother Alvin that has long since slept.[54]

Joseph was amazed when he saw his brother Alvin in the celestial kingdom, as Alvin had died before the gospel was restored. The Lord revealed to Joseph, "All who have died without a knowledge of this gospel, who would have received it if they had been permitted to tarry, shall be heirs of the celestial kingdom of God."[55] Joseph learned also that all children who die before the age of accountability "are saved in the celestial kingdom of heaven."[56]

ABRAHAM:[57] Head of his dispensation and founder of the covenant race that is manifest in the House of Israel. Abraham received the gospel by baptism (the covenant of salvation). The higher priesthood was then conferred upon him, and he entered into celestial marriage (the covenant of exaltation).[58] These events assured Abraham and his wives of eternal increase.[59] He ultimately received the promise that all these blessings would be available to all his posterity.[60] Abraham was extremely blessed with divine revelation regarding the planetary system, the earth's creation, and our premortal spirits. Because of his faithfulness, he has been exalted and enthroned.[61]

1836, 21 January, TWELVE APOSTLES: (Jerusalem) Joseph saw a vision of the celestial kingdom. A small portion is described in the following words: "And finally I saw the Twelve in the Celestial Kingdom of God."[62] They were "especial witnesses of my name, and bear the keys of your ministry"[63] and will "judge the whole house of Israel, even as many as have loved me and kept my commandments, and none else."[64] They are the "stewards of the mysteries of God."[65]

1836, 22 January, JESUS CHRIST: In a meeting with the Council of Twelve and the presidency of the Seventy who were to receive the ordinance (anointing and blessing), the heavens were opened and angels administered to them. Toward the conclusion of the meeting, the gift of tongues fell upon them in mighty power, angels mingled their voices with the brethren, and unceasing praises swelled their bosoms. After the meeting was concluded, the Spirit and visions of God attended Joseph through the night.[66]

1836, 2 April, JESUS CHRIST: Following the Sunday afternoon worship service, Joseph and Oliver withdrew to the Melchizedek Priesthood pulpits on the west side of the temple. The veil was lowered so they could pray privately. Suddenly, "the veil was taken from our minds, and the eyes of our understanding were opened."[67] The Lord himself appeared and accepted the temple. He promised to manifest himself in that holy house "if my people will keep my commandments, and do not pollute this holy house."[68]

MOSES (who led the children of Israel out of Egypt) next appeared and restored "the keys of the gathering of Israel from the four parts of the earth, and the leading of the ten tribes from the land of the north."[69]

ELIAS (see Noah) then appeared and "committed the dispensation of the gospel of Abraham"[70] for the perfecting of the Saints—both individuals and families.

NOAH (Gabriel and Elias): Son of Lamech, he was born 126 years after Adam died and was ten years of age when ordained to the priesthood by Methuselah.[71] Noah holds the keys of the priesthood pertaining to this earth[72] as well as the keys of a dispensation and stands next to Adam in authority. Commanded by the Lord to build an ark, he and his wife, their three sons, and their wives were the only survivors of the flood.

The keys Noah restored have not been revealed but may have to do with the saving of souls at the burning fires.[73] He may be over the four angels spoken of by John: "And I saw another angel ascending from the east, having the seal of the living God: and he cried with a loud voice to the four angels."[74] Is it possible that Noah was the Elias who appeared in the Kirtland Temple on 3 April 1836 and conferred the keys of the dispensation of the gospel of Abraham upon Joseph Smith and Oliver Cowdery?[75] We know that "This Elias was a prophet who lived in the days of Abraham and who held the keys of that dispensation. He came and bestowed the gifts and the blessings that were pronounced upon Abraham's head, both for himself and his posterity after him."[76]

From the New Testament, we know Gabriel appeared to Zacharias.[77] In sequence, Joseph tells us that Gabriel was a messenger to him[78] and that he was Noah. Note that Enos, Cainan, Mahalaleel, Jared, Methuselah, and Lamech knew both Adam and Noah. All were alive at the same time. If we work from the other direction, Nahor (brother of Abraham), Terah, Nahor, Serug, Reu, Peleg, Eber, Salah, Arphaxad, Shem, and Noah lived on the earth at the same time.

ELIJAH then appeared and, in fulfillment of Malachi's prophecy,[79] conferred the sealing power upon Joseph and Oliver:

The spirit, power and calling of Elijah is that ye have power to hold the keys of the revelations, ordinances, oracles, powers and endowments of the fullness of the Melchizedek Priesthood and of the kingdom of God on the earth; and to receive, obtain and perform all the ordinances belonging to the kingdom of God, even unto the turning of the hearts of the fathers unto the children, and the hearts of the children unto the fathers, even those who are in heaven.[80]

This is the great power that gave us the welding link between ourselves and our dead—making it binding in heaven and on earth.[81] It is one of the greatest and most important subjects that God has revealed.[82] Elijah testified that "the keys of this dispensation are committed into your hands" in preparing for "the great and dreadful day of the Lord.[83] (See Chapter 10, **The Priesthood Fullness**.)

1839, July, JESUS CHRIST and **ADAM:** Joseph records the vision seen earlier of Jesus Christ with Adam and his posterity at Adam-Ondi-Ahman.[84]

ADAM: The father of the human race and the first to receive heavenly messengers was Adam. He was the head of the first dispensation and restored all keys for the presidency to the earth.[85] He was 130 years old when Seth was born and lived to be 930 years old. Adam and Eve are the prototype for mortals. The pattern they set is the only one whereby eternal life can be gained.

EVE:[86] Wife of Adam, an equal half of the first eternal unit of our mortal sphere, literally the mother of all living.[87] She has given us one of the most beautiful and glorious explanations of the plan of redemption ever recorded in holy writ. "Were it not for our transgression we never should have had seed, and never should have known good and evil, and the joy of our redemption, and the eternal life which God giveth unto all the obedient."[88]

ABEL:[89] A son of Adam and Eve; a shepherd who offered a more excellent sacrifice to God than his brother Cain. He was murdered by Cain. To know Abel, we must know and understand Seth who was like him.

SETH: A son born to Adam and Eve when they were 130 years old. He was a prophet and a patriarch and was ordained by Adam at sixty-nine years of age. He is called "a perfect man, and his likeness was the express likeness of his father, insomuch that he seemed to be like unto his father in all things."[90]

ENOCH: (See Raphael.) Father of Methuselah, head of a dispensation that was taken to the Lord's bosom.[91] He wrote the book containing Adam's posterity[92] and was 365 years old when he was translated.

RAPHAEL:[93] We do not know his identity in the restoration of all things. This messenger could have been Enoch or someone from that dispensation, as this dispensation is the only one without an identified representative.[94]

METHUSELAH: Son of Enoch. He lived longer than any of the patriarchs.[95] He was a righteous man, a prophet, and an astronomer. When the City of Enoch was taken, he was left on the earth to provide a posterity through which Noah would come.[96]

LAMECH:[97] The ninth from Adam and father of Noah. He was fifty-six years old when Adam died and 182 years old when Noah was born.

ISAAC: The son of promise and heir of the promises was born to Abraham and Sarah in their old age. According to scriptures, Isaac is now exalted and sits upon a throne with Abraham and Jacob.[98]

JACOB: Was the youngest of the twin sons born to Isaac and Rebekah. It was through him that the covenant of Abraham continued.[99] Jacob became the father of twelve sons who were later designated as the Twelve Tribes of Israel. Jacob did "none other thing than that which [he was] commanded" and is today exalted upon a throne in heaven, in company with Abraham and Isaac.[100]

JOSEPH: Was the eleventh son born to Jacob. Joseph obtained the birthright because of his worthiness and because it was his natural right after Reuben, the oldest son, lost the birthright privilege through transgression. Joseph, the firstborn son of Jacob's second wife Rachel, was then next in line for the inheritance. It is through Joseph that the promises remain.[101] Of interest is his experience with prison life. (See Appendix C.) Of Joseph's children, Ephraim and Manasseh, many descendants were among the ten tribes who were lost. A small fragment of his descendants migrated to America about 600 B.C. Their record is contained in the Book of Mormon. It has been basically Joseph's descendants who have been called by the Lord in these last days to carry the gospel to the world in compliance with the covenant God made with Abraham.

The testimony of the fathers is a testimony of being able "to inquire after the knowledge of God; the inquiry . . . always terminated when rightly pursued, in the most glorious discoveries and eternal certainty."[102] This legacy of the fathers has come to us through Joseph.

PAUL:[103] Was known as Saul in his early life. His Latin name, *Paul*, is first mentioned at the beginning of his Gentile ministry. He became an apostle after the death of Jesus Christ. His many epistles cover the entire plan of salvation, with great discourses on the priesthood and the gifts of the Spirit. His fourteen epistles were written to members of the Church who already had some knowledge of the gospel. Paul's works constitute over a third of the New Testament.

NEPHI: Fourth son of Lehi. His family left Jerusalem about 600 B.C. He became a great prophet and the founder of the Nephite nation. It was Nephi who was commanded by the Lord to keep a record of his people after their arrival in the Americas.

MORMON:[104] A Nephite prophet, general, and record keeper. It was he who abridged the records that Joseph Smith, Jr. translated many centuries after they had been buried by Moroni. Mormon knew the heart and soul of all the records, particularly the Book of Mormon.

TWELVE NEPHITE DISCIPLES: They had all things from the beginning unto the end expounded to them.[105] All have a fullness of joy and have sat down with the Father in his kingdom.[106] Three were translated.[107] "The Twelve Apostles and twelve disciples shall judge thy seed."[108]

ZELPH THE LAMANITE: Joseph saw Zelph in vision during the Zion camp march. The event was recorded as follows:

> On June 3, 1834, the brethren ascended a high mound near the Illinois river. On the top of this mound, they found the remnants of three stone altars, one above the other, 'according to the ancient order.' The brethren removed the earth nearby and discovered the skeleton of a man. Between his ribs, the prophet says, 'the stone point of a Lamanitish arrow.' To the prophet it was revealed by the Spirit, 'that the person whose skeleton we had seen, was a white Lamanite, a large, thick-set man, and a man of God. His name was Zelph. He was a warrior and chieftain under the great Prophet Onandagus, who was known from the eastern sea, to the Rocky Mountains.'[109]

Because this messenger was of Lamanite lineage and righteous, he could have told the Prophet much about the Ohio Valley being occupied by the descendants of Lehi. Heber C. Kimball recorded in his journal, "While on the way we felt anxious to know who the person was. . . . It was made known to Joseph that he had been an officer who fell in battle...among the Lamanites. . . . Brother Joseph had inquired of the Lord, and it was made known in a vision."[110]

For Joseph, the great orchestrator of dispensing knowledge was Jesus Christ and his messengers. These messengers always began with reference to Jesus Christ, and through him these angelic voices fulfilled this great declaration, "A prophet would the Lord God raise up among the Jews—even a Messiah, or, in other words, a Savior of the world. And he also spake concerning the prophets, how great a number had testified of these things concerning this Messiah, of whom he had spoken, or this Redeemer of the world."[111] Collectively, these messengers restored all to Joseph Smith. The Prophet's mortal ministry was to lay before us all that had been given him—"Their [the messengers] rights, their keys, their honors, their majesty and glory, and the power of their priesthood; giving line upon line, precept upon precept; here a little and there a little,"[112] into a fullness of the dispensation of times.

Chapter 3

JOSEPH'S LEGACY
OF SCRIPTURES

The unfolding of the scriptural legacy of Joseph Smith, Jr. took his entire prophetic life. The first seven years brought forth the Book of Mormon, which gave him the fullness of the everlasting gospel. Joseph's translation of the Holy Bible, first called the 'Inspired Version', brought forth a purity of doctrinal understanding. The Doctrine and Covenants laid the foundation for the kingdom of God in this final dispensation. An understanding of the sacred mysteries and powers of godliness was given to Joseph through the Book of Abraham. Finally, although not canonized, the *History of the Church* contains the day-by-day dealings of Father, Son, and Holy Ghost with the children of the Covenant.

In July of 1830, the Lord told Joseph, "Behold, thou wast called and chosen to write the Book of Mormon, and to my ministry."[1] Earlier, the Lord had said that Joseph was to "be called a seer, a translator, a prophet."[2] "A seer is a revelator and a prophet also,"[3] and, when necessary, he can use the Urim and Thummim or holy interpreters.[4] There have been many prophets throughout history, but not so many seers. "A seer is greater than a prophet . . . and a gift which is greater can no man have."[5]

Joseph Smith was the great seer of this last dispensation. He was able to translate the Book of Mormon by the gift and power of God. He also used the gift and power of God to translate the Bible by restoring the plain and precious parts. Thus, we now have in our new scriptures Matthew 24, the Book of Moses, and the Joseph Smith Translation. The Book of Abraham completes the legacy of scriptures Joseph left us.

The Most Correct Book on Earth

The Book of Mormon was the first book of scripture to come forth in this dispensation. On 22 September 1823, according to the instructions of the angel, Joseph "went to the place where the messenger had told me the plates were deposited; and owing to the distinctness of the vision which I had concerning it, I knew the place the instant that I arrived there."[6] Joseph raised the stone and looked in "and there indeed did I behold the plates, the Urim and Thummim, and the breastplate, as stated by the messenger."[7]

Joseph was informed by Moroni that "the time for bringing them forth had not yet arrived, neither would it, until four years from that time; but he told me that I should come to that place precisely in one year from that time, and that he would there meet with me, and that I should continue to do so until the time should come for obtaining the plates."[8] Accordingly, Joseph did as he was commanded. He "received instruction and intelligence from him [the angel] at each of the interviews, respecting what the Lord was going to do, and how and in what manner his kingdom was to be conducted in the last days."[9]

Finally, on 22 September 1827, the day arrived for the young prophet to be entrusted with the sacred plates, the Urim and Thummim, and the breastplate.[10] The persecution and constant attempts of godless men to get the plates away from Joseph made it impossible for him to begin the work of translation. He and his wife Emma soon left Palmyra and traveled to Susquehanna County in the state of Pennsylvania to stay with Emma's parents. There, in peaceful surroundings, the work proceeded.

Martin Harris came to Harmony and labored as scribe for Joseph until 14 June 1828. At the end of that time, 116 foolscap pages of translation had been completed. Martin had played a prominent role in the translation of the plates. He gave the Prophet money to travel to Pennsylvania and subsequently provided money on a number of occasions, which made it possible for Joseph to move the work forward. Martin's wife Lucy was bitter about the help her husband gave to Joseph and told everyone she saw that her husband had been duped. In an effort to pacify his wife, Martin asked permission to take the 116 pages of translated manuscript home to show to her and a few others. Joseph inquired of the Lord on two different occasions and received "no" for an answer. Martin continued pleading with

Joseph and, wanting to satisfy this man who had been such a great help and a good friend, Joseph again inquired of the Lord. This time, the Lord granted a "conditional" yes. Martin agreed in writing to show the manuscript to only four or five people. He then left for Palmyra with the only copy of the manuscript.

When Martin failed to return in three weeks, Joseph left for Palmyra to look into the matter. Joseph was devastated to learn that the manuscript had been lost. Filled with self-condemnation and fear, the Prophet cried, "All is lost! all is lost! What shall I do? I have sinned— it is I who tempted the wrath of God. I should have been satisfied with the first answer which I received from the Lord; for he told me that it was not safe to let the writing go out of my possession."[11]

Upon his return to Harmony, Joseph began to pray that the Lord would forgive him for acting contrary to his will. Moroni appeared to Joseph and required him to return the plates; however, he told Joseph that if he would be humble and penitent, he could receive them back. Some time later, the Lord chastised him for negligence and for "setting at naught the counsels of God" but also gave him comfort by telling him that he was still chosen to perform the work of translation if he repented.[12] Joseph did repent, and when Moroni returned the plates and the Urim and Thummim, he "seemed pleased with me . . . and he told me that the Lord loved me, for my faithfulness and humility."[13] Moroni promised Joseph that a new scribe would soon be provided.

With the divine gift returned the following September, Joseph learned through revelation that evil men had set a trap for him by altering the words of the manuscript. If he translated the same material again and had it published, they would say he was unable to do it the same way twice, and therefore the work must not be inspired.[14]

From this experience, Joseph learned obedience and later said, "I made this my rule: When the Lord commands, do it."[15] Rebuked by the Lord and admonished by Moroni, he was submissive to the Father's will, always repentant, and full of optimism.

By now, the Prophet had gained considerable experience in receiving revelation. God the Father, his Son Jesus Christ, and other angelic messengers had talked with him. He had seen visions, enjoyed the promptings of the Spirit, and increased in ability to use the Urim and Thummim and seer stones.

During the winter of 1828-29, Joseph, with the help of Emma and her brother, worked on the translation of the Book of Mormon whenever he could; but trying to earn a living left little time for the work. On Tuesday, 5 April 1829, Oliver Cowdery arrived in Harmony. Joseph recognized him at once as the scribe that had been promised. Two days after Oliver's arrival, Joseph commenced to translate the Book of Mormon with Oliver acting as scribe.[16] With Oliver's help, the work moved forward more rapidly than before. "These were days never to be forgotten," wrote Oliver, "to sit under the sound of a voice dictated by the inspiration of heaven. . . . Day after day I continued, uninterrupted, to write from his mouth, as he translated, with the Urim and Thummim . . . the history, or record, called 'The Book of Mormon.'"[17]

By this time, the persecution had become so relentless in Harmony that Joseph was forced to find new quarters to complete the translation. David Whitmer, a friend of Oliver's in Fayette township, convinced his father, Peter Whitmer Sr., that Peter should invite the Prophet and Oliver to stay with them. The invitation was gratefully received, and on 1 June 1829, Joseph and Oliver moved to Fayette. The translating resumed immediately. It has been estimated that although several years had passed, the actual working time of translation was only about fifty-five days. The Whitmer family was most hospitable in meeting the needs of Joseph, Emma, and Oliver Cowdery.

Shortly after their arrival in Fayette, Joseph filed for and received a copyright for the Book of Mormon by the Northern District of New York.[18] As the translation was nearing completion in late June, the Prophet began negotiations with Egbert B. Grandin, a printer in Palmyra. Grandin was reluctant to commit to printing what was then called the "golden Bible." He finally agreed to do so if Martin Harris would sign a mortgage agreement guaranteeing payment. On 17 August 1829, it was agreed that Grandin would print five thousand copies, a huge amount for a small, local printer at that time, for $3,000.[19] Printing began in the fall of 1829, and on 26 March 1830, the Book of Mormon went on sale in Palmyra.

The Book of Mormon contains the fullness of the everlasting gospel. It puts forth the doctrines of the kingdom, outlines the plan of salvation, and tells men and women what they must do to gain peace in this life and eternal salvation and exaltation in the kingdom of God. As a volume of holy scripture, it is comparable to the Bible. It is a record of God's dealings with the ancient inhabitants of the Americas. Joseph himself said, "The Book of Mormon was the most correct of any book on earth, and the keystone of our religion, and a man would get nearer to God by abiding by its precepts, than by any other book."[20]

A great and beautiful affirmation of the Book of Mormon was given by the Savior himself. He said the Book of Mormon

> contains a record of a fallen people, and the fullness of the gospel of Jesus Christ to the Gentiles and to the Jews also;
>
> Which was given by inspiration, and is confirmed to others by the ministering of angels, and is declared unto the world by them—
>
> Proving to the world that the holy scriptures are true, and that God does inspire men and call them to his holy work in this age and generation, as well as in generations of old;
>
> Thereby showing that he is the same God yesterday, today, and forever. Amen.[21]
>
> By these things we know that there is a God in heaven, who is infinite and eternal, from everlasting to everlasting the same unchangeable God, the framer of heaven and earth, and all things which are in them;
>
> And that he created man, male and female, after his own image and in his own likeness, created he them;
>
> And gave unto them commandments that they should love and serve him, the only living and true God, and that he should be the only being whom they should worship.[22]

It is one thing to have a dispensation in which all things have been restored. It is quite another to apply the knowledge of those doctrines to life. How does it work for the individual? Book of Mormon prophets illustrate the process in various ways. Alma, in talking to his son Corianton, gives a beautiful definition of individual restitution with an entirely different twist. "The meaning of the word restoration is to bring back again evil for evil, or carnal for carnal, or devilish for devilish—good for that which is good; righteous for that which is righteous; just for that which is just, merciful for that which is merciful."[23]

Alma then gives a summary that helps us understand the purpose of a full restoration of that which is necessary for individual eternal life:

[S]ee that you are merciful unto your brethren; deal justly, judge righteously, and do good continually; and if ye do all these things then shall ye receive your reward; yea, ye shall have mercy restored unto you again; ye shall have justice restored unto you again; ye shall have a righteous judgment restored unto you again; and ye shall have good rewarded unto you again.[24]

The Plain and Precious Things

Joseph next worked on the translation of the Bible—the Inspired Version, or a "new translation" as the Lord later called it.[25]

The Church was only two months old when Joseph began the translation of the Old Testament. The Lord declared in December 1830, "And I have given unto him [Joseph] the keys of the mystery of those things which have been sealed, even things which were from the foundation of the world, and the things which shall come from this time until the time of my coming."[26] The King James Version of the Bible was the "starting point," but the Spirit of Revelation was the source of divine intelligence.

Joseph Smith, Jr. and various scribes labored with the Book of Genesis for almost two and a half years because of the many interruptions of persecution and travel. The first revision of the Old Testament was finally completed on 2 July 1833. The scribes for Joseph were Oliver Cowdery, who wrote the major portion, John Whitmer, a small portion, and Sidney Rigdon, the rest of the work.

On 7 March 1831, Joseph received a revelation that stated, "And now, behold, I say unto you, it shall not be given unto you to know any further concerning this chapter [Genesis], until the New Testament be translated, and in it all these things shall be made known."[27] The very next day, 8 March, translation of the New Testament was begun and completed a little over a year later. "I completed the translation and review of the New Testament, on the 2nd of February, 1833 and sealed it up, no more to be opened til it arrived in Zion."[28] Obviously, Joseph was involved in translating either the Old or New Testament continuously from June of 1830 to July of 1833. The two short periods he did not translate were during the month of January 1831 and four months from 19 June 1831 to 12 September 1831.

Joseph's translation of the Bible included numerous corrections and a reintroduction of lost passages that have given us doctrinal information concerning the Father, Jesus Christ, Adam, Cain, Satan, Enoch, and Noah.

There are two major reasons why this biblical work was so important. The first is scriptural. God himself, as well as his prophets, has spoken concerning holy writ. In June of 1830, a revelation given to Joseph Smith disclosed that before Moses wrote what is now the first five books of the Bible, the Lord told him:

> And now, Moses, my son, I will speak unto thee concerning this earth upon which thou standest; and thou shalt write the things which I shall speak.
>
> And in a day when the children of men shall esteem my words as nought and take many of them from the book which thou shalt write, behold, I will raise up another like unto thee; and they shall be had again among the children of men—among as many as shall believe.[29]

A second scriptural witness is the prophet Nephi's vision:

> And after they go forth by the hand of the twelve apostles of the Lamb, from the Jews unto the Gentiles, thou seest the formation of that great and abominable church, which is most abominable above all other churches; for behold, they have taken away from the gospel of the Lamb many parts which are plain and most precious; and also many covenants of the Lord have they taken away.[30]

Nephi's vision not only tells of the loss of the plain and most precious parts that were taken out of the Bible but also tells where and how they will be made available to the true believer.[31]

The second reason could be classified as scholarly. The books of the Old Testament (the old covenant) were written in Hebrew. The original manuscripts have all disappeared. Until the Dead Sea Scrolls were discovered, the earliest Hebrew manuscript of any considerable part of the Old Testament did not go beyond the tenth century A.D.

The Old Testament books did receive reverent and technical care from rabbinical perfection and were handed down to us with less material change since 100 A.D. The changes that did occur usually resulted from man's inefficiency and the frailty of writing materials. The changes came as a matter of course in the process of copying, preserving, and translating the original manuscripts. Words, phrases, and sentences were passed over by the copyist or became obscured in the old manuscripts. The result was either an abbreviated account or else a meaningless skeleton of the original text. In Joseph's translation, over two hundred verses were added and almost seven hundred verses changed in the Old Testament.[32] These corrections show that a few rabbis must have made changes to fit their personal theology.

31

The New Testament (the new covenant) is entirely another matter. The Greek fragments and manuscripts used included those written in uncial (capital letters) and the running hand called minuscule, commonly called cursive. Of all uncial and cursive in existence today, only two fragments (John 18:31-34; 37-38) go back to 125 A.D. It would truly be impossible to get a flawless translation of the New Testament. In the Prophet Joseph's translation, there are three times as many corrections in the New Testament—over 280 verse additions and 2,000 verse changes.

Doctrines and Covenants of Our Dispensation

The Doctrine and Covenants is a collection of revelations given by the Lord for his kingdom on earth. These revelations given to the Prophet consisted of important and timely instructions regarding the doctrines and government of the Church. Shortly after the Church was organized, the Prophet and John Whitmer copied and arranged the revelations received up to that time. With the establishment of the press in Independence, Missouri, came the opportunity to publish them.

The first collection of revelations was voted on at the Elders Conference in November 1831. It was printed at Independence, Missouri, in 1833 with sixty-five sections and was called the "Book of Commandments." Before the work was completed, a mob in Independence destroyed the printing press on 20 July and scattered through the streets five completed signatures or galley sheets, each with thirty-two pages.

A second attempt to publish these scriptures was authorized on 24 September 1834 by a high council in Kirtland. After the preliminary work had been done, approval for publication was given on 17 February 1835. The Book of Doctrine and Covenants was published later that year in Kirtland. It contained 102 sections and included the seven Lectures on Faith that were prepared by Joseph and others and that had been given at the School of the Prophets. This section was called "The Doctrine." The 1844 edition was published in Nauvoo and England. It contained 111 sections. The 1876 edition, published under the direction of the First Presidency, was prepared by Orson Pratt at Salt Lake City and contained 136 sections.[33]

In addition, the Doctrine and Covenants contains some doctrines that are not fully explained. It also contains unique doctrines somewhat intrinsic—such as the destiny of the earth, the origin of man, future conditions of man, resurrection and judgment of man, candidacy for the different glories, eternity of the marriage relationship, and the eternal nature of the family. Finally, the gradual developmental changes and administration of the church unfold.

The two major words in the title of this scripture have great significance. The term "doctrine" occurs toward the end of 2 Nephi when Nephi summarizes the straight and narrow path from baptism to eternal life:

> And now, behold, my beloved brethren, this is the way; and there is none other way nor name given under heaven whereby man can be saved in the kingdom of God. And now, behold, this is the doctrine of Christ, and the only and true doctrine of the Father, and of the Son, and of the Holy Ghost, which is one God, without end. Amen.[34]

In 2 Nephi 32, the heading states, "Men must pray and gain knowledge for themselves from the Holy Ghost," and verse 6 says we can see that Christ did appear to the Nephites at Bountiful in the flesh and gave them additional doctrine.[35] In our dispensation, from the legacy of the Lord's appearance to Joseph comes the great term "doctrine."

The second word, "covenant," is the central theme of the Old and New Testaments. *Covenant* in Hebrew means *testament*. That is why we have the old and new covenant or testament in the Bible. Covenant is given as the second purpose for the Book of Mormon. The title page boldly declares "that they may know the covenants of the Lord that they are not cast off forever." These two title words are profound and, in and of themselves, characterize the great part these revelations play in Joseph's legacy.

Abraham's Knowledge of Heaven and Earth

On 3 July 1835, the Church purchased several rolls of ancient Egyptian papyrus and four mummies from Michael Chandler for $2,400. With W. W. Phelps and Oliver Cowdery as scribes, Joseph "commenced the translation of some of the characters or hieroglyphics, and much to our joy found that one of the rolls contained the writings of Abraham (by his own hand while he was in Egypt)" and also of Joseph of Egypt.[36] This book was first published in the *Times and Seasons*.[37]

Why were the writings of Abraham so important? Elohim, Jesus Christ, and the Holy Ghost had entered into covenants with mankind through the prophets down from the time of Adam. The covenants with Abraham comprised a complete dispensation of gospel covenants.[38] His recorded writings have given us for the first time the specifics of these covenants in a very sacred way. The Lord told Abraham that the Lord would "make of thee a great nation and I will bless thee, and make thy name great; and thou shalt be a blessing."[39] We learn from Nephi in the Book of Mormon, "Wherefore, our father hath not spoken of our seed alone, but also of all the house of Israel, pointing to the covenant which should be fulfilled in the latter days; which covenant the Lord made to our father Abraham, saying: In thy seed shall all the kindreds of the earth be blessed."[40] A need for the writings and works of Father Abraham was emphasized in the New Testament: "They answered and said unto him, Abraham is our father, Jesus saith unto them, If ye were Abraham's children, ye would do the works of Abraham."[41]

A second witness to the importance of the Book of Abraham is contained in the Doctrine and Covenants. On 12 July 1843, Joseph received a revelation relating to the new and everlasting covenant that includes the eternal nature of the marriage covenant and indicates why the writings of Abraham were so necessary: "Go ye, therefore, and do the works of Abraham; enter ye into my law and ye shall be saved."[42] Without this law, we could not be saved, for the fullness of Joseph's great doctrinal knowledge would not have been available.

These beautiful scriptures are a fulfillment of the prophecy the Lord gave to Nephi: "I will be merciful unto the Gentiles in that day, insomuch that I will bring forth unto them, in mine own power, much of my gospel, which shall be plain and precious, saith the Lamb."[43]

The Book of Life of a Living Church

It should be mentioned that although the *Documentary History of the Church* is not scripture, it is primarily the work of Joseph Smith, Jr. Of the seven volumes of documentary history, Joseph was responsible for the first six as assembled by Church Historian B. H. Roberts.

Chapter 4

JAIL
PARTICIPANTS

The primary participants with the Prophet Joseph in the Liberty Jail experience were his brother Hyrum and Sidney Rigdon (constituting the three members of the First Presidency), Caleb Baldwin, Lyman Wight, and Alexander McRae. Their wives who came to visit were Emma Smith, Mary Fielding Smith, Nancy Baldwin, Eunice McRae, Harriet Wight, and Phebe Rigdon. Attorneys who represented the cause of the Prophet and his associates were Peter H. Burnett, Alexander Wm. Doniphan, John A. Gordon, Andrew S. Hughes, Amos Rees (Reese),[1] James S. Rollins, Joel Turnham, and William T. Wood. The law officers were Samuel Hadley, sheriff; James H. Ford, deputy sheriff; Samuel Tillery, deputy sheriff-jailer; and John Tillery, guard.

The Prisoners
Joseph Smith, Jr.

Joseph said of himself, "I have witnessed the visions of eternity, and beheld the glorious mansions of bliss, and the regions and the misery of the damned . . . have heard the voice of God, and communed with angels, and spoke as moved by the power of the Holy Ghost for the renewal of the everlasting covenant."[2] He further said, "It is my meditation all the day, and more than my meat and drink, to know how I shall make the Saints of God comprehend the visions that roll like an overflowing surge before my mind."[3]

Toward the end of the ordeal at Liberty Jail, he wrote to Emma, "With emotions known only to God, do I write this letter, . . . under

Joseph Smith, Jr., RLDS Archives, Independece, MO

these circumstances, defies the pen, or tongue, or Angels, to discribe, or paint, to the human mind being, . . . what we experienced."[4]

Of great solace to his companions were the words he spoke on the march to Independence: "Be of good cheer, the word of the Lord came to me last night that, whatever we may suffer during this captivity, not one of our lives should be taken."[5]

When the group of brethren were brought to Liberty Jail, Joseph wore a suit of black and carried a cloak of dark-colored material over his arm.[6] Many of the inhabitants of Liberty and surrounding areas came to see the prisoners' entrance into the jail. "The gaze of the spectators was concentrated upon Joseph, and his majestic air made a deep impression upon them. One lady in the crowd cried: 'Their Prophet looks like a gentleman!' Another looking at the group expressed the opinion: 'Well, they are fine looking men if they are Mormons.'"[7]

The Prophet was the last one to enter the jail. "He turned partly around, with a slow and dignified movement and looked upon the multitude. Then turning away and lifting his hat he said in a distinct voice, 'Good afternoon gentlemen.'"[8]

Joseph and Sidney Rigdon had left Kirtland earlier that same year. Joseph knew he would not die in the jail as, in addition to the comment made on the march to Liberty, he had told the brethren before leaving Kirtland, "One thing is certain, I shall see you again . . . for I have a promise of life five years, and they cannot kill me until that time is expired."[9]

Joseph remarked about the guards, "We are kept under strong guard, who continually watch day and night as indefatigable as the devil dogs in tempting and laying snares for the people of God."[10] He made mention of the law, the Constitution, and attorneys. Even before the Richmond incarceration, Emma said, "Joseph began to study law from books that were loaned him by Alexander Doniphan."[11] Joseph recognized that many of their problems materialized because of ignorance of the law.

Hyrum Smith

Hyrum Smith, RLDS Archives, Independence, MO

Hyrum Smith was born on 9 February 1800. He was five years older than Joseph and had his thirty-ninth birthday while he was in Liberty Jail. He was a participant with Joseph in most every major event involving the kingdom, and he "watched over his brother lest some harm come to him."[12] Hyrum said of his brother Joseph: "I have been acquainted with him ever since he was born, which was thirty-seven years in December last and I have not been absent from him at any one time not even for the space of six months, since his birth, to my recollection."[13]

Hyrum replaced his father as the Patriarch of the Church in 1841.[14] Hyrum was heir apparent to the Prophet[15] and was a counselor in the First Presidency.[16] It is said by those who knew his soul well that he was "the embodiment of the integrity of heart and the humility of soul that should characterize a latter-day saint. No wonder they discribed him as a perfect 'Mormon.'"[17] The most profound benediction about Hyrum came from the Savior. "Blessed is my servant Hyrum Smith; for I, the Lord love him because of the integrity of his heart, and because he loveth that which is right before me, saith the Lord."[18]

Hyrum gives some insight to events and feelings while he was in the jail: "We are often inspected by fools who act as though we were elephants or dromedarys or sea hogs or some monstrous whale or sea serpents. We have never had our teeth examined like an old horse, but expect [to] every day when . . . a new swarm come[s] that have never seen us."[19]

And, personally, "I traversed my prison house for hours, thinking of their [former friends and mobocrats] cruelty to my family, and the afflictions they brought upon the saints."[20] "I . . . endured almost everything but death, from the nauseous cell, and the wretched food we were obliged to eat."[21]

Hyrum's wife, Jerusha Barden, died in October 1837, leaving him with five small children. He later married Mary Fielding, who had their first child 19 November 1838 at Far West while Hyrum was in the Richmond Jail.

In the meridian of time, the Lord said of John the Baptist, "Among them that are born of women there hath not risen a greater than John the Baptist."[22] In our generation, Joseph could well have said that of his brother Hyrum.

Alexander McRae

Alexander McRae outlived all those who shared the Liberty Jail experience. He was born 7 September 1807 and was the youngest and the tallest of his companions in the jail. "He stood six foot six in his stocking feet. He was broad of shoulder and as far as physical courage was concerned, there was not a cowardly hair in his big red shaggy head. The only fear he had was of doing right himself."[23]

In March 1829, as a young man, Alexander enlisted in the United States Army in South Carolina[24] and served five years.[25] While in the army, or maybe before he enlisted, he learned the trade of a tailor.[26] He married Eunice Fitzgerald[27] in a small town in Kentucky following his discharge. After joining the Church, the McRaes moved to Far West. Alexander was elected a captain in the 23rd Regiment of the Missouri Militia.[28] He took a very active part in the defense of the Saints during the persecutions and mobbings in 1838.

Along with the Prophet and other brethren, Alexander was betrayed into the hands of the enemy. He passed through all the mock trials and hardships to which they all were subjected before their confinement at Liberty Jail. With these experiences, his declaration of the dedication of Joseph to the brethren bears stating. He said of the Prophet, "He always took up for the brethren, when their characters were assailed, sooner than for himself, no matter how unpopular it was to speak in their favor."[29]

Alexander must have had a fine voice because Joseph Smith III remembers a man singing two ballads while Joseph III was at the jail with his mother. He recalls the ballads being "The Massacre at the River Raisin" and the "Mobbers of Missouri," sung to the tune of "Hunters of Kentucky."[30] The singing was attributed to Alexander McRae.[31]

Alexander's wife Eunice visited him twice, once bringing their son John and once bringing her new baby whom the Prophet

Joseph blessed in the jail and gave him the name of Joseph.[32] When Eunice left with the children, instructions to Brigham and the Twelve were carefully concealed in the diapers worn by little Joseph. (See Appendix A.)

Alexander became interested in the Church when he heard the Mormons believed in baptism by immersion.[33] He and Eunice had to walk eight miles to hear the elders preach and made the return journey the same night on foot, carrying their young baby in their arms. When the spirit of conversion rested upon them, they walked sixteen miles to

Alexander McRae, LDS Church Archives, Salt Lake City, UT

the place of baptism, carrying John the whole distance. When they arrived, there were about two hundred men who had gathered on the banks of the stream. They were threatening the elders with violence if they proceeded with the baptism. The elders thought it would be wise to postpone the baptism. Alexander asked if he was worthy to be baptized. He was told that he was. "Then I demand baptism, and as for these men, I am not afraid of all the devils out of hell." He and Eunice were baptized, and none of the two hundred moved to stop them.[34] The McRaes then walked the sixteen miles home.[35]

Following the Liberty Jail confinement, Alexander later established himself as a tailor in Navuoo. He served as a captain of the Nauvoo Legion and was active in the defense of that city. When Joseph was killed, Alexander transferred his allegiance to Joseph's worthy successor and defended Brigham Young with the same zeal he had given to the Prophet Joseph.[36] He and his family went west with the Saints, and Alexander later became the second bishop of the Eleventh Ward in Salt Lake City and served in that calling for thirty-six years.

Liberty Jail had a profound effect on each of the men who were imprisoned there. In the case of Alexander, from that time on, he could never allow anyone to keep a bird in a cage in his home.[37]

Lyman Wight

Lyman Wight was born 9 May 1796 in Fairfield, New York, and was forty-three years old at the time of his imprisonment. He fought in the War of 1812. An early convert to the Church, he was baptized by Oliver Cowdery in November of 1830 and was one of the first to be ordained a high priest.[38] Lyman was elected commanding general at Zion's camp[39] and served as a colonel in the Missouri militia. He was one of the first and the most prominent Mormons to settle at Adam-ondi-Ahman, founding Wight's Settlement on a lovely hillside overlooking the Grand River.[40] He established one of his two cabins at Wight's ferry.[41] He served on the Far West High Council[42] and became one of the militia leaders there. Lyman also served as a counselor to John Smith, president of the stake at Adam-ondi-Ahman.[43] A devoted disciple of Joseph, he was later called as one of the twelve apostles—filling the vacancy created with the death of David W. Patten. In the quorum, he was given the designated name of "Wild Ram of the Mountains."[44]

After the betrayal by Colonel George M. Hinkle at Far West and the arrest by General Samuel Lucas, Lyman Wight was sought out in the evening by General Moses Wilson. An attempt was made to induce Lyman to betray Joseph Smith and swear falsely against him. Lyman adamantly refused. General Wilson said, "Wight, you are a strange man, but if you will not accept my proposal, you will be shot tomorrow morning at 6 o'clock." Colonel Wight replied, "Shoot and be damned."[45] This was the character of Lyman Wight; he was totally loyal to Joseph Smith and would have willingly died for his friends.

One of the best descriptions of their food in the jail came from Lyman:

> The mercies of the jailer were intolerable, feeding us with a scanty allowance on the dregs of coffee and tea from his own table, and fetching the provisions in a basket, without being cleaned, on which chickens had roosted the night before. Five days he fed the prisoners on human flesh, and from extreme hunger I was compelled to eat.[46]

During their time in the jail, Joseph told Lyman that he (Joseph) would not live to be forty years old but that Lyman was not to mention this comment until after Joseph's death.[47] Joseph also discussed with Lyman about Lyman's taking a group of Saints to Texas for colonization.[48] Following Joseph's death, Brigham rescinded the Texas colonization plan and asked that Lyman go west with the body of the

Lyman and Harriet Benton Wight, RLDS Archives, Independence, MO

Saints. Lyman was unable to transfer his allegiance from Joseph to Brigham; and following the outline Joseph had given, Lyman went to Texas, taking 150 members of the Church with him. He was there until his death.

Years later, one of the most profound exchanges of correspondence took place between Lyman and Wilford Woodruff. It teaches so very much and gives a wonderful insight into the life of an apostate apostle and his brethren of the quorum.[49]

President Woodruff was preparing a history of the Quorum of the Twelve and had written Brother Wight. In his letter, Elder Woodruff said:

> I wish Brother Wight you could come and pay us a visit. We will all be glad to see you. We have built up a beautiful City in the valley of the Mountains. Our census makes us about 80,000 souls and increasing fast—Mormonism is as great a trouble to the world as ever. All the Twelve are now in this country except O. Pratt, E. T. Benson, Erastus Snow and John Taylor who are abroad. . . . Mormonism is as good to me to day as it was when I was with you in the old log cabin in Clay County, and milking cows for Sister Wight and making brick for Col. Arthur's house.[50]

Lyman received the letter about a month and a half later. He wanted to know why the apostles had cut him off from the Church. He wrote back:

I received your favor on the 12th inst dated July 1st, 1857. You may be assured it was well received it being the first I have received from any of the twelve for the last 12 years. I had come to the conclusion that they had become so far advanced in the order of the kingdom and become so popular in temporal things that they had entirely forgotten that such an uncouth old plough goger [gouger or codger?] as Lyman Wight had an existence on the face of the earth, but I yet live and am bold to say that of the doctrine of Joseph Smith the Angel of the seventh dispensation there is not a firmer believer or defender on the face of the earth and hold every ordination given me as sacred as I did the day they ware given, and if the death of Br. Joseph gave one of the twelve a supremacy over the others I have it yet to learn, did Brigham Young have any authority at Joseph's death more than he received from Br. Joseph. If you answer no I ask whe[n]ce did he receive authority to disannul revelations given by Br. Joseph? See Book of Doctrine & Covenants p. 396 par 7th concerning building the Nauvoo house and by careful examination you will find that I have a revelation given to me which is not to end while I live on the earth, and no man on the earth has a right to take that mission from me being given of God the highest of all. Yet I did consider it my duty to counsel with the twelve, and the fifties [Council of Fifty] had not circumstances ordered it otherwise the mission I am now on Br. Willford I received of the prophet of God, and it was well known by the twelve at that time that Joseph was striving very hard to come to this very place with 250,000 men he therefore requested me to come and establish a church in this region and such mission was even talked of while in jail where I had the advantage of six months teaching and received many things that is yet unknown to the church. . . . Joseph blessed me many times while in jail and prophesied much on my head and gave me much good instruction which is long to be remembered . . . never having refused to obey the prophet I started in all good faith, had but just got out of hearing before I was accused from the stand by who would be big of beging the mission of Br. Joseph who to passify me gave his consent and that I run away from Nauvoo to get rid of fighting. . . . I soon learnt that I was cut off from the church but never learnt what it was for, after lerning this I found I had no where to go but to my beloved Br. Joseph and to the Saviour with the former I have had many communications face to face without a dimming vail between, and received many good instructions this has been to me full satisfactory.

A postscript was added in which many questions were asked concerning the priesthood. Then, the question was asked:

Can you tell me why I was cut off from the church and such men as Orson Hide, W. W. Phelps; T. B. Marsh received in, have they ever asked Joseph Smith, Hyrum Smith, Sidney Rigdon or myself to forgive them for writing letters to the Governor and swearing against us with a view of swearing away our lives?[51]

Although Lyman's letter was dated 14 August 1857, it did not reach Elder Woodruff until June the following year. In reply, Elder Woodruff wrote:

> We have ever entertained the warmest feelings for you personally, and regret exceedingly that your course has led you from our midst; instead of building up ourselves, we have labored as one man to build up the Kingdom of God; you complain that Pres. Young used the pronoun I too much to suit you. He was the President of the Twelve, and the quorum backed him up and sustained him, you claiming more authority than the Eleven, went your own way, we regret the result exceedingly; it was your duty not only to council with the Twelve, but to take their council.
>
> When Joseph was taken away, the Priesthood continued with the quorum of Twelve, with the fullness of the authority of the Priesthood, and when you turned your heels against it, Satan had you in his sieve, and like chaff you were blown away. Come back again brother Lyman and dwell in Zion, and resume your duty enjoined upon you by the Lord. . . .
>
> You was cut off from the Church in the latter part of 1848, the subject was brought up on the receipt of a pamphlet which you published against the Authorities of the Church.
>
> Brother Lyman come home to Zion, mingle in our midst, confess and forsake your sins, and do right, as we all men have to do, in order to enjoy the favor of God, and the gift of the Holy Ghost, and have fellowship with the Saints."[52]

Lyman never received Wilford Woodruff's letter. Lyman died on 31 March 1858 near Mountain Valley.

Caleb Baldwin

Born 2 September 1791 in Nobletown, Orange County, New York, Caleb Baldwin was the oldest of the group.[53] A veteran of the War of 1812, he served as an ensign in the U.S. Navy. After the war, he moved to Cleveland, Ohio. It was here that he met and married Nancy Kingsbury on 7 December 1914.[54] They heard Parley P. Pratt preach on Mormonism and, after attending several meetings, were impressed with the teachings. On 14 November 1830, just eight months after the Church was organized, they were baptized by Parley P. Pratt.[55] Soon after, they left their home and moved to Jackson County to be with the other Saints.

It was there he took part in the battle of the Big Blue River on 4 November 1833. The skirmish lasted several days. The Baldwins had a home on the Big Blue in the David Whitmer community. Caleb nearly lost his life in this episode. The mob struck in the middle of the night and, pulling Caleb out of bed, severely whipped him, leaving scars he carried for the rest of his life. Their house and barn were burned to the ground.[56]

Caleb was called to serve a mission with Jacob Gates, a new convert, and arrived at Flat Branch, Sangamon County, Illinois, on 18 February 1836.[57] Following his mission, he returned to Far West and became embroiled in the persecution that had become rampant. He was among those betrayed and arrested with the Prophet and was confined in Liberty Jail.

Following the brethren's release, Caleb and his family settled in Nauvoo. He contracted malaria and suffered with it off and on for the rest of his life. When the Saints went west, Caleb and his family were among them. Nine months after their arrival in the Salt Lake Valley, he died in June 1849. He was the thirteenth person buried in the Salt Lake City Cemetery.[58]

Sidney Rigdon

Sidney Rigdon was born in Saint Clair Township, Allegheny County, Pennsylvania, on 19 February 1793.[59] He was forty-five years old during the Liberty Jail period.

Sidney first heard about the Church from Parley P. Pratt. Parley had earlier studied under Sidney Rigdon, who was a prominent minister in Amherst, Ohio. Sidney later helped found the church called Disciples of Christ, or Campbellites. He consented to the elders presenting their message in his church. Many, including Sidney, were converted. When Sidney made a trip east to meet Joseph Smith, the Prophet was impressed with him. Joseph and Sidney were admonished to "strenthen the Church . . . especially in Colesville."[60] It was in Colesville that Sidney's oratorical gifts were first evidenced. He later consecrated and dedicated the land of Missouri unto the Lord. In June of 1838, Sidney gave a heated discourse known as the Salt Sermon and, on July 4, followed with an Independence Day speech. Both of these addresses added fuel to an already explosive relationship with anti-Mormon hostility.

At the time of Liberty Jail, he was a counselor to Joseph in the First Presidency. During their imprisonment at Richmond, Sidney became very ill. He became ill with a fever again in Liberty. He had periods of depression and claimed his suffering was greater than that of Jesus Christ.[61]

On 25 January 1839, after petitioning to have their case heard, the prisoners were brought before Clay County Judge Joel Turnham. Sidney stated that this was the first time since he had been arrested that he heard the evidence behind the charge of treason.[62] He asked to plead his own case and was allowed to do so. His eloquence so touched the crowd of antagonistic Mormon haters that he had them in tears. Alexander Doniphan, their attorney, said of this instance, "Such a burst of eloquence it was never my fortune to listen to, at its close

Sidney Rigdon, RLDS Archives, Independence, MO

there was not a dry eye in the room, all were moved to tears."[63]

The judge then said, "The prisoner is discharged to the custady of the court. Mr. Rigdon is free to go his way." One of the leading men of the crowd picked up his hat and, turning to the bystanders, said, "We came here determined to do injury to this man. He is innocent of crime, as has been made to appear. And now, gentlemen, out with your money and help the man to return to his destitute family." After passing the hat, he placed a hundred dollars in Elder Rigdon's hands and said, "Now, old gentleman, make the quickest possible time to your family, who need you and your help."[64]

Sidney was held by Sheriff Samuel Hadley and jailer Samuel Tillery until they were sure it was safe for him to leave.[65] After dark on 5 February 1839, he was given a horse, a pistol, and a guide who knew the country. Sidney said, "He [Sheriff Hadley] took me by the hand and bade me farewell, telling me to make my escape, which I did with all possible speed."[66]

The Wives

Emma Hale Smith

Emma Hale was born 10 July 1804 to Isaac and Elizabeth Lewis Hale. Her parents farmed near Harmony, Pennsylvania, and operated a country inn. Emma met Joseph Smith, Jr. when he boarded at her

Emma Hale Smith, RLDS Archives, Independence, MO

father's inn while working in the area. Her father bitterly opposed their courtship, but Joseph proposed to Emma; and she, "preferring him to all others" she had met, accepted his offer. They were married in South Bainbridge, New York on 18 January 1827. She bore nine children, four of whom did not live. Among those that died were twins. At the same time, twins were born to the Murdock family, and the mother died. Joseph and Emma adopted these babies.

The Lord called her an "Elect Lady."[67] He told her, "And the office of thy calling shall be for a comfort unto my servant, Joseph Smith, Jun., thy husband in his afflictions."[68] She was given the assignment to compile the first hymnal; and, later, she became the first president of the Relief Society. She said of Joseph, "My husband was my crown," and her greatness and her glory is measured in that context. A letter from Emma in Quincy, Illinois, to Joseph in Liberty Jail written March 1839 may serve best to describe Emma's love as well as her complete and total support during the Liberty Jail incarceration:

> I shall not attempt to write my feelings altogether, for the situation in which you are, the walls, bars and bolts, rolling rivers, running streams, rising hills, sinking valleys and spreading prairies that separate us, and the cruel injustice that first cast you into prison and still holds you there. . . . Was it not for conscious innocence and the direct interposition of divine mercy, I am very sure I never should have been able to have endured the scenes of suffering that I have passed through . . . but I still live and am yet willing to suffer more if it is the will of kind heaven, that I should for your sake . . . and if God does not record our sufferings and avenge our wrongs on them that are guilty, I shall be sadly mistaken. . . . You may be astonished at my bad writing and incoherent manner, but you will pardon all when you reflect how hard it would be for you to write when your hands were stiffened with hard work and your heart convulsed with intense anxiety . . . but I hope there is better days to come to us yet. . . . I am ever yours affectionately. Emma Smith.[69]

Emma endured the trials and tribulations that were heaped upon Joseph right along with him. Her convictions of the great work that was before them was the foundation of her faith and endurance. This dedication is depicted in the following excerpt written by Joseph about Emma from Independence in a letter dated 4 November 1838, just twenty-six days before he was put in Liberty Jail: "My dear and beloved companion, of my bosom, in tribulation, and affliction."[70]

Emma visited her husband three times while he was in the Liberty dungeon. Each time, she had to endure two winter days and a night traveling a distance of forty-one miles by wagon. The brethren were brought to Liberty Jail on 1 December 1838. Seven days later, the first visitors to the jail were Emma Smith and Phebe Rigdon.

The suffering of the Saints cannot be adequately described. Emma's house was entered and ransacked more than once. When word came from Joseph that blankets were needed, she wept as she had none to send him. William E. McLellin had forced his way into the Smith home and taken all the blankets and other valuables. (See Chapter 7.)

Later, in 1842, reflecting on a visit from Emma while Joseph was in great danger and difficulty, Joseph wrote:

> With what unspeakable delight and what transports of joy swelled my bosom, when I took by the hand, on that night, my beloved Emma—she that was my wife, even the wife of my youth, and the choice of my heart. Many were the reverberations of my mind when I contemplated for a moment the many scenes we had been called to pass through, the fatigues and the toils, the sorrows and sufferings, and the joys and consolations, from time to time, which had strewed our paths and crowned our board. Oh what a commingling of thought filled my mind for the moment, again she is here, even in the seventh trouble— undaunted, firm, unwavering—unchangeable, affectionate Emma![71]

Emma's care and kindness to many ill and homeless Saints, along with the care of Joseph's family, his parents, his brothers and sisters, and his nieces and nephews, is legend. Following Joseph's death and the Saints' exodus from Nauvoo a year and a half later, Emma, a forty-one-year-old widow, was left with her aged mother-in-law and five children ranging in age from fourteen years old to fifteen months to care for. Emma endured her tribulations with great patience and never lost her faith in God.

Before his death, "Joseph Smith" and "Companion" Emma Hale Smith received the "second anointing" and were both "ordained to the highest & holiest order of the Priesthood."[72]

Mary Fielding Smith, RLDS Archives, Independence, MO

Mary Fielding Smith

Mary Fielding was born 21 July 1801 at Honidon, Bedfordshire, England. She immigrated to Toronto, Canada, in 1834 to join her youngest brother, Joseph, and her sister, Mercy. After listening to Parley P. Pratt preach about Mormonism, all three of them were baptized. The following spring, the Fieldings moved to Kirtland:

> When she [Mary] and her equally handsome sister, Mercy, came to Kirtland in 1837, trim, straight, dark-haired and dark eyes, with delicately blooming cheeks and finely molded, graceful figures, clad in dainty silks of modern grace, they were the observed of all observers. Their refined and stately ways made them a shining mark in Kirtland Society. Wherever they went they were spoken of as those "lovely English girls." Refinement, strength, courage, integrity, modesty and infinite sweetness and tenderness—these were the prevailing characteristics of the Fielding sisters.[73]

On 24 December 1837, Mary married the widowed Hyrum Smith. She was his second wife and immediately assumed the responsibility of caring for his five motherless children, which she did with unwavering fidelity. They later settled in Far West and suffered the persecution of godless men with the rest of the Saints in Missouri.

Following the extermination order given by Governor Boggs in October 1838, Joseph, Hyrum, and others were arrested and eventually were taken to Liberty Jail. Twelve days after Hyrum's arrest in Far West, she gave birth to her first son on 13 November 1838. Mary became ill with a severe cold, which brought on chills and fever. She was forced to remain in bed for several months. Her sister Mercy stayed with her as Mercy's husband, Robert B. Thompson, had fled ahead of the mob and had not been heard of for three months. Mercy had a five-month-old baby and nursed both Mary's and her own. Mercy also cared for the five children.

While Mary was so ill and her husband was in the Liberty dungeon, an armed mob led by Samuel Bogart, the infamous Methodist preacher, forced its way into the Smith home, broke open Hyrum's trunk, and carried away papers and other valuables. Around 1 February 1839, at Hyrum's request, Mary and Mercy traveled forty miles to Liberty. Mary was too ill to sit up and so was placed on a bed in the wagon. She held her little son, now eleven weeks old, and also Mercy's baby, eight months, much of the time. The weather was extremely cold, and they suffered much on the journey. When they arrived at the prison in the evening, they were admitted to the jail, and the doors were closed upon them. Mercy later wrote:

> It would be beyond my power to describe my feelings when we were admitted into the jail. . . . We could not help feeling a sense of horror on realizing that we were locked up in that dark and dismal den.[74] [It was] a night never to be forgotten. A sleepless night. . . . [A]s long as memory lasts will remain in my recollection the squeaking hinges of that door which closed upon the noblest men on earth. Who can imagine our feelings as we traveled homeward, but would I sell that honor bestowed upon me of being locked up in jail with such characters for good? No! No![75]

After their arrival, Hyrum took his small son in his arms, blessed him, and gave him the name of Joseph Fielding Smith. Joseph F. Smith became the sixth prophet of the Church. His son, Joseph Fielding Smith, became the tenth prophet of the Church and dedicated the Liberty Jail Visitors' Center in September of 1963.

Mary received all of her ordinances and was sealed to her husband. After Hyrum's martyrdom, she went west with the Saints to Salt Lake. The continued hardship of the frontier life proved too much for her. On 11 December 1852, she died in the home of Heber C. Kimball following two months of illness. It was written of her, "Mary Fielding Smith was a Saint, if ever one lived on this troubled earth. She was a heroine in her own right, by reason of her greatness of spirit and soul."[76]

Eunice Fitzgerald McRea

Eunice Fitzgerald was born 7 February 1818 in Newcastle, Henry County, Kentucky. She was the daughter of Joseph Hawkins and Catherine Parkhurst Fitzgerald. While Alexander was working for David Fitzgerald, Eunice's brother, he fell in love with her; and they were married on 2 October 1834 at Newcastle. Alexander was twenty-seven, and Eunice was sixteen.[77] Soon after their marriage, they moved across the Ohio River into Ripley County, Indiana, where their first child, John, was born 30 January 1836.[78] Eunice embraced the gospel of Jesus Christ with her husband. They were baptized in June 1837. In September, they moved to Far West, Missouri. Eunice later said,

Eunice Fitzgerald McRae and youngest daughter, LDS Church Archives, Salt Lake City, UT

"Alexander was a very profane man and was addicted to the use of tobacco, but he made a complete reversal of his life."[79]

After Alexander was incarcerated at Liberty Jail, Eunice wrote: "I visited my husband several times while he was in Liberty jail. I carried letters to and from the Prophet, that were sent by his family."[80] Once, the guards searched her before admitting her, but usually they failed to take this precaution. Once, she took a pistol in without being detected. On another of her visits, she fastened a butcher knife to the inside of her leg and carried the knife in with her. Joseph told her that was just the kind of excuse the Missourians wanted to kill them, so she took the knife home with her. When she carried letters in or out, she put them inside her stockings. Eunice wrote the following experience in the Liberty Jail:

> Several times when I visited, I sat down at the table and ate with them. The food was brought in and we all sat down together. The Prophet always deferred to his brother Hyrum, and as he was the eldest he had Hyrum sit at the head of the table and serve. Any meat that was to be carved was carved by Hyrum. One day a piece of roast meat was brought in that looked very dark, as though it had been burned. Brother Hyrum took the carving knife and fork, put the fork into the meat and they fell from his hands. He picked up the tools again and attempted to carve the meat and they fell from his hands again. After the second attempt, the Prophet said: "Do not touch it, for it is human flesh!" It was afterwards told that the guards boasted they had cut a piece of flesh from the thigh of a dead Negro and had fed it to the Mormons.[81]

Eunice was among the exodus of the Saints driven out of Missouri and was at Quincy, Illinois, when Alexander joined her. Before leaving Far West, she was visited at her home by four men who came there to search for counterfeit money and for dies for making it. She gave them access to all parts of the house, and they searched every part of the cupboards and dresser drawers without success. Then, they tore a hole in the log floor, and two of them got down and began to dig and throw dirt out. When they found nothing, they turned to the door, to be confronted by Mrs. McRae with a pistol in her hand. She said, "Gentlemen, you have had your fun, now put all that dirt back in the hole you took it from, and put the floor down as it was, and clean the floor. The first man who attempts to leave before it is completed will get killed." They had only to look at her to see she meant what she said, and they complied.[82]

Alexander received his endowments 18 December 1845. Eunice was endowed 7 February 1846. They were sealed on 23 March 1848 by Brigham Young.[83]

Nancy Kingsbury Baldwin

Nancy Kingsbury was born 7 December 1814 in Cuyahoga County, Ohio, the daughter of James Kingsbury. She married Caleb Baldwin on 7 Dececmeber 1814.[84] Shortly after their marriage, they made their home in Cleveland, Ohio, and were among the first converts to the Church in Ohio. Nancy had nine children—seven daughters and two sons—the last two being born at Liberty, Clay County, Missouri.[85]

After Caleb's arrest and incarceration at Liberty jail, Nancy visited her husband at the jail twice. (See Appendix A.)

Harriet Benton Wight

Harriet Benton Wight was born 19 March 1801 in Litchfield, Connecticut, the daughter of Dr. John Benton and Sarah Bradley. Harriet was a farmer by trade.[86] She married Lyman Wight on 5 January 1823 in Henrietta, Monroe, New York. She had six children—four boys and two girls—born between 1823 and 1838.[87]

On two different occasions, Harriet was without a roof over her head while giving birth to her babies. Her only protection from the cold was under the cover of blankets that had been hung for that purpose. While her babies were in the birth process, her husband was being pursued by a mob.

She visited her husband at the jail twice. (See Appendix A.) Harriet died 26 February 1889 at Greeley, Nebraska.

Phebe Brooks Rigdon

Phebe Brooks met Sidney Rigdon through Adamson Bentley, a popular Baptist minister of the day whose wife was Phebe's sister. It was Bentley who trained Sidney and started him in a ministry.[88]

Phebe married Sidney on 12 June 1820. She was completely devoted to her husband and his quest for religious truth.[89] Records have been found of ten children to this union,[90] and Van Wagoner in his autobiography of Sidney states that Phebe was pregnant with their eleventh child during January of 1838[91] and "Birthing twelve children, burying several."[92] Their journals show Phebe with much economic and social concern about leaving her husband's congregation and embracing "Mormonism." Sidney asked Phebe, "My dear, you have followed me once into poverty, are you willing to do the same again?" Phebe replied, "I have weighed the matter, I have contemplated on the circumstances in which we may be placed, I have counted the cost, and I am perfectly satisfied to follow you; it is my desire to do the will of God, come life or come death."[93]

Mrs. Rigdon was well educated for her day, with a fine mind and exquisite penmanship.[94] They were married fifty-six years. A great tribute to her is her unfaltering love for Sidney through this time, which included extreme hardships, chronic poverty, mental depressions, and religious intensity. She visited her husband twice at the jail (see Appendix A) and was at the jail a third time, for the well-planned escape, on 5 February, to accompany her husband to safety in the state of Illinois.[95]

The Attorneys

The first encounter the Saints had with Missouri attorneys was in 1833 when Governor Daniel Dunklin advised the brethren to secure legal representation in seeking redress for the losses in Jackson County. From this time on, Joseph and the brethren became closely associated with a few attorneys who had been employed by the Saints. During the eight years in Missouri, they became very good friends. It is interesting that Wm. T. Wood, David R. Atchison, Alexander W. Doniphan, and Amos Rees were all involved in various degrees during the Far West siege, arrest, and trial.

Later, William T. Wood, David R. Atchison, and Alexander W. Doniphan were admitted to practice as attorneys at law in Clay County. It was just in time to be of service to the brethren when they were incarcerated in that county.[96] Joseph makes reference to his first experience with them in his letter to Emma dated Richmond, 12 November 1838. Joseph stated: "The trial will begin today for some of us, Lawyer Reese, and we expect Doniphan, will plead our cause.

We could get no others in time for the trial. They are able men and will do well no doubt."[97]

The amounts of monies paid were unusually high. In 1833, each of the four attorneys were paid $250, a total of $1,000.[98] During the Richmond trials, $5,000 was paid.[99] Joseph commented that he had paid attorneys over $50,000 in Missouri. The attorneys who were used were almost all given appointments by Governor Boggs (see Exhibit 4.4), and almost all were indicted by the courts for betting, along with Hyrum Smith. (See Exhibit 4.1, Exhibit 4.2, and Exhibit 4.3 and transcription.)

Peter H. Burnett, Clay County Archives and Historical Library, Liberty, MO

Peter H. Burnett

Peter H. Burnett was a member of the Missouri militia, serving under Brigadier General Alexander Doniphan. It was Doniphan who refused to carry out the execution order for Joseph and the brethren who had been sentenced to be shot at Far West.[100] Alexander sought Burnett's advice when Alexander was given the execution order and received moral support from him.[101]

Burnett said that Joseph's views were "strange and striking" and that his manner was "so earnest" and apparently "so candid, that you could not but be interested. There was a kind, familiar look about him that pleased you. . . . [He had] the capacity for discussing a subject in different aspects and for proposing many views, even of ordinary matters." He further said of Joseph that he saw Joseph "out among the crowds, conversing freely with everyone, and seeming to be perfectly at ease. In the short space of five days, he had managed so to mollify his enemies that he could go unprotected among them without the slightest danger."[102]

It was the Mormon problems of Missouri that actually helped get Mr. Burnett out of merchandising and back into law.[103]

Burnett was the lead attorney for the prisoners while they were in Liberty Jail, and he visited them at the jail six times. (See Appendix A.)

April Term 1839

State of Missouri
vs
Amos Rees } Indictment for Betting

Now at this day came the Circuit Attorney who prosecutes for the State in this behalf as well as the said defendant in his own proper Person it being forth[with] demanded of him how he will acquit himself of the matters and things in said Indictment alledged against him for Plea thereof saith that he is guilty in manner and form as charged against him in said Indictment Whereupon the Court here doth assess the Punishment of said defendant to a fine of five dollars. It is therefore considered by the Court that the said defendant make his fine to the State of Missouri for the use of the County of Daviess to be rendered of five dollars aforesaid assessed as aforesaid together with her costs by her in this behalf Expended and that she have thereof Execution-

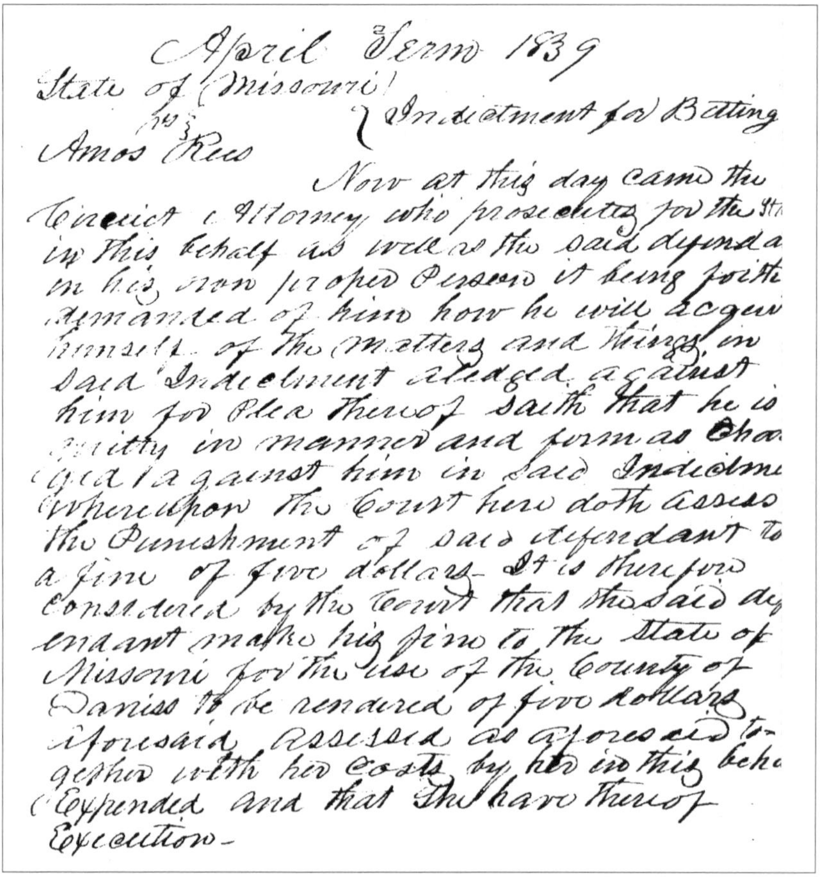

Exhibit 4.1: Betting charge filed against Amos Rees, Daviess County Court Archives, Gallatin, MO

The State of Missouri
vs
Alexander Doniphan } Indictment for Betting

Now at this day came here in open Court Peter H Burnet and acknowledged himself to owe and be indebted to the State of Missouri for the use of the County of Daviess to be levied of his Goods and Chattles Lands and Tenements but to be void upon this condition that the said Alexander Donophan appear by himself or attorney on the first day of the next Term of the Circuit Court to be holden for the County of Daviess, before said Court, then and there to answer the said Indictment, and not depart the said Court without leave thereof-

Exhibit 4.2: Betting charge filed against Alexander Doniphan, Daviess County Court Archives, Gallatin, MO

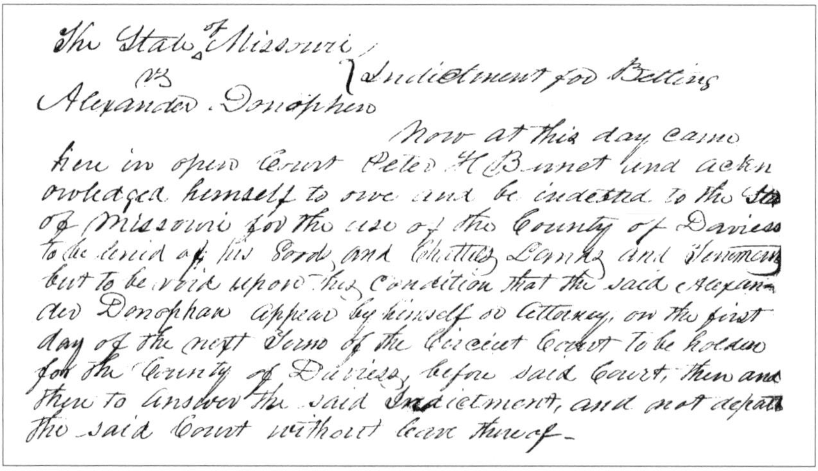

Exhibit 4.3: Betting charge filed against Hyrum Smith, Daviess County Court Archives, Gallatin, MO

TRANSCRIPTION OF EXHIBIT 4.3

State of Missouri	)	**In the Circuit Court**
County of Clay	)	**April Term Eighteen**
Clay County Court	)	**Hundred and Thirty Nine**

The grand jurors of the State of Missouri for the body of the County of Clay aforesaid upon their oath present that Hiram Smith late of said county on the twentieth day of December Eighteen Hundred and Thirty Eight with force and arms at the county aforesaid did bet a large sum of money to wit. the sum of twenty five cents upon a game then and there played by means of a pack of playing cards then and there being which said pack of playing cards was there and then a gambling device adapted devised and designed for the purpose of playing a game of chance for money and property against the form of the statute in such and as made and provided against the peace and dignity of the state.

William T. Wood

Circuit Attorney

Of these visits, he said:

> We apprehended that we may be mobbed, our clients taken from
> us and hung. . . . We determined to do our duty at all hazards
> and to sell our lives as dearly as possible if necessary. . . . We
> armed ourselves and had a circle of brave faithful friends armed
> around us at the hearing. I made the opening speech; Doniphan
> made the closing argument. As he arose to speak, I whispered to
> him: "Doniphan, let yourself out, my good fellow; and I will kill
> the first man that attacks you." He did let himself out, in one of
> the most eloquent and withering speeches I ever heard. The
> maddened crowd foamed and gnashed their teeth, but only to
> make him more and more intrepid. He faced that terrible storm
> with the most noble courage. All the time I sat within six feet of
> him with my hand on my pistol, calmly determined to do as I
> had promised him.[104]

Mr. Burnett again defended the brethren when they were
remanded back to Daviess County in Gallatin. He was appointed
circuit attorney for the Fifth Judicial Circuit a year later, April 1840.
(See Exhibit 4.4.) His distinguished career eventually took him to
California where he became its first governor and later a supreme
court judge.[105] He was the governor of California when Deseret
applied to be admitted to the Union as East California in 1850.[106]

Peter Burnett and Alexander Doniphan were close friends in
this early frontier setting. Mr. Burnett later dedicated his book, "Old
Pioneer," "To Col. Alexander W. Doniphan—The Xenophon of the
Mexican War, The able and eloquent advocate, the man of undoubted
integrity. This work is dedicated, as evidence of the admiration and
esteem of his old friend. The Author." [107]

W. Alexander Doniphan

W. A. Doniphan was born in Mason County, Kentucky, 9 July
1808. His father had come to Kentucky with Daniel Boone.
Alexander's mother was bright and trained Alexander well, as there
was no school. He received his formal education at the Methodist
College in Augusta, Kentucky. Alexander studied law in the office of
the Honorable Martin P. Marshall, a kinsman of Chief Justice John
Marshall of the Supreme Court of the United States. In 1830,
Alexander immigrated to Lexington, Missouri, with a license to
practice law. Three years later, he moved to Liberty in Clay County
and practiced law for thirty years.[108] Doniphan never was a
prosecutor; he always took the part of the defendant. In Liberty, he
established residences at two locations. He was a state legislator for
Missouri in 1836, 1840, and 1854 and loved the region very much.

Monday April the 20th AD 1840
This day Peter H Burnett Presented to Court a Commission
from the Governor of the State of Missouri as follows to wit
Lilburn W Boggs Governor of the State of Missouri
To all who shall see these presents Greeting Know ye that repos-
ing Especial trust and confidence in the integrity and abil-
ities of Peter H Burnett I do hereby appoint and commission
him Circuit Attorney within and for the fifth Judicial
Circuit of the State of Missouri And do authorize and
empower him to discharge the duties of said Office according to law to hold said Office with all the powers and
privileges and emoluments to the same [illegible] ap-
pertaining until the legal termination thereof
In Testimony Whereof I have hereunto set my
hand and caused the great seal of the State of Missouri to be affixed at the City of Jefferson this thirteenth day of March in the year of our Lord one
thousand Eight hundred and forty of the Indepen
of the United States the sixty fourth and of this
State the Twentieth
Lilburn W Boggs
by the Governor
Jas L Minor Secretary of State
on which Commission is the following endorse-
ment . I Peter H Burnett do Solemnly Swear
that I will support the Constitution of the United
States and the Constitution of the State of Missouri
And that I will faithfully demean my self in
Office Peter H Burnett
Sworn and Subscribed to in Open Court this
20th day of April AD1840
Saml Tilley Clerk

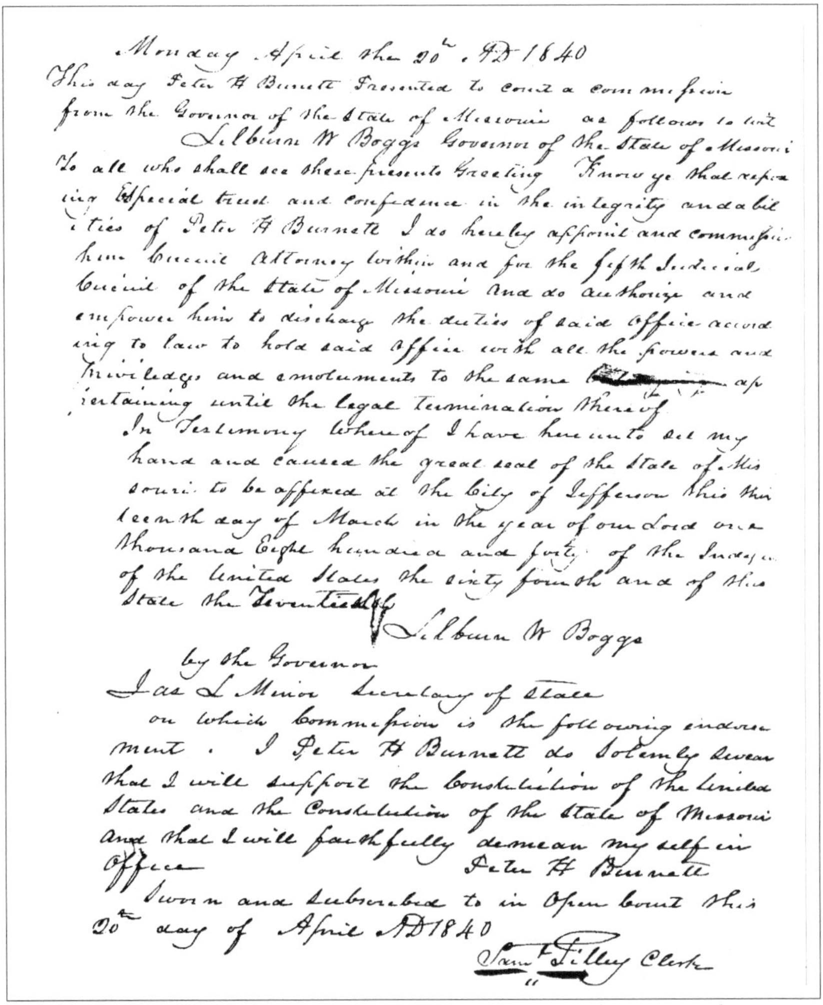

Exhibit 4.4: Peter H. Burnett's appointment by Governor Boggs to the position of circuit attorney in 1840, Clay County Court Archives, Liberty, MO

Colonel Doniphan once commented:

> It was a common error (and not just of Mormons) to think that the first emigrants (southerners) were wanting in education and the higher order of intelligence. No greater mistake was ever made. The drones never migrate, but live and die near the old homestead. The thinking, energetic, self-reliant ones dare to encounter and overcome the hardships of frontier life. Sloth and stupidity never achieve conquests; the successful factors are energy and intellect.[109]

By befriending and defending the Mormons against expulsion from Jackson County in 1833, Doniphan jeopardized his standing

Alexander W. Doniphan (Circa 1849), Daniel J.
Bortko, Liberty, MO

with the community. During his first term, he was successful in persuading the Missouri legislature to create Caldwell County for the Mormons. He was better acquainted with the various causes of difficulties between the citizens and Mormons than any other nonmember. In November 1838, when anti-Mormon militia surrounded Far West and arrested the Prophet and six other men, Doniphan was given the order to execute them. He refused to obey the order, thus risking the possibility of court martial. This valiant response preserved the lives of Joseph and the other brethren. By putting his own safety and career in peril, he became a true friend and hero to the Mormon people.[110] When Judge Austin King, the circuit court judge from 1837-45, who later became governor of the State of Missouri, declared there was no law for the "Mormons" in the state of Missouri, Doniphan told Joseph, "Though a legion of angels from the opening heavens should declare your innocence, the courts and populace have decreed your destruction."[111]

Doniphan visited the jail three times. (See Appendix A.) On another occasion, he had Joseph brought to his office for consultation. It was at this time that Joseph prophesied to Alexander about the purging that would come to Jackson County, Missouri—that it would be one hundred times worse than what the Missourians had done to the Mormons. (See Chapter 13.)

Alexander was once asked by a reporter what kind of a people the Mormons were. He replied:

> They were northern people, who, on account of their decline to own slaves and their denunciation of the system of slavery, were termed "free soilers." The majority of them were intelligent, industrious, and law-abiding citizens. . . . While they resided in Clay County, they were peaceful during their stay with us; not one was ever accused of a crime of any kind.[112]

In April 1846, at the outbreak of the Mexican War, Doniphan recruited 856 troops for the governor. This group of recruits became known as the Colonel Doniphan Expedition and was the most colored and publicized of the entire war.

That he was highly revered by Joseph and Emma is found in the name given to their son. Alexander Hale Smith was born 2 June 1838 at Far West, Missouri, and was named after the Missouri attorney.

John A. Gordon

Mr. Gordon represented Joseph in the court action against Wm. McLellin. (See Exhibt 4.5 and transcription.) He visited Liberty Jail on 16 January and 1 March. (See Chapter 7 and Appendices A and B.)

Andrew S. Hughes[113]

Andrew S. Hughes, a general in the Missouri militia, was involved at Far West.[114] After Dr. Alvord testified, General Hughes was brought in as counsel at Richmond. As a sleeper seated among the prisoners, he proved very effective. Later, Hughes visited the brethren at Liberty Jail on 18 January 1839, as a consultant for their attorneys.

Amos Rees (Reese)

At Richmond, Andrew S. Hughes,[115] Amos Rees, and Alexander Doniphan were the main attorneys, with Peter Burnett present but not helping.[116] Although it is not known if Rees ever visited Liberty Jail, he was helpful in working with the prisoners in trying to obtain witnesses. Rees is shown on the 1830 census of Clay County as between twenty and thirty years of age with no other family.

During the siege of Far West in October of 1838, Amos Rees is mentioned by Liliburn Boggs, commander in chief of the Missouri Militia, in a letter to General John B. Clark. Governor Boggs identifies Rees as the source of information that put the Mormons in such bad light, the one impetus that started military action. (See Exhibit 4.6.) Rees had his residence at Richmond[117] but later moved to Daviess County, which many court records show.[118] Living in the county and being familiar with proceedings, Rees and Peter Burnett were the counsel during these legal proceedings at Gallatin held in a rough log school house of twenty-five square feet.[119]

James S. Rollins

James T. Rollins from Boone County was an attorney for the defendants.[120] He later became a state legislator from that county, and he had sympathy for the Mormon petitions and voiced it. But he was overruled by the tremendous pressures of the mob lobbyist.[121]

Exhibit 4.5 (Continued on next page)

appertain to him but contriving and
fraudulently intending craftily and
and subtilly to deceive and defraud
the said plaintiff in this behalf hath
not as yet delivered the said Library
of books, cloth calico or other articles
or any part thereof to the said plaintiff
(although often requested so to do) but
so to do hath hitherto wholly refused
and still refuses. And afterwards to
wit on the tenth day of September
in the year eighteen hundred and thir
-ty eight at the county of Clay afore-
-said converted and disposed of the
said library of books, cloth calico
and other articles to his the said defen-
-dants own use to the damage of
the said plaintiff of five hundred
dollars and therefore he brings
suit &c

J. A. Gordon

Att Pl'ff

Exhibit 4.5: Lawsuit filed by Joseph Smith, Jr. against E. McCleland (McLellin) filed by J.A.
Gordon, Attorney for Plaintiff, Clay County Archives and Historical Library, Liberty, MO

TRANSCRIPTION OF EXHIBIT 4.5

STATE OF MISSOURI

Clay Circuit Court
 April Term 1839
Clay County to wit

Joseph Smith Jr. complains of William E. McCleland being in the custody of Li J a plea of trespass on the case. For said whereas the said plaintiff here before to wit on the first day of September in the year of our Lord eighteen hundred and thirty eight at the county of Clay a — =Jones and was lawfully prophicited as of his own property of certain goods and chaffles to wit of a Library of books part of which were in the Hebrew and _____languages the balance in the english language treating of history, divinity and general literature, twenty yards of broad cloth, 20 yards of linen and forty yards of calico with various other articles value to wit of the value of five hundred dollars lawful money of Missouri and being so prophisied thereof so the said plaintiffs afterwards to wit on the day and year first above mentioned at Clay county aforesaid causually lost the said library of books, cloth, calico and other articles out of his possession and the same afterward to wit on the day and year last aforesaid at the county afore said come to the proposition of the said defendant by finding yet the said defendant well knowing the said library of books, cloth, calico and other articles to be the property of said plaintiff and a right to belong and appertain to him but contriving and fradulently intending craftily and outtilly to deceive and defraud the said plaintiff in this behalf hath not as yet delivered the said library of books, cloth, calico or other articles or any part thereof to the said plaintiff (although often requested so to do) but so to hath hitherto wholly refused and still refuses, and afterwards to wit on the tenth day of September in the year eighteen hundred and thirty-eight at the county of Clay aforesaid mentioned and disposed of the said library of books, cloth, calico and other articles to his the said defendant's own use to the damage of the said plaintiff of five hundred dollars and wherefore he brings just do.

J. A. Gordon
At-Plaff

Joel Turnham

JoelTurnham was the state judge who tried the brethren at Liberty on 25-30 January. He eventually released Sidney Rigdon. He, along with Justice of the Peace Abraham Shafer, tried the seven visiting brethren for involvement in an escape attempt on 7 February 1839. (See Exhibit 4.7 and Chapter 6, **The Outside Break**.) Turnham visited the jail on 8 January, 1 February, and 2 February. Although not an attorney, he was used for consultation at various times.[122]

William T. Wood

William T. Wood was one of the first defending lawyers for the Latter-day Saints. He is the first listed along with A. W. Doniphan, Peter H. Burnett, and two others as the committee to conduct negotiations for the 1835 Platte Purchase movement.[123] He was a distinguished lawyer from Lexington and had been the Clay County court clerk in 1829 where h e probably got his early training. Wood later became a circuit court judge at Lexington.[124]

Wood was among the attorneys listed as helping the Saints as early as 1833. William Wood, along with Rees (Reese), Doniphan, and Atchison, was the first to sign a formal letter about finances, fees, challenges, and expectations involving legal matters concerning the Saints in Missouri.[125] He strongly denied that the brethren were ever given human flesh: "As to the Mormon beef, human flesh of some of the brethren—All bosh!"[126]

Sheriffs, Jailer, and Guards

Joseph said, "Nearly all of the officers of the law, if not in league with the mob, were in terror of its power."[127] They seemed to be fair, helpful, and informative until the attempts to escape were made. Then, some of the guards changed their whole demeanor toward the prisoners. Because of the deep animosity, even hatred of the mob, they feared if the prisoners got away, it would be the law officers who would pay the consequences.

The last experience Joseph and his associates had with the law officers in Gallatin, Missouri, in April 1839 supported this belief very vividly. Sheriff William Morgan and his assistant, William Bowman, the ex-Sheriff of Daviess County, acting under direct orders from court officials, county and state, allowed the prisoners to escape. When the officers got back to Gallatin, the mob rode Sheriff Morgan out of town on a rail and dragged their ex-sheriff around the town square by the hair of his head.[128]

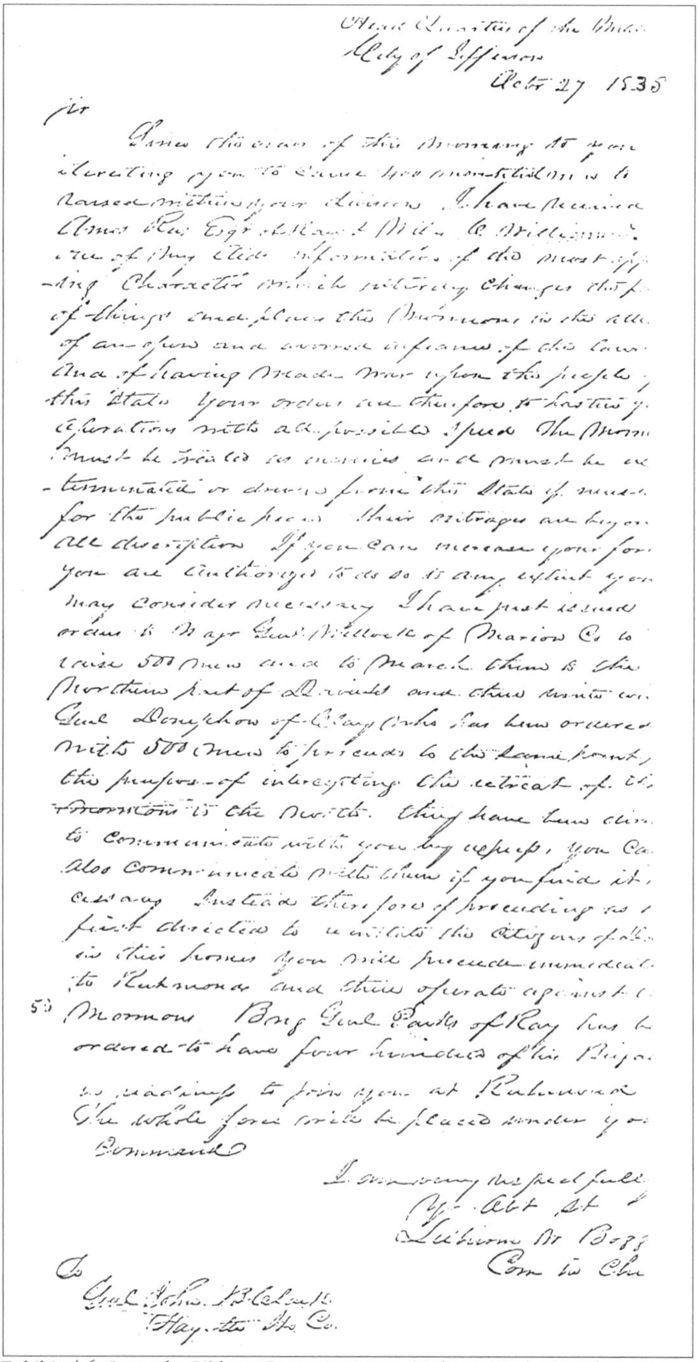

Exhibit 4.6: Letter by Liliburn Boggs to General John B. Clark identifying Rees as the source (also known as Governor Bogg's Exterminating Order), Missouri State Archives, Jefferson City, MO.

TRANSCRIPTION OF EXHIBIT 4.6

General John B. Clark:

Sir—Since the order of this morning to you, directing you to cause four hundred mounted men to be raised within your division, I have received by Amos Reese, Esq., of Ray county, and Wiley C. Williams, Esq., one of my aids, information of the most appalling character, which entirely changes the face of things, and places the Mormons in the attitude of an open and avowed defiance of the laws, and of having made war upon the people of this state. Your orders are, therefore, to hasten your operation with all possible speed. The Mormons must be treated as enemies, and must be exterminated or driven from the state if necessary for the public peace—their outrages are beyond all description. If you can increase your force, you are authorized to do so to any extent you may consider necessary. I have just issued orders to Maj. Gen. Willock, of Marion county, to raise five hundred men, and to march them to the northern part of Daviess, and there unite with Gen. Doniphan of Clay, who has been ordered with five hundred men to proceed to the same point for the purpose of intercepting the retreat of the Mormons to the north. They have been directed to communicate with you by express, you can also communicate with them if you find it necessary. Instead therefore of proceeding as at first directed to reinstate the citizens of Daviess in their homes, you will proceed immediately to Richmond and then operate against the Mormons. Brig. Gen. Parks of Ray, has been ordered to have four hundred of his brigade in readiness to join you at Richmond. The whole force will be placed under your command.

> I am very respectfully,
> your ob't serv't,
> Liliburn W. Boggs,
> Commander-in-Chief.

Exhibit 4.7: Certification of court proceedings by Justices of the Peace Abraham Shafer and Joel Turnham, Clay County Court Archives, Liberty, MO

Sheriff Samuel Hadley

Samuel Hadley, sheriff of Clay County, certified the mittimus sent to him by Judge Austin A. King, judge of the Fifth Judicial Circuit Court of Missouri, to be true. This was the document that sent Joseph and party to Liberty Jail.[129] Mr. Hadley signed the document as the jailer. He was sheriff for five terms through 1838-48 and 1850-58.[130] He was out of office two years when he was defeated by nine votes, 654 to 645, by A. Doniphan's brother-in-law.[131] The 1850 census shows him as "50, farmer, two females 40 & 37 and two children 14 and 11," Hyrum said of him, "At the time of his death he was survived by his widow Thebe, three sons and two daughters."[132] Mr. Hadley seemed to be kind to the women when they came. Emma stated he was in charge of the jail and told her, "All the authorities are waiting for is for you to get out of the state . . . [and] the prisoners will be let out. There is no reason for detaining them other than the unreasonable orders given."[133] (See Exhibit 4.8.)

I Samuel Hadley Sheriff of Clay County do certify that I Executed the within Writ by taking into Custody Alanson Ripley Watson Barbow, Erastus Snow, David Holeman W. D. Huntyngdon and bringing them before Abraham Shafer & Joel Turnham two Justices of the Peace for Liberty Township in Clay County on the 8th day of Februery 1839
Given under my hand this 8th day of Februery 1839
Samuel Hadley
Sheriff of Clay Cty

Sheriff fee $5.00

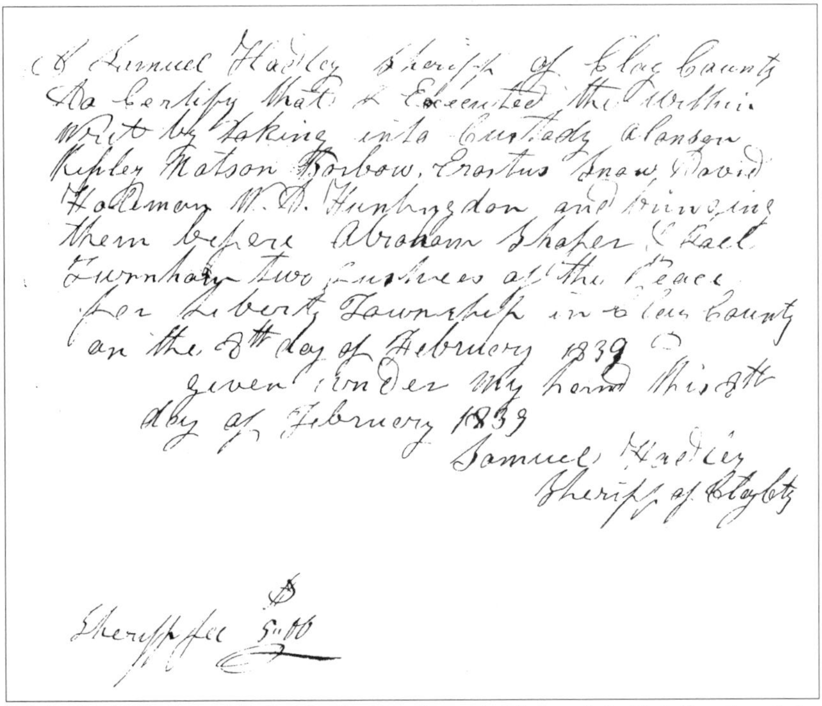

Exhibit 4.8: Writ of arrest against five brethren housed with Joseph Smith, Jr. for attempted Jail break, Clay County Court Archives, Liberty, MO

TRANSCRIPTION OF EXHIBIT 4.8

I Samuel Hadley Sheriff of Clay County do certify that I executed the within writ by taking into custody Alanson Ripley, Watson Barlow, Erastus Snow, David Holeman and W.D. Huntington and bringing them before Abraham Shafer and Joel Turnham, two Justices of the Peace for Liberty Township in Clay County on the 8th day of February, 1839.
Given under my hand this 8th day of February, 1839.

Samuel Hadley
Sheriff of Clay County

Sheriff Fee $5.00

No. 2 Examination of James H. Ford

OATH.

You do solemnly swear in the presence of God and these witnesses, that you will truly and faithfully answer such questions as may now be asked you, and that you will tell the truth, the whole truth and nothing but the truth. So help you GOD.

What is your name? Answer: James H. Ford

Where do you now reside? Answer: Clay Co

What is your age? Answer: 50 years

Where were you born? Answer: Ky

How long have you resided in Missouri? Answer: 30 years

How long have you resided in this county? Answer: 30 years

How long have you resided in this election district? Answer: 30 years

Are you well acquainted with the terms of the 3d Section of the 2d Article of the Constitution of the State of Missouri? Answer: I am not

Will you now recite the general nature of the requirements of that Section? Answer:

Have you during the late rebellion been truly and loyally on the side of the Government of the United States and against all its enemies? Answer: I dont know that I have

With whom did you sympathize during the rebellion? Answer: With the Rebellion

How did you manifest your loyalty to the Government during the war? Answer:

What acts of loyalty did you do during the war?

How did you oppose the enemies of the Government? Answer:

Whom did you then consider the enemies of the Government of the United States? Answer:

Did you ever belong to any secret organizations during the war? Answer:

What were the names of such organizations?

What was the object or design of such organizations? Answer:

Did you at any time during the rebellion leave this State? If so, for what cause? Answer:

When did you so leave and when return? Answer:

Did you, during the rebellion, write or send letters to any person then serving in the rebel armies? Answer:

Did you, during the rebellion, receive letters from any such persons? Answer:

Did you at any time during the rebellion feed or lodge or harbor any person or persons then engaged in armed hostility to the United States Government, either in the rebel service or engaged in what was commonly called "bushwhacking?" Answer:

Did you furnish a horse, a saddle, a bridle, a blanket, a gun, a pistol, powder, shot or other ammunition, or clothing, or any of these articles to any person who entered the rebel service, or engaged in what was commonly called "bushwhacking?" Answer:

Were not yourself at any time during the rebellion in the rebel service, or engaged in what was commonly called "bushwhacking?" Answer: I was

Did you ever send or give any information of any kind to persons who were in the rebel service, or engaged in bushwhacking? If so, what kind of information? Answer:

Were you at any time during the rebellion arrested by the military authorities of the Government or State? If so, state when, and for what reason, and how long you were thus kept under arrest? Answer:

Had you a son, or brother, or other near relative in the rebel army or service or engaged in what was commonly called bushwhacking during the rebellion? If so, state his name, the position he held, and his present whereabouts. Answer:

Was such son, brother or other near relative advised or urged by you to go into the rebel or bushwhacking service? Answer:

Did you help outfit such son, brother, or other near relative, by furnishing him with money, a horse, bridle, saddle, blanket, clothing or anything else? Answer:

Did you, while such person was in the rebel or bushwhacking service, send him any money, clothing, food or other articles? Answer:

Did you at any time during the rebellion become security upon the bond of any person who had been arrested by the military authorities, and who was released on oath and bond? If so, state for whom. Answer:

Did you at any time during the rebellion advise, counsel or urge any person whomsoever to enter into the rebel service, or to engage in bushwhacking? Answer:

What were your feelings when you first heard of the defeat of the Federal army at Bull Run, Va., in July, 1861? Answer:

What were your feelings when you heard of the capture of General Mulligan and his army at Lexington, Mo., by General Sterling Price? Answer:

Were you at any time during the rebellion assessed by the military authorities to help rebuild bridges burnt by rebels? Or were you assessed by such authorities for any other purpose? If so, state for what amount, and whether you paid it? Answer:

[illegible], in the enrollment made by order of the U. S. military authorities were you enrolled as loyal or disloyal? Answer: I was not enrolled at all I was in the Rebel Service

Do you consider the Constitution of this State commonly known as the "New Constitution" to be valid and binding upon the people of Missouri until declared void by the proper Judicial Tribunals? Answer: I considered it the law of the land

Do you believe the "Oath of Loyalty," which you are required to take in order to be registered, to be valid and binding upon you? Answer: I do not

Do you believe that to take that oath falsely involves perjury? Answer:

Do you believe that in taking the "Oath of Loyalty" you make a statement of facts while calling upon God to bear witness to the truth or falsity of such statements? Answer:

In taking the "Oath of Loyalty" do you do it "without mental reservation or evasion?" Answer:

Do you believe that a mental reservation, or that any human law or any human decision or tribunal can absolve you from your responsibility to God if in taking the "Oath of Loyalty," you state that which is not true? Answer:

Are you now willing to take and subscribe the Oath of Loyalty? Answer: I am not

Jas. H. Ford (Signature of Deponent.)

Sworn and subscribed before me this .... *day of* .... *1866.*

.... *Register.*

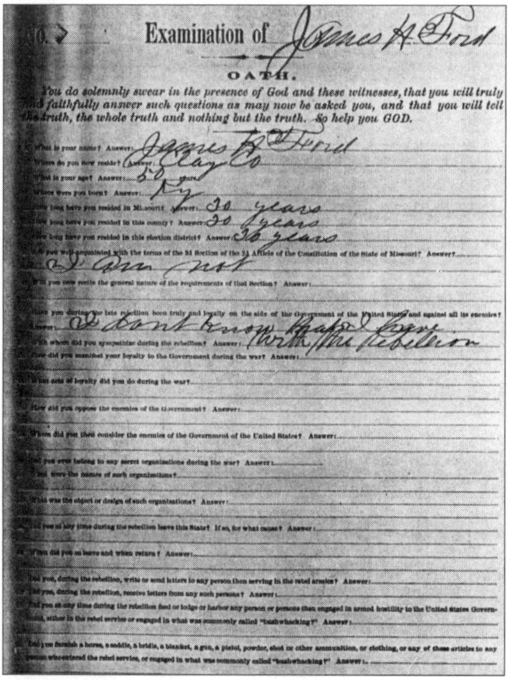

Exhibit 4.9: "Loyalty Oath" filled out and signed by James H. Ford, Clay County Archives and Historical Library, Liberty, MO

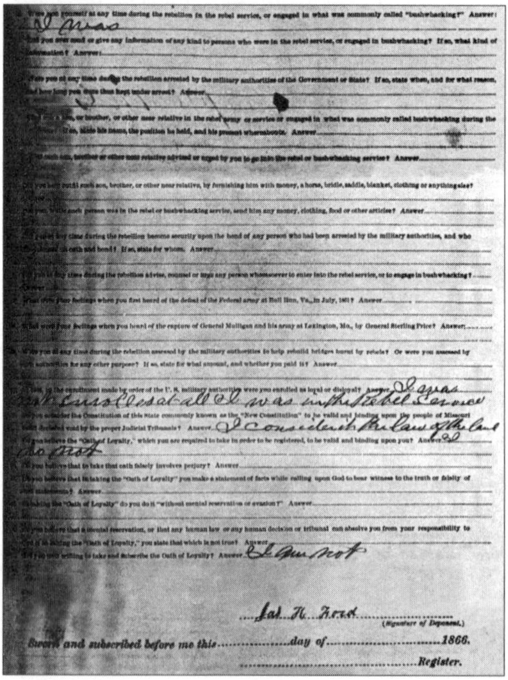

Deputy Sheriff James H. Ford

James H. Ford is listed on the 1840 Clay County census as having two males between twenty and thirty years with no family. He was one of two witnesses of Samuel Tillery's last will and testament in 1857. Being a Confederate, he was arrested and transported from Missouri by Union soldiers in 1861.[134] On the Civil War oath that he answered and signed in 1866, he stated he had lived in Clay County for twenty years and was fifty years old. As to the oath, he wrote during the rebellion that he was not sympathetic to the government of the United States. To the question, "With whom were you sympathetic?" he wrote in bold hand, "With the rebellion." To the last question, "Are you willing to take and subscribe the Oath of Loyalty?" his answer was "I am not."[135] (See Exhibit 4.9 on facing page and Exhibit 6.4 in Chapter 6.)

Jailer Samuel Tillery, Esq.

Samuel Tillery served as clerk of the court and then as justice of the peace. In June of 1827, he became ex-officio county judge for a short time.[136] In 1831, he was the commissioner who purchased the first public school lands.[137] Although referred to as "the jailer" by Hyrum and Lyman in their testimonies, Samuel Tillery must have had at this time a dual role, for he signed documents as "Dep'y sheriff & Jailer for Clay County."[138]

Lyman Wight mentioned they were "under the care and direction of Samuel Tillery."[139] It was probably Tillery who tried to put chains on the prisoners after their attempted jail break. Caleb Baldwin, who gave the jail-break account,[140] called the person "Judge Tillery." The title of "judge" does not fit the occasion. The law officers were known to be in fear of the prisoners escaping, which they knew would bring great repercussion to themselves. Chaining the prisoners was to their benefit. In addition, there is only one known account of a judge visiting them—Judge Turnham—and his visit was before and not after the escape attempt. (See Appendices A and C.)

Concerning Far West, Tillery explained that the whole plan was conceived by Governor Boggs and that Generals Atchison, Wilson, Lucas, and Gillium, along with or all the way down to the lowest judge in that upper county, were all involved. Toward the end of their incarceration, Tillery told the brethren, "But, you need not be concerned, for the governor has laid a plan for your release." He told them that Squire Birch, the state's attorney, had instructed the judge to fix the papers to clear them from any incumbrance.[141]

Liberty Jail, RLDS Archives, Independence, MO

John Tillery

John Tillery was a guard at Liberty Jail. His existence is documented in history when he makes his appearance after the attempted escape on 7 February 1839. Tillery gave testimony at the trial of the brethren, who were charged with an attempted escape. (See Exhibit 6.3 in Chapter 6.)

Summary

A knowledge of the background and personality of the people involved in the Liberty Jail experience enhances the drama of this trying episode. The participants become real and give the reader a greater understanding concerning their actions and reactions.

Jail

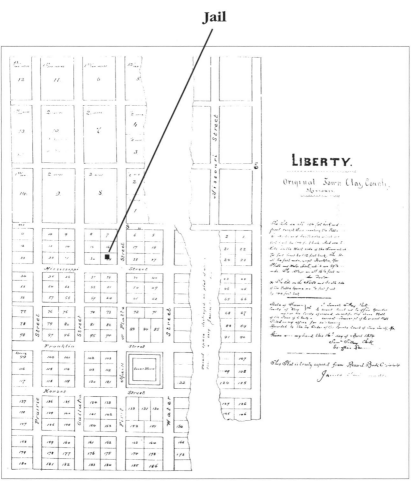

Plat of Liberty, Clay County, Missouri, 1834, Clay County Archives and Historical Library, Liberty, MO

Jail

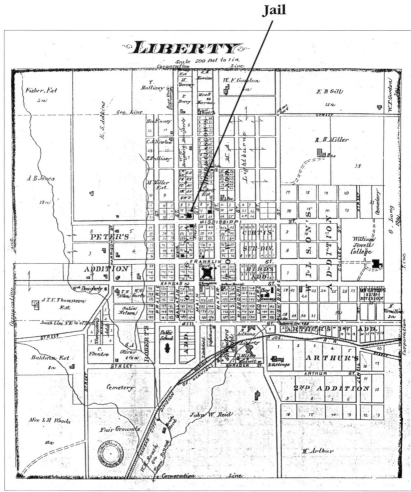

Plat of Liberty, Clay County, Missouri, Clay County Archives and Historical Library, Liberty, MO

Chapter 5

LIBERTY JAIL

The town of Liberty, Missouri, evolved from a ferry port on the Missouri River about three miles northeast of the river. It developed into a thriving little community by expanding its resources to meet the needs of a growing frontier society. A great demand developed for outfitting trappers, explorers, settlers, and pioneers. Liberty became one of the outfitting centers for those going west through the Oregon-California and Santa Fe Trails. Five trading posts were in close proximity near the river.[1] By 1822, Liberty had become the seat of justice for Clay County. With this new judicial status came the need for a county jail.

The Dungeon Gaol (Jail)

The jail was first built about 1830 of hewn oak logs. Its dimensions were 14 by 14 1/2 feet in the clear.[2] Soon after its construction, Solomon Fry contracted to put in a stone wall and fill the space between the oak logs and stone wall with loose rocks for $600.[3] He was once asked what year he built the jail. He replied, "I know it was built the same year the stars fell [1833],"[4] having reference to the great celestial phenomenon that occurred when the Saints were driven out of Jackson County.

It was used as the jail for Clay County for twenty-three years but was declared unsafe when it began to deteriorate because of poor mortar. After the jail was abandoned, the dungeon area was used as an ice house for a dozen or so more years, but the building was finally deserted altogether.

Liberty Jail, Dora Dunyon Nelson, Salt Lake City, UT

The jail resembled a square box. The outside dimensions were 22 1/2 feet long, 22 feet wide, and 12 feet high to the square. The door in or out was on the east end, facing the street, and was 5 1/2 feet high and 2 1/2 feet wide. For those early days, this outside door was almost impregnable. It had a pair of heavy, strapped door hinges that were made of hand-forged iron. The lock was extra-heavy iron consisting of an iron hasp and iron lock holder.[5] This door opened into the upper chamber of the jail, which was above the dungeon.[6]

The upper and lower quarters measured about 14 1/2 feet from east to west and 14 feet from north to south. From the floor of the dungeon to the ceiling of the upper room was about 14 feet, two feet of which was under ground, for the ground had a sharp fall.[7] Two-foot-wide limestones were laid on the outside of the building, and large, 12-inch-square, hewn oak hardwood made up the interior. There was a one-foot space left between the logs and the limestones, which was filled with loose rocks. Thus, the walls were four feet thick. The upper-chamber ceiling had large rocks laid on top of it, making all levels of the jail, if not escape proof, very formidable.

The only way into the dungeon from the upper room was through a trap door in the floor. The floor of the dungeon was made of jagged, coarse stones. It was covered with straw. The only openings giving light and ventilation to the dungeon were two very small grated windows through the four-foot walls—one on the south side and another on the north side. These openings, each of which had a heavy, square iron bar running horizontally through the middle, were two feet wide and six inches high. The bar was encased in an iron frame.[8] The window size and iron made an escape through the lower windows virtually impossible.

The dungeon space was furnished with two small, wooden benches, small stools, a small table, and a few blankets.[9] Because of the width of the walls, the prisoners' view through the openings was a straight line. They could not see up or down or left or right. The physical light was dismal; but, as was recorded in the journals of the valiant men in the jail, the windows of heaven were always open, bright, and magnified. Each prisoner stated that when needed, he could see as wide as the heavens with the revelatory knowledge they revealed.

A beautiful, scriptural foundation of this attitude is found in Psalms:

> Oh that men would praise the Lord for his goodness, and for his wonderful works to the children of men!
>
> For he hath broken the gates of brass, and cut the bars of iron in sunder. . . .
>
> Then they cry unto the Lord. . . .
>
> He sent his word, and healed them, and delivered them from their destructions.[10]

Joseph often mentioned other great prophets of the past who had suffered similar experiences. Joseph of Egypt, Jeremiah, Hosea, the two Johns, Peter, Paul, Abinadi, Alma, Ammon, Amulek, and Aaron had previously endured the discomfort and pain that Joseph came to know. (See Appendix C.)

Charged with treason, Joseph Smith, Jr., his brother Hyrum, Caleb Baldwin, Lyman Wight, Alexander McRae, and Sidney Rigdon were brought to this miserable place of confinement on 1 December 1838. (See Exhibit 5.1 for transcription of charge.)

Prison Dialogue

It would be difficult to comprehend the conditions that were imposed upon the brethren who were enclosed within this dungeon-prison for 128 days. It was a dark, dismal, filthy, wet, foul-smelling,

State of Missouri, Ray County.

To the Keeper of the Jail of Clay County; Greeting:
Whereas, Joseph Smith., Junior, Hyrum Smith, Lyman Wight, Alexander McRae, and Caleb Bladwin, as also Sidney Rigdon, have been brought before me, Austin A. King, Judge of the fifth judicial circuit in the State of Missouri, and charged with the offense of treason against the State of Missouri, and the said defendants, on their examination before me, being held to answer further to said charge, the said Joseph Smith, Junior, Hyrum Smith, Lyman Wight, Alexander McRae, and Caleb Baldwin to answer further in the county of Daviess, and the said Sidney Rigdon to answer further in the county of Caldwell for said charge of treason, and there being no jail in said counties: These are therefore to command that you receive the said Joseph Smith., Junior, Hyrum Smith, Lyman Wight, Alexander McRae, and Caleb Bladwin, and Sidney Rigdon into your custody in the jail of the said county of Clay, there to remain until they be delivered there from by due course of law.
Given under my hand and seal the 20th day of November, 1838.

Austin A. King

Exhibit 5.1: Transcription of charge of treason, signed by Austin A King. Original document is from the Daviess County Circuit Court Record, State Historical Society of Missouri, Columbia, MO.

vermin-infested hole. The only sanitation facilities were slop buckets. Journals speak of the physical trauma—toothaches, earaches, pneumonia, hunger, cold, unsanitary conditions, stinging eyes, etc.

Of the many trials of the Prophet, imprisonment for five months (four of them at Liberty Jail) was certainly one of the most severe. As personally unpleasant as incarceration conditions were to endure, they were to him not nearly as weighty a matter as were the hardships of the Saints he loved. The reports of cruelties—the whippings, the beatings, the rapes, and the plundering of homes and farms—were overwhelming. Then, finally, the enforced march out of the state in wintertime caused him to ask, "How long shall they suffer these wrongs and unlawful oppression?"[11]

Their food was very coarse and was so filthy that "We could not eat it until we were driven to it by hunger."[12] "Orin P. Rockwell brought us refreshments many times; and Jane Bleven and her daughter brought cakes, pies, etc. and handed them in at the window."[13] Every prisoner expressed great joy for these small comforts.

Words used to describe the jail are "dungeon," "prison," "temple," "place of tutoring higher education," and "place of confinement that brought introspection," "pondering," "contemplation," and "doctrinal fullness." It certainly became a revelatory center with spiritual depths as high as the heavens themselves when the Savior and other angelic ministers were giving enlightenment to the prophet. Brother B. H. Roberts put it in beautiful perspective: "It was more temple than prison, so long as the prophet was there."[15]

Joseph's feelings were tenderly expressed:

> [W]hen we read those letters they were to our souls as the gentle air is refreshing. . . . And we need not say to you that the floodgates of our hearts were lifted and our eyes were a fountain of tears, but those who have not been enclosed in the walls of prison without cause or provocation, can have but little idea how sweet the voice of a friend is.[16]

As the year came to a close, the Saints were impoverished and scattered. Their prophet was confined to a dark and loathsome dungeon. "The earth was wrapped in gloom for the people of God when the sun sank for the last time upon the year 1838; but beyond and above this sphere was the star of eternal faith, whose light no prison wall could shut out from trusting souls."[17]

At this time, Joseph wrote: "Thus, in a land of liberty, in the town of Liberty, Clay County, Missouri my fellow prisoners and I in chains and dungeon saw the close of 1838."[18] To open 1839, Joseph expressed these feelings:

> Tuesday, January 1, 1839, dawned upon us as prisoners of hope, but not as sons of liberty. O Columbia, Columbia! How art thou fallen! "The land of the free, the home of the brave!" "The asylum of the oppressed"—oppressing thy noblest sons, in a loathsome dungeon, without any provocation, only that they have claimed to worship the God of their fathers according to his own word and the dictates of their own consciences.[19]

Because Joseph was in constant communion with the heavens while he was in prison, his presence lifted the spirits of the brethren and gave them hope. He sent letters full of instructions and encouragement to the leaders among the Saints. His cheerful courage under such difficult circumstances sustained the members and gave them the energy and determination to carry on.

Notable Events

The prisoners' legal experiences while in Liberty Jail were many. The last of January gave them the most expansive experience, for they were all involved. It lasted for eight days, from 22 January until

30 January. Through this period, they were visited by four, and possibly seven, attorneys. (See Appendix B.)

As all legal attempts to gain their freedom had failed, they began to think of a way they could escape. Hyrum asked that Joseph pray and ask the Lord if it was his will that they should leave the prison. The reply came to the Prophet that if they were all agreed in faith and purpose, they might escape that night. When these conditions were made known to the brethren, all but Lyman Wight agreed they should make the attempt that night. It was planned that "when the jailer came with our supper"[20] (6 February)[21] they would overpower the existing guard, rush the relief guard, and take control of the jail at this time.

Their plan was really set up perfectly for that night:

> [T]he jailer came alone with our supper, threw the door wide open, put the supper on the table, and went to the back part of the room, where a pile of books lay, took up a book, and went to reading, leaving us between him and the door, thereby giving us every chance to go if we had been ready.[22]

But Lyman said he could not go that night and insisted on waiting until the next night. His companions would not leave him, as the Lord's promise was based upon their unity. They then decided they would wait until the following night. The delay caused them to fail in their attempt, as the Lord had promised success for the previous evening. (See Chapter 6, **The Outside Break**.)

Brother McRae describes the very contentious aftermath when many of the citizens were aroused by a shot and quickly appeared:

> I should judge, from the number, that all the town, and many from the country, gathered around the jail and every mode of torture and death that their imagination could fancy, was proposed for us, such as blowing up the jail, taking us out and whipping us to death, shooting us, burning us to death, tearing us to pieces with horses, etc. But they were so divided among themselves that they could not carry out any of their plans, and we escaped unhurt.[23]

The authorities brought charges against those who had come to visit, locked them up, and made threats against them and their property. (See Exhibit 6.1 and transcription in Chapter 6.) The Prophet told the brethren who were arrested not to fear because not a hair of their heads should be harmed and because those who had come to comfort them should not lose any of their personal belongings—not even a horse or a saddle.[24]

Liberty Jail Front Wall, Clay County Archives and Historical Library, Liberty, MO

Brother Erastus Snow inquired of Joseph whether Erastus should hire a lawyer. The Prophet told him to plead his own case. "But," said Brother Snow, "I do not understand the law." Joseph asked him if he did not understand justice. Erastus thought he did. "Well," said Joseph, "go and plead for justice as hard as you can, and quote Blackstone and other authors now and then, and they will take it all for law."[25]

When the time of this trial arrived, Brother Erastus Snow pleaded their cause as Joseph had advised him to do. He presented their argument in such a forcible and eloquent manner that orders of discharge in some cases and orders for bail in others were immediately entered. The lawyers who heard his defense assumed that he was trained in the law.[26]

Some enemies of the Prophet were allowed by the guards to visit him while he was in prison. In most cases, the visitor would charge Joseph with murder. A few accused him of having killed their sons at the battle of Crooked River. Others who were of no relation to each other blamed him for the death of their brothers in the same battle. These were the kinds of accusations made against him in and out of court. Only one Missourian was killed at Crooked River; thus, it was impossible for so many to have lost sons and brothers there. Joseph had not been anywhere near the scene of that battle.[27]

Alexander McRae told of an attempt by the guards to poison the prisoners. It was probably administered in either tea or coffee. All but Alexander, who did not drink it, were sorely afflicted, and some were blind for two or three days. It was only because of their faith and prayers that the effect was overcome.[28]

The Lord set the stage for knowledge during the first great trial-test of the Saints in Missouri in 1833:

> For he will give unto the faithful line upon line, precept upon precept; and I will try you and prove you herewith. . . .
>
> [B]e not afraid of your enemies, for I have decreed in my heart, saith the Lord, that I will prove you in all things, whether you will abide in my covenants unto death, that you may be found worthy.[29]

Faith was definitely tested, leading to the third and final attribute of spiritual fulfillment: Many are called, some are chosen, and a few are found faithful. These brethren were not found wanting in their faith.

Shortly after leaving the jail, although pertaining to another subject, Joseph expressed a beautiful truism that seems to relate well to his experience in the jail. Joseph was of the pure seed of Abraham. In June of 1839, he said:

> It is more powerful in expanding the mind, enlightening the understanding, and storing the intellect with present knowledge, of a man who is of the literal seed of Abraham, than one that is a Gentile, though it may not have half as much visible effect upon the body; for as the Holy Ghost falls upon one of the literal seed of Abraham, it is calm and serene; and his whole soul and body are only exercised by the pure spirit of intelligence; while the effect of the Holy Ghost upon a Gentile, is to purge out the old blood, and make him actually of the seed of Abraham. That man that has none of the blood of Abraham (naturally) must have a new creation by the Holy Ghost. In such a case, there may be more of a powerful effect upon the body, and visible to the eye, than upon an Israelite, while the Israelite at first might be far before the Gentile in pure intelligence.[30]

Joseph himself put these concepts in his own words when he said: "[U]ntil finally all enmity, malice and hatred and past differences, misunderstanding and mismanagement be slain victims at the feet of hope and when the heart is sufficiently contrite, then the voice of inspiration steals along and whispers, my son, peace be unto thy soul."[31]

Endurance, sacrifice, and faithfulness seem to be some of the essential elements or steps of spiritual development and maturity. Joseph said, "For my part, I think I never could have felt as I now do if I had not suffered the wrongs that I have suffered. All things shall work together for good to them that love God."[32]

It was the last of March, the fourth month of confinement for the prisoners, when the Lord finally revealed Sections 121, 122, and 123 of the Doctrine and Covenants. The last two verses of Section 121 state:

> Let thy bowels also be full of charity towards all men, and to the household of faith, and let virtue garnish thy thoughts unceasingly; then shall thy confidence wax strong in the presence of God; and the doctrine of the priesthood shall distill upon thy soul as the dews from heaven.

> The Holy Ghost shall be thy constant companion, and thy scepter an unchanging scepter of righteousness and truth; and thy dominion shall be an everlasting dominion, and without compulsory means it shall flow unto thee forever and ever.[33]

The life of Joseph Smith, Jr. manifested every aspect of these principles. The confidence, the companionship and the power, and, above all, the scepter of righteousness and truth flowed to him without compulsory means—as shown by the knowledge he imparted to us almost immediately after he left the jail.

The principle of virtue as given by the Lord to the brethren while in Liberty Jail seemed to be well understood by Joseph. A beautiful statement expressing his comprehension was given during the return from Washington, D.C., where some of the brethren had gone to petition the president and Congress for redress in 1839. On his return, while in the Philadelphia area, Joseph visited a family named Wilkinson. While with them, he bestowed a blessing upon the family in the form of a written note in the front of one of their books. It is perhaps the most salient commentary on D&C 121:45 we have:

> Virtue is one of the most prominent principles that enables us to have confidence in approaching our Father who is in heaven in order to ask wisdom at his hand therefore if thou wilt cherish this principle in thine heart thou mayest ask with all Confidence before him and it shall be poured out upon thine head and thou shalt not lack any thing that thy soul desires in truth.[34]

Before being driven out of Missouri, Brigham Young, Heber C. Kimball, and George A. Smith went to see the Prophet in prison. They visited him twice while they were in Liberty; and when they left,

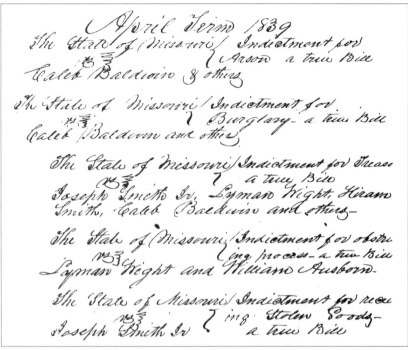

Exhibit 5.2: Indictments executed against Joseph and others in Daviess County Criminal Court, Daviess County Court Archives, Gallatin, MO

they were determined to do something to get the brethren released. After they had done everything they could do and expressed their failure to the Prophet, Joseph told them to be of good cheer. "We shall be delivered; but no arm but that of God can save us now. Tell the brethren to be of good cheer and to get the Saints away from Missouri as soon as possible."[35]

Brother McRae, writing for the *Deseret News* on 1 November 1854, revealed a test of their faith. Fear for their lives was paramount until Brother Joseph told them the Lord had revealed to him they were "not to fear, that not a hair of their heads should be hurt."

> We never suffered ourselves to go into any important measure without asking Brother Joseph to inquire of the Lord in relation to it. Such was our confidence in him as a Prophet, that when he said "Thus saith the Lord," we were confident it would be as he said; and the more we tried it, the more confidence we had, for we never found his word fail in a single instance.[36]

A short time before they were to go to Daviess County for trial, General Doniphan or General Atchison offered to raise a military force to protect them. The offer was discussed by the brethren (except Joseph), and they concurred that it would be best to accept the offer. Brother Hyrum asked Joseph for his opinion. Joseph hung his head a few moments and seemed in deep thought. Then, he said, "Brother Hyrum, it will not do; we must trust in the Lord; if we take a guard with us we shall be destroyed."[37]

This answer caught them by surprise. Brother Hyrum then said, "If you say it in the name of the Lord, we will rely on it. Said Brother Joseph, "In the name of the Lord, if we take a guard with us, we will be destroyed; but if we put our trust in the Lord, we shall be safe, and no harm shall befall us and we shall be better treated than we have ever been since we have been prisoners."[38]

The matter was settled. They would request no extra guard. On 6 April 1839, the prisoners were taken from Liberty Jail and, under guard of ten or fifteen men, were moved to Gallatin, where formal charges were again brought upon them. (See Exhibits 5.2 and 5.3.) It was a tedious journey, for their long confinement and the deprivations they had endured greatly enfeebled their bodily powers. Hyrum said, "I feel my body broken down and my health very much impaired . . . so that I have not been able to perform any labor since I have escaped."[39] Joseph, on the other hand, must still have been in fair shape. Upon persistent coaxing from the crowd for some friendly competition in wrestling, Joseph threw the Gallatin champion wrestler flat on his back in a pool of water.[40]

When they arrived at the location where the court was held, there began to be a feeling that this time Joseph had been mistaken, "for the people rushed upon us en masse, crying, 'Kill them: —— — — them, kill them.' There seemed to be no chance of escape. At this, Brother Joseph, at whom all seemed to rush, rose up and said, 'We are in your hands; if we are guilty, we refuse not to be punished by the law.'"[41] Upon hearing this, two of the most "bitter mobocrats in the country," William Peniston and Mr. Kinney or McKinney, stood up on benches and began to talk to the people. "Yes, gentlemen, these men are in our hands; let us not use violence, but let the law have its course; the law will condemn them, and they will be punished by it. We do not want the disgrace of taking the law into our own hands."[42]

In a few minutes, the crowd had quieted down and suddenly seemed friendly. "This took place in the court-room (a small 12 by 12 foot cabin), during the adjournment of the court."[43] From that time

April Term 1839

recieved, but upon condition that the said Hira.
G Parks appear by himself or attorney, on the first
day of the next term of the Circuit Court to be holden
for the County of Daviess before the said Court on
then and there to answer said Indictment, and not
depart the said Court without leave thereof –

The State of Missouri
vs } Indictment for Treason

Joseph Smith Jr, Lyman Wight, Hiram Smith
Caleb Baldwin and Alexander McCray
                    Motion to Admit to Bail
overruled by the Court –

The State of Missouri
          vs   } Indictment for Treason
Joseph Smith Jr, Lyman Wight, Hiram Smith
Caleb Baldwin and Alexander McCray an
others –

          The Judge of this Court having
been Counsel in this Cause, and the Parties here
in not Consenting to a Trial thereof, in this Co.
But the said Defendants, Joseph Smith Jr,
Lyman Wight, Hiram Smith, Caleb Bald
win and Alexander McCray, objecting
thereto for the reason that the Judge of the
Court has been of Counsel in this Cause;
It is therefore ordered by the Court here that s.
Cause as to the said Joseph Smith Jr, Lyman
Wight Hiram Smith, Caleb Baldwin and Alexan
der McCray be removed to the Circuit Court of
County of Boone in the Second Judicial Circui
in this State – It is further ordered by the Court here t.
The Sheriff of the County of Daviess, do and he is
Commanded to remove the Bodies of the said
Joseph Smith Jr, Lyman Wight, Hiram Smi.
Caleb Baldwin and Alexander McCray to th
Jail of the County aforesaid and there deliv
them to the keeper of said Jail together wi
the warrant or process by which they are

Exhibit 5.3: Court Transcripts of Joseph and others in Daviess County Criminal Court, Daviess County Court Archives, Gallatin, MO

84

Home Built over Liberty Jail Dungeon, Ralph Brant, Liberty, MO

on, the jail personnel could not put a guard over the brethren without facing a situation in which the guard would become very friendly with the prisoners. Under these circumstances, the guards had to be changed frequently.

Two days later, a grand jury that was presided over by Thomas C. Burch brought indictments of riot, arson, burglary, treason, and receiving stolen goods and denied bail. Objecting on the grounds of extreme prejudice, the prisoners were granted a change of venue. En route to the new location at Boone County, the sheriff, having been directed by his superiors, allowed them to escape during the night. After a difficult journey of "much fatigue and hunger," they arrived in Quincy, Illinois, on 22 April 1839 and rejoined their families and friends.

Chapter 6

JAIL BREAKS

Three primary legal experiences occurred in Liberty Jail consisting of (1) the indictment and trial in January, (2) the court action against the brethren accused of aiding an attempted jail break, and (3) the McLellin robbery of the Prophet's home.

The eight-day trial in January involved all the prisoners (Joseph and Hyrum, Sidney Rigdon, Caleb Baldwin, Lyman Wight, and Alexander McRae). As the trial progressed, they gained a great deal of insight concerning their attorneys and also concerning their fate if it were left to the county and state officials they had been dealing with for eight years. Alexander McRae said, "We . . . had tried every means we could to obtain our liberty by the law, without effect"[1] (except for Sidney). The prisoners came to the justifiable conclusion they would never obtain a release through the legal process. They had been told in the beginning, and it had proved to be true, that there was no law for the Mormons in Missouri.

This conclusion became evident when Joseph related that they had witnesses they wanted to call before Judge Turnham. "[B]ut he utterly refused to hear any of our witnesses, which we had been at a great trouble in providing. Our lawyer also refused to act, being afraid of the people."[2] "Nearly all of the officers of the law, if not in league with the mob, were in terror of its power."[3]

In that environment, even the attorneys themselves were at risk in helping the prisoners, although the attorneys had done much to protect the prisoners and had tried to make their confinement as

The State of Missouri
To the Sheriff of Clay County Greeting:
Whereas Samuel Tillery of Clay County
hath this day given information upon oath
to me Abraham Shafer a Justice of the peace
within & for said County of Clay that on the
7th day of February last past at the County
aforesaid one Alanson Ripley, Watson
Barlow, W. D. Huntington, David Holeman
& Erastus ~~Snow~~ Snow attempted by force to set
at liberty & rescue certain prisoners in the
Custody of him the said Samuel Tillery as
the deputy Jailor of Samuel Hadley who is
Sheriff and jailor of Clay County to wit. Joseph
Smith Jr Alexander McRay Hiram Smith
Caleb Baldwin & Lyman Wight charged
with the Crime of Treason against the
State of Missouri.
These are therefore to Command
you forthwith to apprehend the said Alanson
Ripley, Watson Barlow, W. D. Huntington
David Holeman & Erastus ~~Snow~~ Snow and bring
them ~~before~~ me or some other Justice of the
peace for this County to answer the premises
and further to be dealt with according to law
Given under my hand & seal at the
County of Clay aforesaid this 8th
day of February in the year of our
Lord Eighteen hundred and thirty
nine
Abraham Shafer J. P. Seal

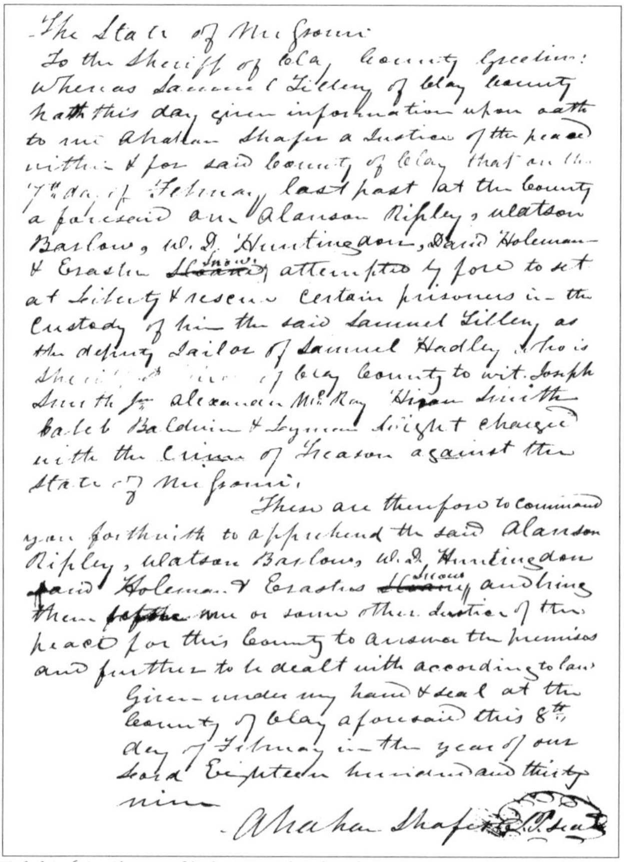

Exhibit 6.1: Charges filed against five brethren for trying to break Joseph Smith, Jr. out of Liberty Jail, Clay County Court Archives, Liberty, MO

TRANSCRIPTION OF EXHIBIT 6.1

The State of Missouri
To the Sheriff of Clay County Greetings:
Whereas Samuel Tillery of Clay County hath this day given information upon oath to me, Abraham Shafer, a Justice of the Peace, within and for said county of Clay, that on this seventh day of February last past at the county aforesaid one Alanson Ripley, Watson Barlow, W D. Huntington, David Holeman, and Erastus Snow attempted by force to set at liberty and rescue certain prisoners in the custody of him the said Samuel Tillery as the deputy jailer of Samuel Hadley who is sheriff and jailer of Clay County to wit. Joseph Smith Jr., Alexander McRay, Hiram Smith, Caleb Baldwin, and Lyman Wight charged with the crime of treason against the State of Missouri.
These are therefore to command you forthwith to apprehend the said Alanson Ripley, Watson Barlow, W. D. Huntington, David Holeman, and Erastus Snow and bring them before me or some other Justice of the Peace for this county to answer the premises and further to be dealt with according to law.
Given under my hand and seal at the county of Clay aforesaid this 8th day of February in the year of our Lord eighteen hundred and thirty nine.
Abraham Shafer (J. P. SEAL)

pleasant as possible. At this point, the brethren must have felt they were well represented, although Joseph did remark, "[W]e should have been liberated at the time Elder Rigdon was, on the writ of habeas corpus, had not our own lawyers interpreted the law, contrary to what it reads against us; which prevented us from introducing our evidence before the mock court."[4] Sidney was ordered released after his testimony on 30 January, but it was not until 5 February (six days later) that it was deemed safe enough for him to leave. Even then, Sidney had to plan an escape, and the sheriff and jailer helped him carry it out.

After Sidney's departure, McRae described their situation by saying "that it had been stated in the public street, by the most influential men in that part of the country" that no release would ever occur.[5] Finally, the brethren collectively decided they would have to resort to other measures to obtain their freedom.

Two jail breaks were attempted—one on 7 February and another on 1 March. Research has revealed conflicts in reporting that make it difficult to know exactly what happened. Discrepancies between Church records and county records will be noted in the following accounts.

The Outside Break

The first attempt took place on 7 February, two days after Sidney's release. The brethren planned to make their break in the evening at the changing of the guards. Usually, there was only one guard on duty at night and one replacement. This night, as the door opened, two relief guards came in, followed by six of the brethren who had come to visit the prisoners. Alexander McRae gives a very vivid description of what happened during this escape attempt:

> It looked like a bad chance to get away, but we were determined to try it; so when the jailor started out, we started too. Brother Hyrum took hold of the door, and the rest followed; but before we were able to render him the assistance he needed, the jailer and guard succeeded in closing the door, shutting the brethren in with us, except Cyrus Daniels, who was on the outside.

> As soon as the attempt was made inside, he took two of the guards, one under each arm, and ran down the stairs. . . . When he reached the ground they got away from him; and seeing we had failed to get out, he started to run, but put his foot in a hole and fell, a bullet from one of the guards passed very close to his head, and he thinks the fall saved his life.[6]

Church records mention six brethren who went to the jail to visit: Alanson Ripley, David Holman, Watson Barlow, Wm. Huntington Jr., Erastus Snow, and Cyrus Daniels.[7] Civil records show that five were charged by the county. (See Exhibit 6.1 and transcription.) Emanuel Murphy and John Outhouse signed as security for the $150 bail. (See Exhibit 6.2.) The court records do not show C. Daniels as charged or involved but do mention the name of Jonathan Tilatson as one charged.

Testimony was given by John Tillery, replacement guard, (Exhibit 6.3), James H. Ford, deputy sheriff, (Exhibit 6.4), and Samuel Tillery, deputy jailer, (Exhibit 6.5a and transcription and Exhibit 6.5b) that others were seen outside the jail whom they thought were part of the planned escape. John Tillery said, "[O]ne of the strangers came out being the same that made his escape." Most likely, that person was C. Daniels.

During Mr. Ford's testimony, he was asked why he did not fire at the escaping man. Mr. Ford replied, "The pistol was only half cocked and I thought it was cocked, therefore it would not go off."

The court records show the testimony of Theodore Turley and Philander S. Frost as witnesses in behalf of the defendants. (See Exhibit 6.6.)

Following the charges of assisting the prisoners in an escape attempt, four of the five visitors were held in the jail from 8 February to 13 February. The Prophet told them that they had risked their lives to bring joy to himself and companions and that the Lord would bless them. This promise was fulfilled.[8] They were released 13 February.

Some of the indicted brethren employed lawyers to defend them. Those with attorneys were tried separately but on the same days and used some of the same testimony.

The charge was made on 8 February 1839 to the sheriff of Clay County. Jailer Samuel Tillery gave to Judge Shafer, under oath on 7 February, the names of Ripley, Barlow, Huntington, Holeman, and Snow, "who attempted by force to set at liberty and rescue certain prisoners in his custody with orders to apprehend them. Signed Abraham Shafer J. P." (See Exhibit 6.7.)

The following record is taken from the actual document (see Exhibit 6.8):

State of Missouri, County of Clay

Be it remembered that on this 8th day of February in the year of our Lord eighteen hundred and thirty nine at a criminal court of inquiry held before us Abraham Shafer & Joel Turnham two of the Justices of the peace within and for the afore said county:At his courthouse in the Town of Liberty herein to wit David Holeman, Erastus Snow, Jonathan Tilatson [this name is not mentioned anywhere else],Watson Barlow,William D.Huntington & Alanson Ripley.The following named persons . . . and these brought before us being charged with having attempted by force to rescue and set at liberty certain prisoners in the custody of this jailor of said county & the said defendants to wit: David Holeman, Erastus Snow,Watson Barlow,William D.Huntington & Alanson Ripley not being ready for their case to be taken up. This court then adjourned until the 11th February A.D. 1839.

All were fined $150.(See Exhibit 6.2.)They then cross signed as security for each other.All signed as security for Alanson Ripley as principal:"Witness our hand and seals this 13th day of February,A.D. 1839." On the same day, documents were signed by Erastus Snow, and Emanuel Murphy as security for Watson Barlow.Another document showed David Holeman,John Outhouse, Erastus Snow,and Emanuel Murphy as security, with David Holeman as principal. Still another was signed by Snow and Murphy with Ripley as the principal.

From the original records,we learn the following (see Exhibit 6.8):

February 11th, 1839.The Court met pursuant to adjournment.

The State of Missouri Vs David Holeman, Erastus Snow,Alanson Ripley and William D. Huntington.

Alanson Ripley & David Holeman made their motion to have a separate trial or examination from the others these defendants which is granted them—

The State of Missouri Vs Erastus Snow,Watson Barlow & W. D. Huntington.This Court is continued until tomorrow morning.

The State of Missouri Vs Alanson Ripley & David Holeman.

The Inside Break

Twenty-eight days had elapsed since the first attempt to escape. As to the exact day,a notation from Church history,under the date of 25 February, reads: "Determination of the Prisoners to Escape." Following that notation is the statement, "[O]ur course . . . was to escape out of their hands as soon as we could,and by any means we could."[9]

The labor of escape began on 1 March,[10] after Porter Rockwell had smuggled a "wood auger into the window and an iron bar."[11] The brethren labored extensively. Lyman Wight wrote: "March 3. This morning hard at work for our deliverance."

The timber of the wall was so hard that the auger handles gave out and delayed them longer than expected. Hyrum explained why: "The logs were so hard that the handles would slip and we had to make new ones with our fire wood. We had to bore the hole for the shank with my pen knife which delayed time."[12] A friend was asked to get them new handles.

On 4 March, Lyman penned these comments:

> This morning I walked out and returned about ten o'clock. We expect to make our escape this afternoon without fail. We got all ready to go out, and Shoemaker felt so tickled to think that he was our assistant that he made a confidant of Doctor Moss. The thing leaked out and there were ten guards called for.

What a disappointment for these brethren. They had everything ready but the last stone and could have made their escape in one minute had it not been for the indiscretion of their friend.[13]

Even after this attempt, Hyrum said that the "Jailor and sheriff had no bad feeling but the Baptist, Presbyterian and Methodists were very much excited."[14]

Joseph remarked:

> The sheriff and jailer did not blame us for our attempt; it was a fine breach, and cost the county a round sum; but public opinion says that we ought to have been permitted to have made our escape; that then the disgrace would have been on us, but now it must come on the state.[15]

With the unsuccessful escape attempts, the faith of these valiant men was further tested. Only after this additional trying test did the beautiful, enlightening revelations come. Liberty Jail is remembered, not as a place of suffering, but as a "prison temple" where God talked to a living prophet and gave significant and meaningful teachings for all mankind.

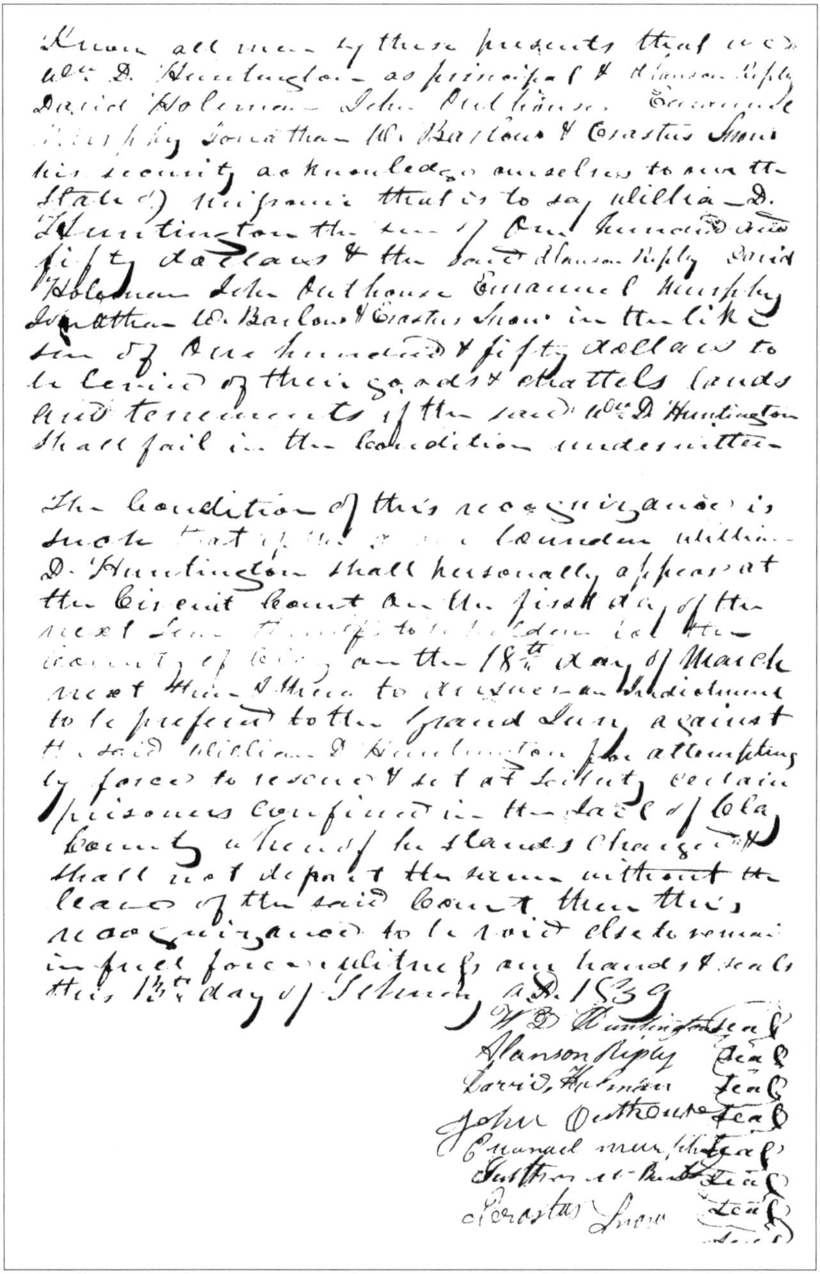

Exhibit 6.2: Recognizance Agreement for bail for those charged in trying to break Joseph Smith, Jr. out of Liberty Jail, Clay County Court Archives, Liberty, MO

TRANSCRIPTION OF EXHIBIT 6.2

Know all men by these presents that we Wm. D. Huntington, as principal and Alanson Ripley, David Holeman, John Outhouse, Emanuel Murphy, Jonathan W. Barlow and Erastus Snow his security acknowledge ourselves to owe the State of Missouri that is to say: William D. Huntington the sum of one hundred and fifty dollars and the said Alanson Ripley, David Holeman, John Outhouse, Emanuel Murphy, Jonathan W. Barlow and Erastus Snow in the like sum of one hundred and fifty dollars to be levied of their goods and chattels lands and tenements if the said Wm. D. Huntington shall fail in the condition underwritten.
The condition of this recognizance is such that if the above bounden William D. Huntington shall personally appear at this circuit court on the first day of the next term thereof to be holden for the county of Clay on the 18th day of March next then and there to answer an indictment to be prefered to the Grand Jury against the said William D. Huntington for attempting by force to rescue and set at liberty certain prisoners confined in the jail of Clay County whereof he stands charged and shall not depart the same without the leave of this said court then this recognizance to be void else to remain in full force. Witness our hands and seals this 13th day of February, A.D. 1839

> Wm. D. Huntington (seal)
> Erastus Snow (seal)
> Alanson Ripley (seal)
> David Holman (seal)
> John Outhouse (seal)
> Emanuel Murphy (seal)
> Jonathan W. Barlow (seal))

TRANSCRIPTION OF EXHIBIT 6.3

John Tillery a witness on behalf of the State being produced sworn & examined deposeth & saith that on last Thursday evening he went to the jail as one of the guards from the house of Samuel Tillery and that three strange persons started and the then deputy jailer and myself and these strangers were admitted into the jail and also three other strangers was admitted into there. Five of them are the prisoners at the bar and one of them eased? out and made his escape. I did not go into the jail but handed the part of the supper carried up into the jail doors. Then I stepped back and closed the inside jail door and I afterwards opened it to let in Mr. Ford and then closed it again and some short time after Mr. Sam Tillery who was in the jail called to me to open the door and I done so. At that time one of the strangers came out being the same that made his escape and stood on the platform before the jail door and shortly after I heard a scuffle in the jail and heard Samuel Tillery holler out once or twice shoot and James Ford who was on the platform went into the doorway and the stranger who had came out of the jail took hold of him and I immediately pulled him from Ford and it did not require much force to pull him away and as soon as pulled away he fled and that at the time of the scuffle he saw Sam Tillery trying to shut the jail doors but could not. (Signed) John Tillery
At this time the testimony on behalf of the State closed. The court then adjourned until tomorrow morning 9 o'clock.

John Tillery a witness on behalf of the
State being produced sworn & examined deposeth & saith that on last
thursday evening he went to the Jail
as one of the guard from the house of
Saml. Tillery & that 3 / Strange persons
Started with the the deputy Jailor & himself
~~[illegible]~~. & the Strangers were admitted into the Jail & also 3 other strangers
was admitted into the. 5 of them are
the prisoners at the Bar and one of them
came out & made his escape, I did
not go into the Jail but handed the
part of the supper carried, in into
the Jail door. then stepped back &
& closed the inside Jail door & I afterwards
opened it to let in Mr. Ford & then closed
it again & some short time after Mr. Sam
Tillery who was in ~~the~~ Jail called to
me to open the door & I done so, at
that time one of the strangers came out
(being the same that made his escape)
& stood on the platt form before the
Jail door — & shortly after I heard a
scuffle in the Jail & heard Saml. Tillery
hallow out once or twice short & Sam
Ford who was on the platform went
into the door way & the stranger who
had come out of the Jail took hold
of him — & I immediately pulled him —
from Ford & it did not require much
force to pull him away & as soon
as pulled away he fled — & that at
the time of the scuffle he saw Sam
Tilley trying to shut the Jail door
but could not ~~he was either held or some person held hold of the door~~

John Tillery

at this time the Testimony on behalf
of the State closed

Exhibit 6.3: John Tillery's testimony during court proceedings of the attempted escape, Clay County Court Archives, Liberty MO

James Ford a witness on behalf of the
State produced sworn & examined
deposeth & saith that on the twenty of
February last past myself and Mr. Samuel Tillery
started in the evening from Mr. Tillerys house
to carry supper up to the prisoners in jail
when we started three of those prisoners at
the bar started with us and went into the
Jail with Mr. Tillery after they had entered a
short time two more men I beleave Two of
those prisoners at the bar came to the Jail
and was admitted to go in upon their request
after a short time one other person came
and was admitted upon his request to go in to
the Jail after the prisoners was done their
supper the things was taken up and carried
out as usual after which Mr. Tillery got
up and told the prisoners at the bar that
they must come out upon which they got
up and Hiram Smith took hold of
Mr. Tillery and one of the prisoners at
the bar also took hold Mr. Tillery which
one I cannot say, one of those who
had went in before this time and after the
Came out and that
Scuffle and took hold of me after some
Scuffling Mr. Tillery told us to flee when
they in the house gave way so that the door
was closed and the man out of doors
made his Escape the man who took
hold of Mr. Tillery I thought at the time
was Mr. Coleman other of the prisoners at the
bar but Mr. Tillery thought not
while we were at the Jail there was circumstances that made me suspect there was a
plot Conspiracy to release the prisoners one is that the 3 of the
prisoners in Jail had their hats on &
an other is that some person went & peeped
into the guard house & & I then hailed him

Exhibit 6.4 (Continued on next page)

96

Exhibit 6.4: James H. Ford's testimonies (2) during court proceedings of the attempted escape, Clay County Court Archives, Liberty MO

TRANSCRIPTION OF EXHIBIT 6.4

James Ford a witness on behalf of the State produced sworn & examined deposeth & saith that on the seventh of February last past thyself and Mr. Samuel Tillery started in the evening from Mr. Tillery's house to carry supper up to the prisoners in jail. When we started three of those prisoners at the bar started with us and went into the jail with Mr. Tillery. After they had entered a short time two more men I believe two of those prisoners at the bar came to the jail and was admitted to going upon their request after a short time. One other person came and was admitted upon his request to go into the jail after the prisoners was done their supper the things was taken up and carried out as usual. After which Mr. Tillery got up and told the prisoners at the bar they must come out. Upon which they got up and Hiram Smith took hold of Mr. Tillery and one of the prisoners at the bar also took hold of Mr. Tillery which one I cannot say. One of those who had went in before this time came out and after the scuffle took hold of me. After some scuffling Mr. Tillery told us fire when they in the house gave way so that the door was closed and the man out of doors made his escape. The man who took hold of Mr. Tillery I thought at the time was Mr. Holeman one of the prisoners at the bar but Mr. Tillery thought not. While we are at the jail there was circumstances that made me suspect there was a plot on foot to release the prisoners in jail. One is that three of the prisoners in jail had their hats on and another is that some person went and peeked? in the guard house and I then hailed him and he told me he was waiting for a gentlemen and he did not wish him to pass the rode without seeing him and shortly after a man came riding and he stopped him and they both went back together. This one walked and the other riding but I do not know whether they were Mormons or not. The jail is on the public street and that this was the first person I had ever seen come & peep into the guard house.

(Signed) James H. Ford

Samuel Tillery a witness on behalf of the
State produced sworn & examined deposeth
and saith that on the 7 day of February last past
at the time I was going to give the prisoners in
Jail their Supper the defendants Hoolman & Ripley
with others were by permission admitted in the Jail
on the plea of having business with the prisoners
that after Supper was over there was some
talk privately with the prisoners. I did not hear
the purport. I then told those in the Jail
that they must go out and the door being
opened one man went out I do not know
his name. Mr Baldwin one of the prisoners
advanced and asked leave to go out with me
to do some business I told him he could
not during the time he was talking to me
they had all crowded close to me & I was
standing close to the door with my right hand
on the door as I believe I then told them
all to stand back and let them go out that
had to go. At that moment Hiram Smith
rushed towards me and said some thing in
a low smothered voice to let him pass or
let him out and the same time he caught
hold by the left arm and tried to shove me
away from the door some one else had
hold of me but I do not know which one
the door was pulled open at the same
time I ordered the guard to fire on them
and they rather retired I then ordered
them to shoot down any one that attempted
to come towards the door they retired to
the right and left and one Mr Barlow
had hold of the door I ordered him to let
it go, he did not do it and I ordered the
^or said I would do it myself
guard to fire on him he then let
go the door and I closed it during
this time there was a scuffle in the
door way but what it was I am not
able to say as I never looked behind
me — & that some person touched me
during the time that the door was
held but I cannot say that it was
either ~~and did not~~ David Holman
or Alanson Ripley there was various things
and circumstances ^before that took place that induced
led me to Suspect there was a Conspiracy

Exhibit 6.5a (Continued on next page)

98

Exhibit 6.5a: Samuel's Tillery's testimony during court proceedings of the attempted escape, Clay County Court Archives, Liberty MO

TRANSCRIPTION OF EXHIBIT 6.5a

Samuel Tillery a witness on behalf of the State produced sworn & examined deposeth and saith that on the 7 day of February last past at the time I was going to give the prisoners in jail their supper the defendant Holeman & Ripley with others were by permission admitted in the jail on the plea of having business with the prisoners. That after supper was over there was some talk privately with the prisoners. I did not hear the purport. I then told those in the jail that they must go out and the door being opened one man went out. I do not know his name. Mr. Baldwin, one of the prisoners, advanced and asked leave to go out with me to do some business. I told him he could not during the time he was talking to me they had all crowded close to me. I was standing close to the door with my right hand on the door as I believe. I then told them all to stand back and let them go out that had to go. At that moment Hiram Smith rushed towards me and said some thing in a low smothered voice to let him pass or let him out and the same time he caught me by the left arm and tried to shove me away from the door. Some one else had hold of me but I do not know which one. The door was pulled open at the same time I ordered the guard to fire on them and they rather returned. I then ordered them to shoot down any one that attempted to come towards the door. They retired to the right and left and a Mr. Barlow had hold of the door. I ordered him to let it go. He did not do it and I ordered the guard to fire on him or said I would do it myself. He then let go the door and I closed it. During this time there was a scuffle in the door way but what it was I am not able to say as I never looked behind me and that some person touched me during this time that the door was held but I cannot that it was either David Holeman or Alanson Ripley. There was various things and circumstances before I & at that took place that induced(?) me to suspect there was a conspiracy among the afore said persons. One circumstances was there tying their horses very near the jail's door which had never been done before. Another was a great silence after we entered the jail. Another was one of the guards came to the door and told me to be on my guard that there was something wrong going on that there had been since he entered the jail two persons being(?) about the jail and when challenged by said guard and did not answer satisfactory and that when the said defendants were going to the jail were wrapped up more than in my opinion the coldness of the evening required to be comfortable. (Signed) Samuel Tillery

With the crime of Treason against the State
When Mr. Samuel Tillery was produced on the
part of the State as a witness and was duly
Sworn did depose and Say as stated in
his testimony on the tryals of David Holeman
and Alonson Riply with this addition
Ques.d by the accused.
at the time the Scuffle commenced between Yan and Hiram Smith, was Caleb Baldwin between Yan and the Prisoners at the bar
and in advance of them?
Answer he Baldwin beckoned to me to advance
as though he wished to speak to me I did
advance one step and he spoke low to me
I answered the Prisoners were Close along side
of Baldwin he rather in front I drew back
and Smith then seized me he Baldwin
being on the right of the door as you
go in and to my right hand further
this deponent saith not
Sam.t Tillery

Mr. Samuel Tillery being Call.d to the bar On again
the part of the prisoners deposeth and saith
further upon being asked by the prisoners Council
whether at the time these prisoners are charged
of committing the crime of attempting to write
the the prisoners in Jail charged with treason
whether he was deputy Sailor and whether
he was Sworn in as such answered
that he was deputy Sailor and that he
had not been Sworn in as such —
Sam.t Tillery

Exhibit 6.5b: Samuel's Tillery's two additional testimonies during court proceedings of the attempted escape, Clay County Court Archives, Liberty, MO

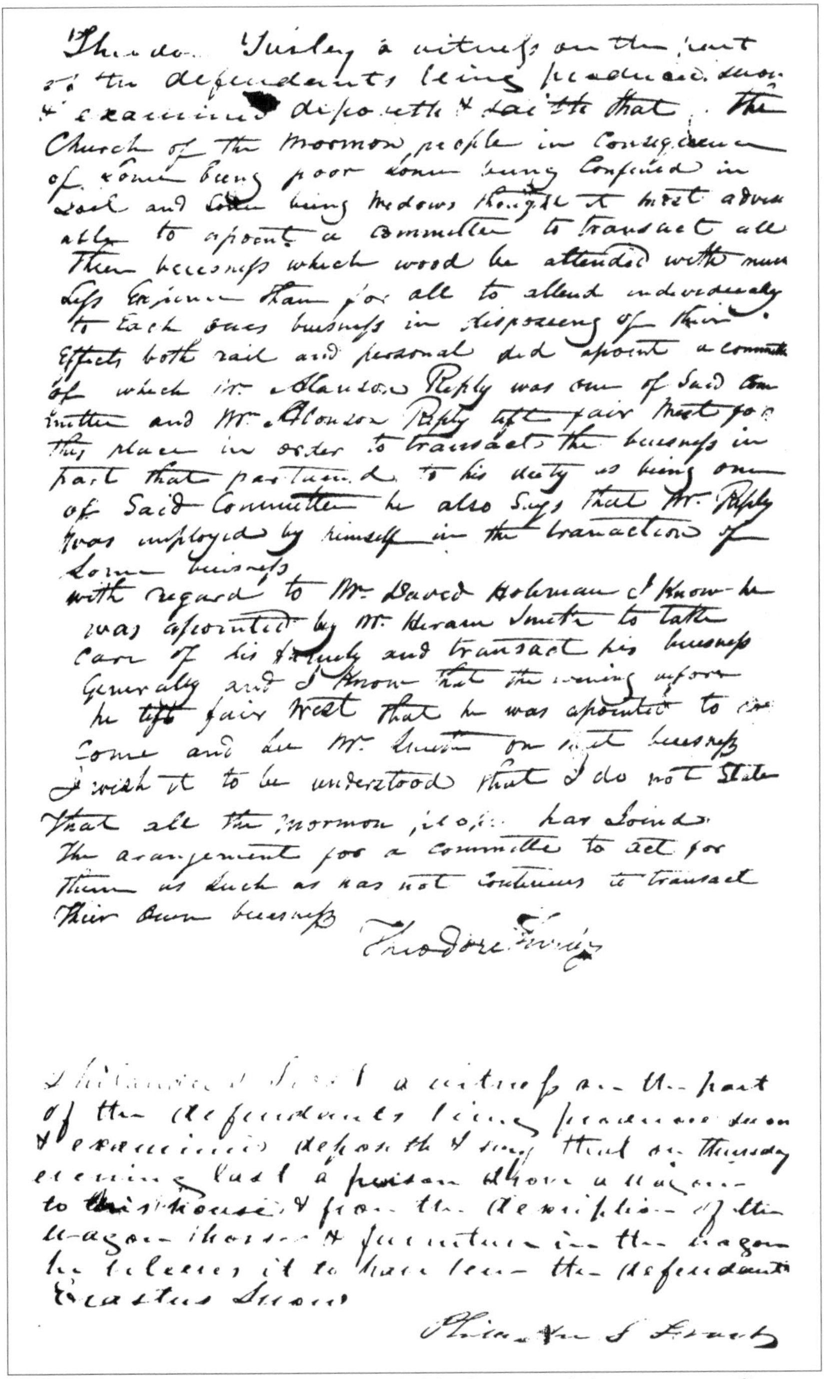

[Handwritten testimony — partially legible cursive script]

Theodore Turley a witness on the part of the defendants being produced, sworn & examined deposeth & saith that the Church of the Mormon people in consequence of some being poor some being confined in jail and others being widows thought it most advisable to appoint a committee to transact all their business which would be attended with much less expense than for all to attend individually to each ones business in disposing of their effects both real and personal did appoint a committee of which Mr. Alanson Ripley was one of said committee and Mr. Alanson Ripley left fair West for this place in order to transact the business in part that pertained to his duty as being one of said committee he also says that Mr. Ripley was employed by himself in the transaction of some business

with regard to Mr. David Holman I know he was appointed by Mr. Hiram Smith to take care of his family and transact his business generally and I know that the evening afore he left fair West that he was appointed to come and see Mr. Smith on said business I wish it to be understood that I do not state that all the Mormon people has joined the arrangement for a committee to act for them as such as has not continued to transact their own business

Theodore Turley

Philander S. Frost a witness on the part of the defendants being produced sworn & examined deposeth & say that on thursday evening last a prison [person] above a wagon to this house & from the description of the wagon horses & furniture in the wagon he believes it to have been the defendants Erastus Snow

Philander S. Frost

Exhibit 6.6: Testimony of Theodore Turley and Philander S. Frost during court proceedings concerning the attempted escape of Joseph Smith, Jr., Clay County Court Archives, Liberty, MO

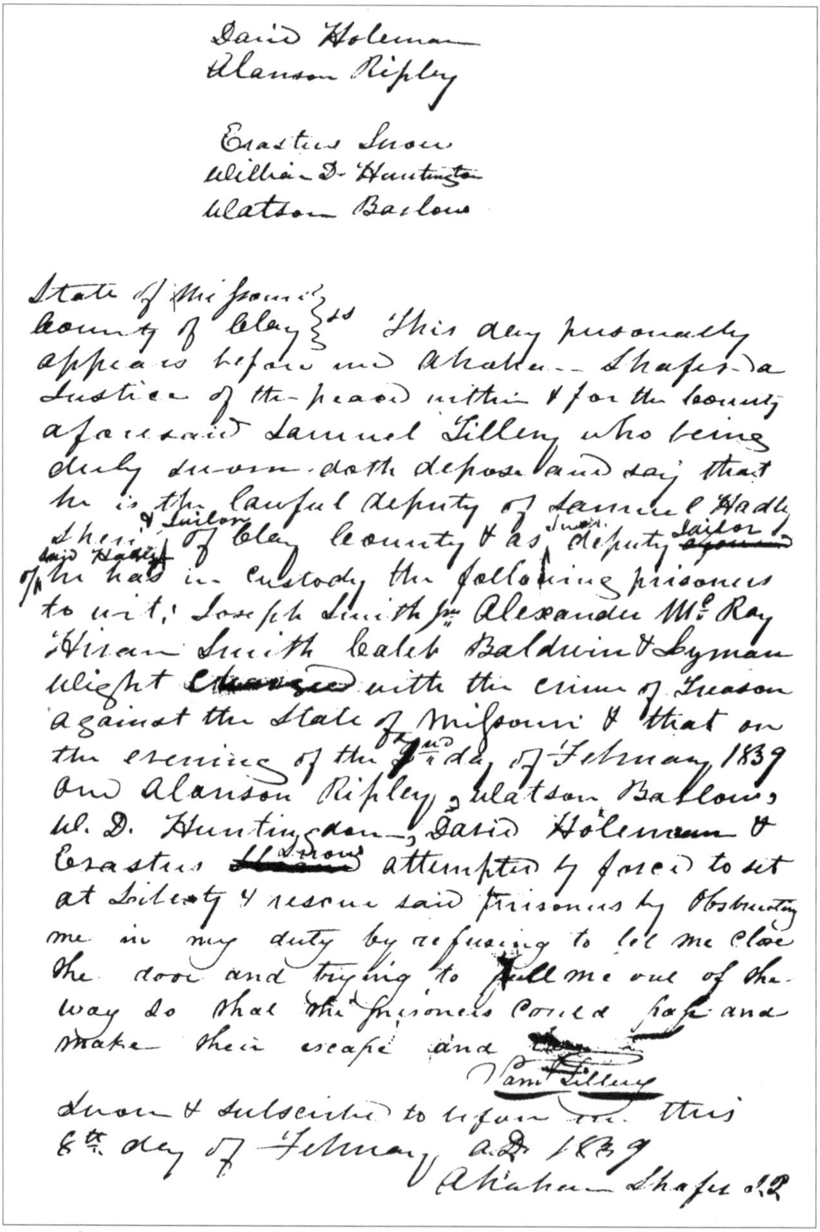

Exhibit 6.7: Charge against brethren for attempting to "set at liberty and rescue said prisoners" (Joseph Smith, Jr. and companions), Clay County Court Archives, Liberty, MO

TRANSCRIPTION OF EXHIBIT 6.7

David Holeman
Alanson Ripley

Erastus Snow
William D. Huntington
Watson Barlow

State of Missouri)
County of Clay   )
This day personally appears before me Abraham Shafer a Justice of the Peace
within and for the county aforesaid Samuel Tillery who being duly sworn doth
depose and say that he is the lawful deputy of Samuel Hadley Sheriff and Jailer of
Clay County and as said deputy Jailer of said Hadley he has in custody the
following prisoners to wit: Joseph Smith Jr, Alexander McRay, Hiram Smith, Caleb
Baldwin, and Lyman Wight charged with the crime of treason against the state of
Missouri and that on the evening of the 7th day of February 1839 one Alanson
Ripley, Watson Barlow, W. D. Huntington, David Holeman, and Erastus Snow
attempted by force to set at liberty and rescue said prisoners by obstructing me in
my duty by refusing to let me close the door and trying to pull me out of the way
so that the prisoners could _____ and make their escape and _____.
                                        Samuel Tillery
Sworn and subscribed to before me this 8th day of February A.D. 1839.
                                        Abraham Shafer J.P.

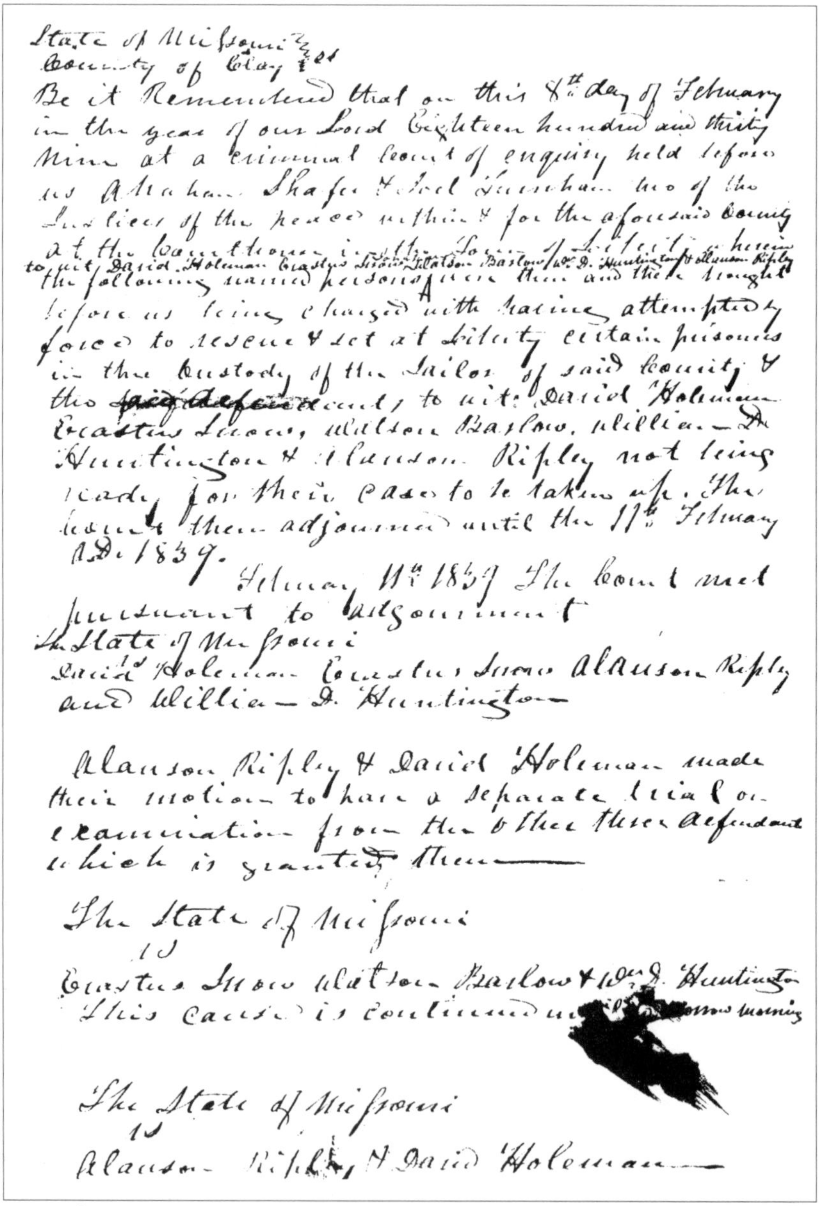

Exhibit 6.8: Charge against brethren trying to rescue Church leaders, Clay County Court Archives, Liberty, MO

Chapter 7

PEOPLE AND SPIRITUAL ATTRIBUTES

Antagonistic Apostates

The most damaging testimony against the brethren contributing to their imprisonment came from former close associates. All had been prominent Church leaders while the Saints were in Missouri. Among the antagonistic apostates were Dr. Sampson Avard, John Corrill, W. W. Phelps, George M. Hinkle, and John Whitmer.[1] In the minutes of the conference at Quincy, Illinois, on Sunday, 17 March 1839, Elder George W. Harris made some remarks about those who had deserted the Saints in their time of "perils, persecutions and danger" and who were continuing to act against the Church. He said that if they would not repent of their sins and turn to God, they could no longer be held in fellowship.

After those at the conference had fully expressed themselves, it was unanimously voted that the following persons be excommunicated: George M. Hinkle, Sampson Avard, John Corrill, Reed Peck, William W. Phelps, Frederick G. Williams, Thomas B. Marsh, Burr Riggs, John Whitmer, and several others.[2] On 17 March 1839, over the signature of "Brigham Young, President," and "Robert B. Thompson, Clerk," these men (with the exception of John Whitmer) and several others were excommunicated from The Church of Jesus Christ of Latter-day Saints.[3]

Affidavits Signed by Thomas B. Marsh and Orson Hyde

During the preliminary hearing after the brethren's arrest at Far West, Judge King, a Methodist, asked many questions about the views of the Church concerning the prophecy of Daniel: "In the days of these

105

kings shall the God of heaven set up a kingdom which shall break in pieces all other kingdoms, and stand forever. . . . and the kingdom and the greatness of the kingdom, under the whole heaven, shall be given to the Saints of the Most High."[4]

He made note that their belief in this prophecy could be used as evidence of Joseph's intention to take over the world. However, the most damaging testimony against the prisoners were two affidavits charging treason signed by Thomas B. Marsh and Orson Hyde on 24 October 1838 in Richmond, Missouri. They claimed that it was the intent of the leaders of the Church to overthrow the governments of Missouri, of the United States, and, eventually, of the world.[5] Marsh wrote out the charges in an affidavit stating the prevarications. Orson Hyde's affidavit of the same day simply said, "The most of the statements in the foregoing disclosure I know to be true: the remainder I believe to be true,"[6] and then he signed it.

Orson Hyde later confessed his mistakes and wrongdoing and within a year and a half was back in full fellowship within the Quorum of Twelve Apostles. Although he was restored to his former position, his action toward Joseph and the brethren cost him the presidency of the Church. Before his death, Brigham Young realigned the quorum, placing Orson's seniority to conform with the date he was reinstated.

The major points in the affidavit of Thomas B. Marsh are as follows:

> They have among them a company, considered true Mormons, called the Danites, who have taken an oath to support the heads of the Church in all things that they say or do, whether right or wrong. Many, however, of this band are much dissatisfied with this oath, as being against moral and religious principles. On Saturday last, I am informed by the Mormons, that they had a meeting at Far West, at which they appointed a company of twelve, by the name of the "Destruction Company," for the purpose of burning and destroying, and that if the people of Buncombe came to do mischief upon the people of Caldwell, and committed depredations upon the Mormons, they were to burn Buncombe; and if the people of Clay and Ray made any movement against them, this destroying company were to burn Liberty and Richmond. . . . The Prophet inculcates the notion, and it is believed by every true Mormon, that Smith's prophecies are superior to the laws of the land. I have heard the Prophet say that he would yet tread down his enemies, and walk over their dead bodies; and if he was not let alone, he would be a second Mohammed to this generation, and that he would make it one gore of blood from the Rocky mountains to the Atlantic ocean;

that like Mohammed, whose motto in treating for peace was, "the Alcoran or the Sword." These last statements were made during the last summer. The number of armed men at Adam-ondi-Ahman was between three and four hundred. (Signed) Thomas B. Marsh.

Following his apostasy, Marsh

lived upon husks for more [than] a score of years, and finally wandered a miserable object of pity, poor, naked, destitute and disconsolate, and appeared before a congregation of 8,000 Saints, and humbly asked them to forgive him and let him at least dwell in our midst; they did forgive him, and permitted him to be baptized, and he remained a member, a living, palsied, limping spectacle of the fruits of apostasy.[7]

W. W. Phelps

The W. W. Phelps case was extremely fascinating and is a tremendous example of repentance, change, forgiveness, and love. According to a *History of the Church* footnote in connection with the Prophet's letter to W. W. Phelps:

When the great offense of Elder William W. Phelps is taken into account—amounting as it did to a betrayal of the Prophet and the Church in Missouri during the troubles of the Saints in that state—this letter to the Prophet asking for forgiveness is rather remarkable. The Prophet's frank forgiveness of his erring brother, gently chiding his wrong-doing, but at the same time remembering in a large way that brother's former devotion and labors; the Prophet's willingness to have the prodigal return and occupy his former high standing among the Saints . . . exhibits a broad-mindedness and generosity that can only come from a great soul, influenced by the spirit of charity enjoined upon his disciples by the teachings of the Son of God. One of the surest evidences of Joseph Smith's greatness of mind and of the inspiration of God upon him is to be seen in his treatment of those who had fallen but were willing to and did repent of their sins. His capacity to forgive under these circumstances seemed boundless.[8]

In Joseph's response to W. W. Phelps letter and request for forgiveness, Joseph wrote:

It is true, that we have suffered much in consequence of your behavior—the cup of gall, already full enough for mortals to drink, was indeed filled to overflowing when you turned against us. One with whom we had oft taken sweet counsel together, and enjoyed many refreshing seasons from the Lord—"had it been an enemy, we could have borne it." "In the day that thou stoodest on the other side, in the day when strangers carried away captive his forces, and foreigners entered into his gates, and cast lots upon [Far West], even thou wast as one of them." . . .

However, the cup has been drunk, the will of our Father has been done, and we are yet alive, for which we thank the Lord. And having been delivered from the hands of wicked men by the mercy of our God, we say it is your privilege to be delivered from the powers of the adversary, be brought into the liberty of God's dear children, and again take your stand among the Saints of the Most High, and by diligence, humility, and love unfeigned, commend yourself to our God, and your God, and to the Church of Jesus Christ.

Believing your confession to be real, and your repentance genuine, I shall be happy once again to give you the right hand of fellowship, and rejoice over the returning prodigal. . . .

Come on, dear brother, since the war is past, For friends at first, are friends again at last.[9]

The exceptional accomplishments of W. W. Phelps in the Church in ensuing years gave efficacy to his genuine change of heart. He paid Joseph the highest tribute by writing the hymn, "Praise to the Man." Four days after the death of Joseph and Hyrum, "A Word of Consolation" was written to The Church of Jesus Christ of Latter-day Saints and signed by W. W. Phelps, Willard Richards, and John Taylor.[10] This document is certainly worth the reading. At that time, John Taylor was still recovering from the wounds he received in Carthage Jail.

Deeply impressed for the welfare of all, while mourning the great loss of President Joseph Smith, our "Prophet and Seer," and President Hyrum Smith, our "Patriarch," we have considered the occasion demanded of us a word of consolation.

As has been the case in all ages, these saints have fallen martyrs for the truth's sake, and their escape from the persecution of a wicked world, in blood to bliss, only strengthens our faith, and confirms our religion as pure and holy.

We, therefore, as servants of the Most High God, having the Bible, Book of Mormon, and the Book of Doctrine and Covenants, together with thousands of witnesses, for Jesus Christ, would beseech the Latter-day Saints, in Nauvoo and elsewhere, to hold fast to the faith that has been delivered to them in the last days, abiding in the perfect law of the gospel.

Be peaceable, quiet citizens, doing the works of righteousness, and as soon as the Twelve and other authorities can assemble, or a majority of them, the onward course to the great gathering of Israel, and the final consummation of the dispensation of the fullness of times will be pointed out, so that the murder of Abel, the assassination of hundreds, the righteous blood of all the holy Prophets, from Abel to Joseph, sprinkled with the best blood of the Son of God, as the crimson sign of remission, only carries conviction to the bosoms of all intelligent beings, that the cause is just and will continue; and blessed are they that hold out faithful to the end, while apostates, consenting to the shedding of innocent blood, have no forgiveness in this world nor in the world to come.

Union is peace, brethren, and eternal life is the greatest gift of God. Rejoice then, that you are found worthy to live and die for God. Men may kill the body, but they cannot hurt the soul, and wisdom shall be justified of her children. Amen. [Signed] W. W. Phelps, Willard Richards, John Taylor, July 1, 1844.

William Earl McLellin

William E. McLellin was teaching school in Illinois when he

William McLellin, LDS Church Archives, Salt Lake City, UT

heard David Whitmer testify "to having seen an Holy Angel." He followed Mormon missionaries to Jackson County and was baptized into the Church on 20 August 1831 by Hyrum Smith. He later served missions to the East with Hyrum, Samuel H. Smith, and Parley P. Pratt. At age twenty-nine, McLellin was ordained one of the original twelve apostles on 15 February 1835 by Oliver Cowdery, David Whitmer, and Martin Harris at Kirtland, Ohio. He was excommunicated from the Church at Far West on 11 May 1838.

During the trial in Richmond, McLellin and others plundered and robbed the houses of Sidney Rigdon, George Morey, the widow Phebe Ann Patten, and others. While the brethren were imprisoned in Richmond it is said that

> McLellin, who was a large and active man, went to the sheriff and asked for the privilege of flogging the Prophet. Permission was granted on condition that Joseph would fight. The sheriff made known to Joseph McLellin's earnest request, to which Joseph consented, if his irons were taken off. McLellin then refused to fight unless he could have a club, to which Joseph was perfectly willing; but the sheriff would not allow them to fight on such unequal terms.[11]

While Joseph was in Liberty Jail, McLellin entered Emma and Joseph's house in Far West and plundered it, taking "one roll of linen cloth, quantity of valuable buttons, one piece of cashmere, a number of very valuable books of great variety, a number of vesting with

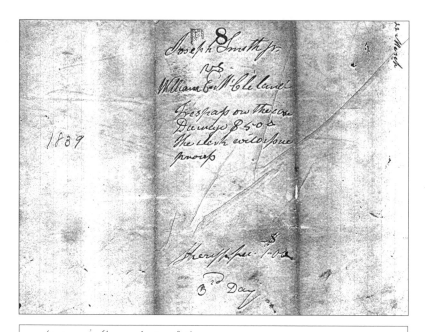

Exhibit 7.1: Cover sheet and summons of William Earl Mceland (McLellin) for action of trespass and damages brought by Joseph Smith, Jr., Clay County Archives and Historical Library, Liberty, MO

various other articles."[12] He also took from Joseph's stable "one gig and harness, with some other articles."[13] Court action was taken against William McLellin, and he was summoned to Liberty to answer the charges. (See Exhibit 7.1.) Emma claimed that he and his associates took blankets, which caused her great distress when Joseph requested she send blankets to the jail and she had none to send.

Alanson Ripley

It would be an impossible task to enumerate the many men and women who were closely involved with Joseph and his companions and who played important and meaningful roles during this period of confinement. One who has come to light and who is not given recognition for his many acts of assistance is Alanson Ripley. Alanson and Heber C. Kimball were appointed liaisons between the Prophet and the brethren. Alanson visited the jail five different times: 23 January, 7 February, 14 March, 22 March, and 31 March. His name appeared at the top of the signatures on the 15 March petition to the Supreme Court. He appeared before Judge Abraham Shafer with the others who signed to affirm the petition. When he visited the jail on 22 March, he took the "package of letters for Quincy." The first time the prisoners attempted to escape, he was among the six visiting brethren who had come to see them and, when charged, spent several days in the jail as a prisoner. (See Exhibit 7.2.)

Transcription of this criminal court case is filed in the Clay County Court House at Liberty, Missouri, under the name of Alanson Ripley in Criminal Case Record, Box 4, 1839.

After the Saints arrived in Quincy, Illinois, and four days after the brethren had left Liberty Jail, Alanson Ripley wrote a passionate letter to them dated 10 April. The following is an excerpt from that letter:

> Dear brethren, I am at your service, and I await your counsel at Quincy, and shall be happy to grant you the desire of your hearts. I am ready to act. Please to give me all the intelligence that is in your power. If you take a change of venue, let me know what county you will come to, and when, as near as possible, and what road you will come: for I shall be an adder in the path.
>
> Yes, my dear brethren, God Almighty will deliver you. Fear not, for your redemption draweth near; the day of your deliverance

The Court then distinctly informed the prisoners of the charges [redacted] made against them & that they were at liberty to refuse to answer any question put to them & thereupon the defendants Alanson Ripley & David Holeman made the following statement: Alanson Ripley states that he was one of the committee on the part of part of the Mormon Church to sell their lands in Caldwell County & that he had come to Liberty to make some arrangements with the prisoners in the jail of Clay County whose families were about to leave the State of Missouri & that they wanted the prisoners in the jail of Clay County to furnish them the means of so doing. ~~That the families which at the court.~~ That 4 of the prisoners breakfasted at Thos. Farmer's & one of them had stayed all night at Farmers to wit Erastus Snow, & ~~that he the~~ said Ripley does not recollect of stating to Thos. Farmer his business in Liberty & that he knew of Rigdon's being [remitted to Clay jail if unguarded before he left Caldwell County] [redacted] & that he had not seen Rigdon since bailed. & that he believes the deposition of Samuel Tillery to be true except that he thinks but one person who was Hiram Smith that had hold of said Tillery while in jail & that he knew of no combination or plot to release the prisoners in Clay County jail & that he remonstrated against too many persons coming from Caldwell coming to Clay County for the purpose of selling the lands in Caldwell county for the reason that it would probably produce great excitement

Alanson Ripley

Firm sufficient security

Exhibit 7.2: Alanson Ripley's testimony during the court proceedings on charges of assisting in the attempted jail break of 7 April 1939, Clay County Court Archives, Liberty, MO

is at hand. Dear brethren, I have it in my heart to lay my body in the sane, or deliver you from your bonds; and my mind is intensely fixed on the latter.

Dear brethren, you will be able to judge of the spirit that actuates my breast; for when I realize your sufferings, my heart is like wax before the fire; but when I reflect upon the cause of your afflictions, it is like fire in my bones, and burns against your enemies, and I never can be satisfied, while there is one of them to stand against a wall, or draw a sword, or pull a trigger. My sword has never been sheathed in peace for the blood of David W. Patten and those who were butchered at Haun's Mill, crieth for vengeance from the ground.

Therefore, hear O ye heavens! and write it, O ye recording angels! bear the tidings ye flaming seraphs! that I from this day declare myself the avenger of the blood of those innocent men, and of the innocent cause of Zion, and of her prisoners; and I will not rest until they are free, who are in prison, as I am.

Your families are all well and in good spirits. May the Lord bless you all. Amen

Brother Amasa Lyman and Watson Barlow join in saying, Our hearts are as thy heart. Brother Joseph, if my spirit is wrong, for God's sake correct it. Brethren, be of good cheer, for we are determined, as God liveth, to rescue you from that hellish crowd, or die in the furrow. We shall come face foremost. [signed] Alanson Ripley[14]

Emanuel Masters Murphy

Don Murphy, a visitor to the Liberty Jail Visitors' Center in the summer of 1996, shared the following account of his great-great-grandfather:

Emanuel Murphy joined the Church and moved to Far West to be with the Saints. He sold Joseph a beautiful black horse. The Prophet paid cash for part of the amount and wrote an I.O.U. for the balance.

Not long after this transaction, Joseph was arrested and eventually taken to Liberty Jail. Emanuel went to visit him. The jailer wanted to know his reason for seeing the prisoner. Acting upset, he replied, "Because he owes me money." The jailer asked if he could prove it. Taking the I.O.U. from his pocket, he showed it to the jailer and was then allowed to see Joseph.

Once in the presence of Joseph, Emanuel, who had a $5 gold piece in the palm of his hand, transferred it to the Prophet Joseph when they shook hands. Joseph was most grateful and told Emanuel that he didn't know when he would be able repay him or pay for the horse. Murphy told him to "put it on the temple." (See Appendices A and B.)

There are many stories such as this that depict the love of the Saints for the Prophet and for each other.

Emanuel seems to be forgotten as one who was involved with the court case of 8 April 1839. Court documents show he was security for recognizance four times. These documents show that Emanuel Murphy and others signed as security for the sum of $150, the sum levied against the brethren for "attempting by force to rescue and set at liberty certain prisoners confined in the jail." (See Exhibits 7.3 and transcription and Exhibit 7.4 and transcription.) Emanuel Murphy was one of the many valiant and great souls within this time period.

Heber C. Kimball and Theodore Turley

Many of the brethren were filled with the desire to rescue Joseph and his companions from their incarceration in the dungeon. Untiring effort was made with the hope it could be accomplished. On 25 March, Elders Heber C. Kimball and Theodore Turley started their journey to see the governor. They called on the sheriff of Ray county to get a copy of the mittimus by which the prisoners were held in custody. The sheriff told them he had none. The brethren had been held for several months without even a mittimus and for crimes supposedly committed in another county. They then went to Judge King, and "he made out a kind of mittimus."[15] Elders Kimball and Turley took it, along with the petition to the state supreme court judges, and traveled to Jefferson City (the capital). The governor was away. They were treated kindly by the secretary of state. When presented with the papers, he found it hard to believe that those were the only documents by which the prisoners were being held, as the documents were illegal:

> The Secretary was astonished at Judge King acting as he did, but said he could do nothing in the premises, and if the governor were present, he could do nothing. . . .
>
> The brethren then started to find the supreme judges, and get writs of habeas corpus; and after riding hundreds of miles to effect this object, returned to Liberty on the 30th of March . . . but did not obtain the writ of habeas corpus.[16]

Theodore Turley also testified before Joel Turnham in defense of the brethren. (See Exhibit 6.6 in Chapter 6.)

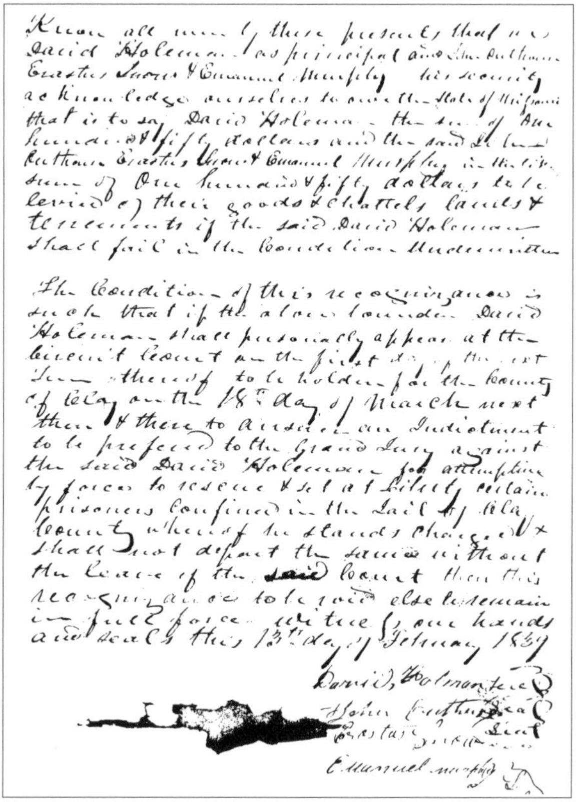

Exhibit 7.3: Recognizance Agreement of David Holeman principal with John Outhouse, Erastus Snow and Emanuel Murphy, Clay County Court Archives, Liberty, MO

TRANSCRIPTION OF EXHIBIT 7.3

Know all men by these presents that we David Holeman as principal and John Outhouse, Erastus Snow and Emanuel Murphy his security acknowledge ourselves to owe the state of Missouri that is to say David Holeman the sum of one hundred and fifty dollars and the said John Outhouse, Erastus Snow and Emanuel Murphy in the like sum of one hundred and fifty dollars to be levied of their goods and chattels lands and tenements if the said David Holeman shall fail in the condition underwritten.

The condition of this recognizance is such that if the above bounden David Holeman shall personally appear at the circuit court on the first day of the next term thereof to be holden for the county of Clay on the 18th day of March next then and there to answer an indictment to be prefered to the Grand Jury against the said David Holeman for attempting by force to rescue and set at liberty certain prisoners confined in the jail of Clay County whereof he stands charged and shall not depart the same without the leave of this said court then this recognizance to be void else to remain in full force. Witness our hands and seals this 13th day of February, 1839

David Holeman (seal)
John Outhouse (seal)
Erastus Snow (seal)
Emanuel Murphy (seal)

Exhibit 7.4: Recognizance Agreement of Alanson Ripley principal with
Erastus Snow and Emanuel Murphy, Clay County Court Archives, Liberty MO

TRANSCRIPTION OF EXHIBIT 7.4

**Know all men by these presents that said Alanson Ripley as principal and Erastus
Snow and Emanuel Murphy his security acknowledge ourselves to owe the state of
Missouri that is to say: Alanson Ripley the sum of one hundred and fifty dollars
and the said Erastus Snow and Emanuel Murphy in the like sum of one hundred
and fifty dollars to be levied of their goods and their chattels lands and tenements
if the said Alanson Ripley should fail in the condition underwritten.**
**The condition of this recognizance is such that if the above bounden Alanson
Ripley should personally appear at the circuit court on the first day of the next
term thereof to be holden for the county of Clay on the 18th day of March next
then and there to answer an indictment to be (prefered ?) to the Grand Jury
against the said Alanson Ripley for attempting by force to rescue and set at liberty
certain prisoners confined in the jail of Clay County whereof he stands charged
and shall not depart the same without the leave of this said court then this
recognizance to (be) void else to remain in full force. Witness our hands and seals
this 13th day of February, A. D. 1839**

Alanson Ripley (seal)
Erastus Snow (seal)
Emanuel Murphy (seal)

The Saints

Following the Liberty Jail experience, Joseph Smith wrote a beautiful tribute to the Saints which should be included in this portion:

> The conduct of the Saints, under their accumulated wrongs and sufferings, has been praiseworthy; their courage in defending their brethren from the ravages of the mobs; their attachment to the cause of truth, under circumstances the most trying and distressing which humanity can possibly endure; their love to each other; their readiness to afford assistance to me and my brethren who were confined in a dungeon; their sacrifices in leaving Missouri, and assisting the poor widows and orphans, and securing them houses in a more hospitable land; all conspire to raise them in the estimation of all good and virtuous men, and has secured them the favor and approbation of Jehovah....Their attention and affection to me while in prison, will ever be remembered by me; and when I have seen them thrust away and abused by the jailer and guard, when they came to do any kind office, and to cheer our minds while we were in the gloomy prison-house, gave me feelings which I cannot describe.[17]

The rendering of pure love, concern, and service to Joseph, the brethren with him, and their families must have been a sustaining factor to the Saints—one that brought joy and relief.

Records and letters give us an insight to the feelings and emotions of the Saints who lived during this period. Only a small representation of what is available has been used to demonstrate how people acted and reacted to the afflictions heaped upon the members of the Church. Before the restoration, we had little access to the personal lives, emotions, and feelings of those who were keeping the records. Primarily, we had only the recorded word. Joseph Smith was the first prophet whose day-to-day experiences and teachings were preserved and are available to those who live now. We can get to know Brother Joseph through the wealth of information that has come to us. Certainly, we can know for ourselves that he is the great prophet of the last dispensation.

Following Joseph's martyrdom, John Taylor wrote, "Joseph Smith, the Prophet and Seer of the Lord, has done more, save Jesus only, for the salvation of men in this world, than any other man that ever lived in it."[18]

All the journals, letters, and records verify this statement and provide a literal treasure of information concerning the Prophet Joseph Smith, Jr.

Chapter 8

CORRESPONDENCE AND THE GAOL (JAIL)

December 1838 Correspondence

"Pen or tongue of angels" cannot reconstruct the time spent in the jail, but much can be pieced together from the letters, journals, and testimonies of those who lived the experience.

1 December: Joseph wrote to Emma to let her know he was now at Liberty Jail and in good spirits.[1] (See Exhibit 8.1.)

16 December: Joseph wrote to the Church in Caldwell County.[2] The letter opened with Joseph's giving a prophecy of tremendous assurance: "We believe that that God who seeth us in this solitary place, will hear our prayers, and reward you openly."[3] He then expressed his concern for the Saints' well being and gave encouragement to them. Following are excerpts:

> May grace, mercy, and the peace of God be and abide with you not withstanding all your sufferings, we assure you that you have our prayers and fervent desires for your welfare, day and night. . . . Therefore God has made our shoulders broad that we can bear it. We glory in our tribulation because we know that God is with us, that he is our friend and that he will save our souls.

Included was a prophecy concerning mobocracy and its effect upon faithful Saints:

> But we want you to remember Haman and Mordecai: you know Haman could not be satisfied so long as he saw Mordecai at the king's gate, and he sought the life of Mordecai and the people of the Jews. But the Lord so ordered it, that Haman was hanged upon his own gallows.

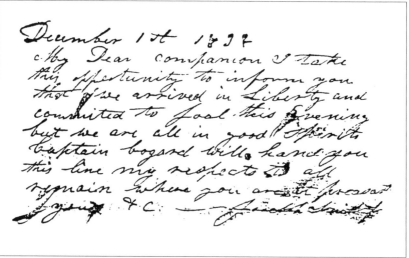

Exhibit 8.1: Letter from Joseph Smith, Jr. to Emma Smith dated 1 December 1838, LDS Church Archives, Salt Lake City, UT

So shall it come to pass with poor Haman in the last days. Those who have sought by unbelief and wickedness, and by the principle of mobocracy, to destroy us and the people of God, by killing them and scattering them abroad, and wilfully and maliciously delivering us into the hands of murderers, desiring us to be put to death, thereby having us dragged about in chains and cast into prison, and for what cause? It is because we were honest men, and were determined to save the lives of the Saints at the expense of our own. I say unto you, that those who have thus villously treated us like Haman, shall be hanged on their own gallows; or in other words, shall fall into their own gin and snare, and ditch and trap, which they have prepared for us, and shall go backwards and stumble and fall, and their names shall be blotted out, and God shall reward them according to all their abominations.

Joseph then closed with "Be of good cheer, for the keys that I gave unto you are yet with you. And now brethren—and when we say brethren, we mean those who have continued faithful in Christ, men, women and children—we feel to exhort you in the name of the Lord Jesus, to be strong in the faith in the new and everlasting covenant."[4]

This letter is closed with Joseph's firm declaration about Zion: "Zion shall yet live though she seem to be dead."

January 1839 Correspondence

16 January 1839: The First Presidency wrote to Heber C. Kimball and Brigham Young,[5] giving a great declaration about the work of the Lord.[6]

> Joseph Smith, Jun., Sidney Rigdon and Hyrum Smith, prisoner's for Jesus' sake, send greetings. . . . Inasmuch as we are in prison, for a little season, if need be, the management of the affairs of the Church devolves on you, that is the Twelve. . . . If we live, we live; and if we die for the testimony of Jesus, we die; but whether we live or die, let the work of God go on."

Members of the presidency, although in a dungeon, were in control of the kingdom and were exercising the authority vested in them:

> It will be necessary for you to get the Twelve together, ordain such as have not been ordained, or at least such of them as you can get, and proceed to regulate the Elders as the Lord may give you wisdom. We nominate George A. Smith and Lyman Sherman to take the places of Orson Hyde and Thomas B. Marsh. . . .
>
> Brethren, we remain yours in hope of eternal life. Sidney Rigdon, Joseph Smith, Jr., Hyrum Smith
>
> N.B. Appoint the oldest of those of the Twelve, who were first appointed, to be the president of your quorum. J.S., S.R., H.S.

24 January: Joseph wrote a petition to the Missouri Legislature.[7] The following are excerpts:

> We ask the sympathies of no one. We ask sheer justice; tis all we expect, and all we merit, but we merit that. . . . We know that much of the prejudice against us is not so much to be attributed to a want of honest motives amongst the citizens as it is to misrepresentation. . . . It is a difficult task to change opinions once formed.

This petition was directed to James M. Hughes with an interesting postscript that read: "Will you be so kind as to present this to the House. The community here would, I believe, have no objection for the trial of these men being transferred to St. Louis. [Signed] P.H.B."

It would be difficult to ascertain who "P.H.B." was, but the initials fit Presendia Huntington Bull (Buell), who visited the jail once with her father (14 January) and once with Frederick G. Williams (no date). She carried the correspondence.

February 1839 Correspondence

26 February: In response to a letter written by Isaac Galland to D.W. Rogers[8] on 11 February informing of land, cabins, etc. available in Commerce, Illinois, Mr. Galland inquired what had happened to Joseph Smith and expressed an interest in knowing more about the Church:

> I desire very much to know how your captive brethren in Missouri are faring. I should like to know if Joseph Smith, Jun. is at liberty or not, and what his prospects are. . . . I wish to serve your cause in any matter which Providence may afford me the opportunity of doing. . . . Accept, dear sir, for yourself and in behalf of the Church a people, assurance of my sincere sympathy in your sufferings and wrongs, and deep solicitude for your immediate relief from present distress, and future triumphant conquest over every enemy. Yours truly, [signed] Isaac Galland.

March 1839 Correspondence

3 and 4 March: Lyman Wight wrote about a plan to escape and its failure. (See Chapter 6, **The Inside Break**.) Lyman informs us of the escape attempt that was started on 1 March and identifies where the leak came from that led to their discovery and failure. It also confirms what Joseph and Hyrum mentioned about having freedoms of leaving the jail.

15 March: Joseph wrote, "To Honorable Judge Tompkins, or either of the judges of the Supreme Court for the state of Missouri."[9] Excerpts follow:

> The petitioners, Alanson Ripley, Heber C. Kimball, Joseph B. Noble, William H. Huntington, and Joseph Smith, Jun. beg leave respectfully to represent to your honor, that Joseph Smith, Jun., is now unlawfully confined and restrained of his liberty in Liberty jail, Clay county, Missouri; that he has been restrained of his liberty nearly five months. . . . [T]he cause of his confinement is unlawful from the first to the last. He was taken from his house by a fraud being practiced upon him by a man of the name of George M. Hinkle. . . . [H]e was forced, contrary to his wishes, and without knowing the cause, into the camp, which was commanded by General Lucas of Jackson county, and thence sent to Ray county, sleeping on the ground, and suffering many insults and injuries, and deprivations, which were calculated in their nature to break down the spirit and constitution of the most robust and hardy of mankind. . . . [He] was deprived of the privilege of being examined before the court as the law directs; that witnesses on the part of the state were taken by force of arms, threatened with extermination or immediate death, and were brought without subpoena or warrant, under the awful and glaring anticipation of being exterminated if they did not swear something against him to please the mob or his persecutors. . . . [T]he commitment was an illegal commitment, for the law

requires that a copy of the testimony should be put in the hands of the jailer, which was not done. . . . [T]he prisoner has been denied the privilege of the law in a writ of habeas corpus. . . . [I]mmediately after the prisoner was taken, his family were frightened and driven out of their house, and that too, by the witnesses on the part of the state, and plundered of their goods; that the prisoner was robbed of a very fine horse, saddle and bridle, and other property of considerable amount. . . . Therefore your petitioners pray your honor to grant to him the state's writ of habeas corpus, directed to the jailer of Clay county, Missouri, commanding him forthwith to bring before you the body of the prisoner, so that his case may be heard before your honor. . . . [Signed] Alanson Ripley, Heber C. Kimball, William Huntington, Joseph B. Noble, Joseph Smith, Jun.[10]

15 March: Hyrum Smith[11] and Caleb Baldwin made a similar petition.[12] Lyman Wight's petition was similar but was addressed "To the Honorable Judges of the Supreme Court for the State of Missouri."[13] Alexander McRea's was addressed "To the Judge Tompkins, of the Supreme court for the State of Missouri."[14]

15 March: Joseph wrote to Mrs. Norman Bull (Presendia H. Buell).[15] She visited the jail twice and was refused entrance on the second visit. Knowledge of this refusal prompted a letter from the Prophet. Excerpts follow:

> My heart rejoiced at the friendship you manifested in requesting to have conversation with us. . . . [E]nclosed in the walls of a prison for five months it seems to me that my heart will always be more tender after this than ever it was before my heart bleeds continually when I contemplate the distress of the Church. . . . I never could have felt as I now do if I had not suffered the wrongs that I have suffered all things shall work together for good to them that love God. . . . I wanted to communicate something and I wrote this. [Signed] J. Smith, Jun.

16 March: Letter from Hyrum to Mary F.[16] Excerpts follow: "Mary my dear companion I again once more sit down to write a few lines to you of our circumstances. . . . Bro. Ripley and Kimball were here yesterday. We have done all we could to make our escape from the prison and not to endanger our lives."

Hyrum then wrote of their second attempt to escape and its failure. (See Chapter 6, **The Inside Break**.) He mentioned Mary's living in the country where things would be less expensive. He had sorrow upon sorrow, "but what can I do or what can I say?" He then asked about little healthy boy Joseph F.

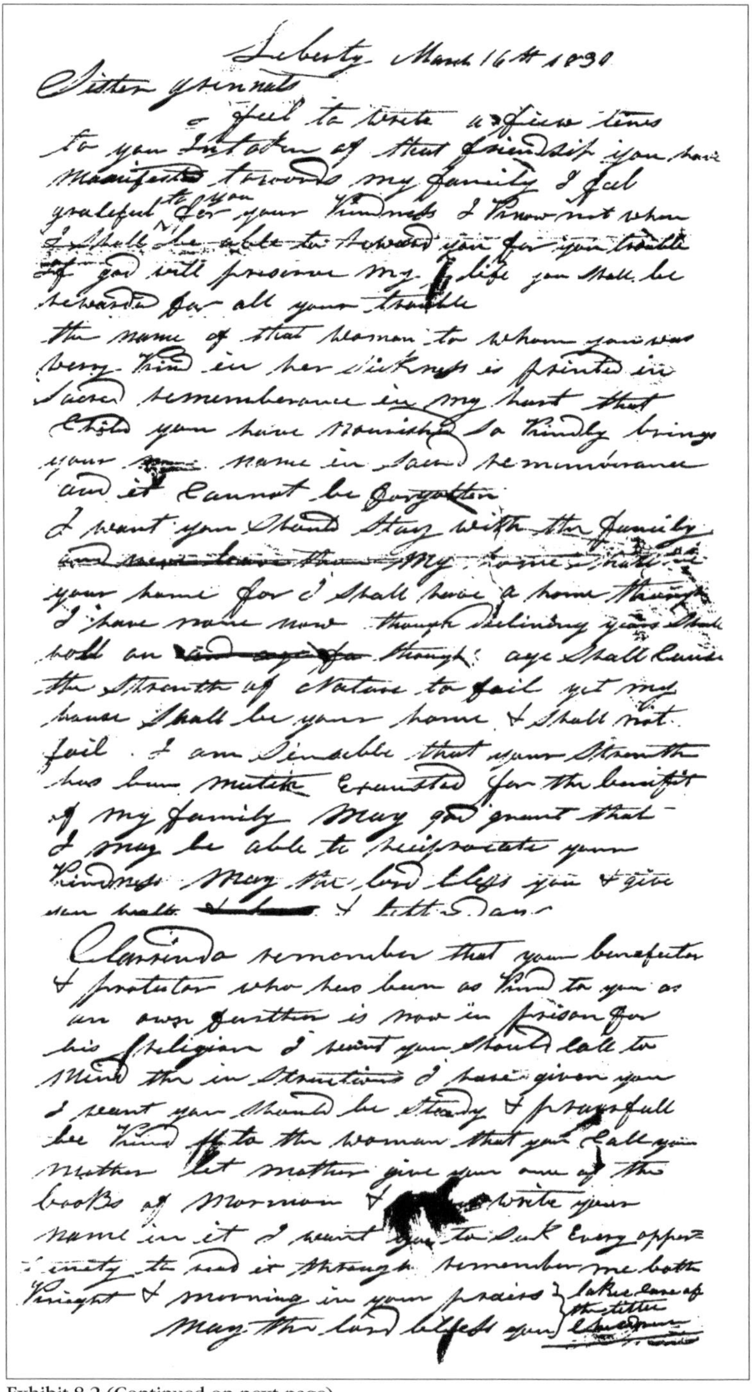

Exhibit 8.2 (Continued on next page)

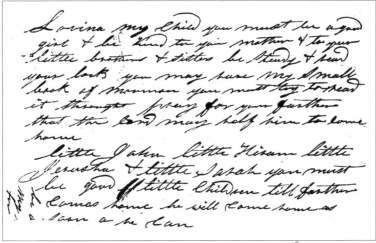

Exhibit 8.2: Letter from Hyrum Smith to a Sister Grinnals from Liberty Jail, LDS Church Archives, Salt Lake City, UT

TRANSCRIPTION OF EXHIBIT 8.2

Liberty, March 16, 1839
Sister Grinnals;
I feel to write a few lines to you in token of that friendship you have manifested towards my family. I feel grateful to you for your kindness and know not when I shall be able to reward you for your trouble. If God will preserve my life, you shall be rewarded for all your trouble.
The name of that woman to whom you was very kind in her sickness is printed in sacred remembrance in my heart. That child you have nourished so kindly brings your name in sacred remembrance and it cannot be forgotten.
I want you should stay with the family and never leave them. My home shall be your home for I shall have a home though I have none now. Though age shall cause the strength of nature to fail, yet my house shall be your home. I shall not fail. I am sensible that your strength has been much exhausted for the benefit of my family. May God grant that I may be able to reciprocate your kindness. May the Lord bless you and give you health and better days.
Clairinda, remember that your benefactor and protector who has been as kind to you as an own father is now in prison for his religion. I wish you should call to mind the instructions I have given you. I want you should be steady and prayerful. Be kind to the woman that you call your mother. Let mother give you one of the Books of Mormon and write your name in it. I want you to seek every opportunity to read it through. Remember me both night and morning in your prayers. May the Lord bless you. Take care of the little children.
Lovina, my child, you must be a good girl and be kind to your mother and to your little brothers and sisters, be steady and read your book. You may have my small Book of Mormon. You must try to read it through. Pray for your father that the Lord may help him to come home. Little John, little Hiram, little Jerusha and little Sarah, you must be good little children till father comes home. He will come as soon as he can.

(Hyrum Smith)

16 March: Letter from Hyrum to Sister Grinnals, who had been so kind to his family by taking care of his sick wife Mary, the baby, and their five children. The letter also had instructions to his oldest children. (See Exhibit 8.2 and transcription.)

19 March: Four letters were received at the jail. One was from Bishop Partridge (5 March).[17] The other letters were from Don Carlos Smith to Joseph and Hyrum,[18] Wm. Smith to Joseph and Hyrum (6 March),[19] and the fourth was from Emma to Joseph (7 March).

On this same day, Hyrum wrote to Mary F. as follows:

> Mary my dear: [He had received a letter from Brother Partridge through the hand of Brother Rogers. He had only scraps of paper to write on.] I was somewhat disappointed that I did not hear from you and the family by your own hand. Bro. Partridge says he informed you of the opportunity of sending by Bro. Rogers. I do not know but you were sick. [He expressed feelings of anxiety.] [A]nd perhaps some kind angel or brooding spirit may manifest all things to me by dream or vision. God has said that he would deliver us from the power of our enemies in his own due time. We try to be as patient as possible. I desire to hear from you by your hand if it is possible. You must excuse my form writing. My nerves are somewhat effected and my hands are this evening quite swollen and fingers are stiff and painful with the rheumatism We have appealed to the supreme judges habeas corpus. We think they will set us free. Pray for us. Pray for me. My affection? for you is incessant. Your in the bands of true friendship and love till death.

20 March: Joseph and the brethren started an epistle addressed to the "Church scattered abroad, and to Bp. Partridge in particular." It contained D&C Sections 121, 122, and 123.[20]

The scribe was Alexander McRae. (See Exhibit 8.3.) Hyrum wrote to Mary F:

> Mary my dear companion, this morning Bro. Rogers came in to see us and thinks he will not return under two weeks. I wrote a short line this evening to you not knowing that I would have an opportunity of writing this morning. They thought they would be at liberty before this time and would be with you so have written much. Our guards are very strict and have been since Elder Rigdon went away from here. The people have been suspicious that he would send a strong force to set us at liberty so they have been more strict. I slept a good day and night but our freedom is close at hand. God is with us and we know the will of God. . . . [T]he people our enemies must be left without excuse. Those that seek our hurt will see their folly sooner or later. I feel a conscience void of offense towards God and I know that my Redeemer lives and I shall see him face to face when he comes to make up his jewels.

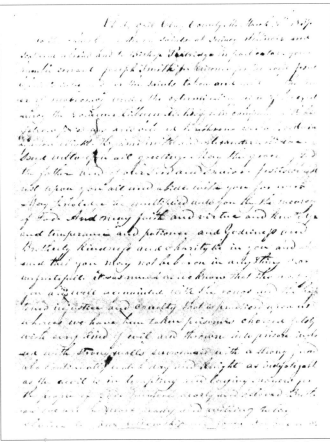

Exhibit 8.3: Letter from Jospeh Smith to the Church at Quincy, Illinois from Liberty Jail (Scribe Alexander McRae), LDS Church Archives, Salt Lake City, UT

He then referred to the suffering of Daniel in the lion's den, the Hebrew children that were cast into the fire or furnace, and the depredations of the Saints and how they joyfully endured the spoiling of their goods at the time of their persecution at Jerusalem when they (the Saints) were scattered.

> After these troubles leave us they will fall on the wasted and they must perish without hope whiles we have a hope of Everlasting life. We shall have joy when they have naught but sorrow if we fail not in hearkening to the Spirit word of God. . . . Bro. Rogers informed us this morning that he called on you and informed you that he was coming here but you gave him no answer. I do not wish to sorrow your feelings if they are innocent but I thought it strange that you did not send one word to me when I thought you knew that I was so anxious to hear from you.

127

Liberty Jail. Cly C⁰ M⁰ 1839 March 21
m[y] Affectionate Wife
                              I have sent an Epistle
to the church directed to you because
I wanted you to have the first reading
of it and then I want Father and
Mother to have a coppy of it keep
the original yourself as I dictated
the matter myself and shall send
an other as soon as posible I want
to be with you very much but the
powers of mobocray is to many
for me at present I would
ask if Judge Cleaveland will be
kind enough to let you and the
children stay there untill we learn
something futher concerning my ⸮
fate I will reward him well if
he will and see that you donot
suffer for any thing I shall have
a little money left when I come
my Dear Emma I very well know
your toils and simpethise with you
if God will spare my life once more
to have the privelege of taking care
of you I will ease your care and
indeavour to comfort your heart

I want you to take the best care
of the family you can which I believe
you will do all you can I was sorry to learn
that Frederick was sick but I trust he is
well again and that you are all well I
want you to try to gain time and write to
me a long letter and tell me all you can
and even if old major is alive yet and what
those little prattlers say that cling around
your neck do you tell them I am in prison
that their lives might be saved
I want all the church to make out
a bill of damages and apply to the united States Court as soon as posible
however they will find out whatcan
be done themselves you ere present my

Exhibit 8.4 (Continued on next page)

128

Exhibit 8.4: Letter from Joseph Smith, Jr. to Emma Smith dated 21 March 1839, LDS Church Archives, Salt Lake City, UT

He next expressed concern that Mary may have no feelings for her husband and disappointment at not receiving information

> concerning the little babe or those little children that lies near my heart although my heart feels wounded today wist I write yet my heart is tender like that of a child's not withstanding my experienced manhood and age.The tears do obstruct my writing hand on my weakness. My desire has been to make you as comfortable as possible but you know I have been prevented. Be assured you have my warmest affections and ever will till death. . . . This brother knows nothing of the family except yourself.You were upstairs and did not come down to see him nor to give him any information only he learned by others that your health was improving.This fact was good news.Time will bring about all things and we must be patient in tribulations and wait the will of God be done. I have no fears of my salvation for God is my judge.

21 March: Joseph wrote to Emma in response to a letter from her and mailed his letter along with the epistle to the Church. He told her,"I have sent an epistle to the Church directed to you because I wanted you to have the first reading of it." (See Exhibit 8.4.)

22 March: Joseph wrote to Isaac Galland about land in Commerce.As requested in Mr. Galland's letter,Joseph told him about the Church. Joseph also described some of the jail conditions. Excerpts follow:

> We have not the privilege of cooking for ourselves,we have been compelled to sleep on the floor with straw, and not blankets sufficient to keep us warm; and when we have a fire, we are obliged to have almost constant smoke. . . .To deprive some fifty thousand, of the right of citizenship,and for what? . . .And finally was it for any thing? no sir,not for any thing,only,that Mormonism is truth; and every man who embraced it felt himself at liberty to embrace every truth: consequently the shackles of superstition, ignorance, and priestcraft, falls at once from his neck; and his eyes are opened to see the truth, and truth greatly prevails over priestcraft; hence the priests are alarmed. . . . We believe that we have a right to revelations,visions,and dreams from God,our heavenly Father; and light and intelligence, through the gift of the Holy Ghost, in the name of Jesus Christ, on all subjects pertaining to our spiritual welfare.

23 March: Hyrum to his wife Mary,postmarked 23 March 1839, Liberty.

> Dear Companion:I feel to set down this morning to write to you a few reflections of my mind in verse and send them to you the first opportunity for you to peruse in your lonely moments whilst I am in prison.

When shivery Novembers chilling blast
made fields and forests bare
one evening as I wandered forth
Along in the pleasant air
I spied a man whose aged step
his face was furrowed over with years
white and hoary was his hair
young Stranger, whither wanderest thou
Said the revered Sage to me
Pocs(?) thirst of wealth thy step constrain
as youthful pleasures rage
or haply, prest with cares and woes
too soon thou hast began
to wander forth with me to mourn
the miseries of man

the sun that over hangs the world
out spredding far and wide
where hundreds labour to suport
A lordlings(?) haughty pride
I have seen your weary winter sun
most porty(?) times return
and every time has added proofs
that man was made to mourn

O man! while in thy early years
How prodiyal of time!
Mispending all they precious time
thy glorious youthful prime
Alternate follies take the Sway
Licentious passions burn
which tenfold force gives nature's Law
that man was made to mourn

Look not alone on youthful prime
as manhood's active might
kman than is useful to his kind(?)
Supported in his right.

But See him on the Edge of life
With larcs(?) and sorrows worn
then age and want, ah, Ill matehtd(?) pair
Show man was made to sorrow and to mourn

A few seems favourites of fate
In pleasures Sap lasest
Yet, think, not all the rich and greate
are likewise truly blest
but hark! what crowds in every land
Are wretched and forlorn
Thro weary life this lesson learns
that man was made to mourn

Many and sharp the numerous ills
in weven with our frame
More printed still we make our selves
Regret, remorse, and shame
And man, whose heaven Erectell face
the smiles of god adore
Tis mans inhumanity to man
that makes countless thousands mourn

That man was made to bear sorrow & grief in all his days if he will be saved in the world to come and all these apprehnsions by the harm of his fellow man although they are of the same blood. Descendants of the same progenitor yet they are? when they get the advantage of one another and thus man causes his fellow man to mourn. My health is still on the gain. The lawyers came in to see today for the first time for many weeks. They appear to be more friendly than usual. I have sent several scrapts of writing to you but I do not know that you will ever get them. If you do I do not know that you can read them. Please excuse me for bad writting and bad spelling &al conposition for my confinement is so farinfull? to me that I cannot write nor compose my mind. Do not neglect to write to me on the receipt of this. Yours in the bonds of love. [Signed] Hyrum Smith

Mary Smith. NB? a letter mail to Liberty Post office will be brought right to my hand? without inspection. It has been so long since I have heard from you that I am exceedingly anxious to hear from you. I have continued scrabling till I have run out no out side paper so I will have to take another half sheet.

April 1839 Correspondence

3 April: Hyrum's diary entries this date mention letters to Sister Walton and Jacob Scot (Stollings).

4 April: Letter from Joseph to Emma two days before they left Liberty Jail. He spoke of his feelings about leaving, of his love for the children, and of not wanting them to forget him. He reminded Emma of her responsibility in teaching them and of other tender feelings about friends and enemies.[21]

> Dear and affectionate wife. Thursday night I set down just as the sun is going down, as we peak throw the great of this lonesome prison, to write to you, that I may make known to you my situation. It is I believe [it is] now about five months and six days since I have been under the grimace, of a guard night and day, and within the walls grates and screeking of iron dors, of a lonesome dark durty prison. With immtions known only to God, do I write this letter, the contemplations, of the mind under these circumstances, defies the pen, or tounge, or Angels, to discribe, or paint, to the human being, who never experiance[d] what we experience. This night we expect; is the last night we shall try our weary Joints and bones on our dirty straw couches in these walls, let our case hereafter be as it may, as we expect to start to morrow, for David Co, for our trial. We shall have a change of Venue to some of the lower counties, for the final trial, as our Lawyers generaly say, if law can be adheared to in Davis, as it grants us the privaliege. But you are awere what we may expect, of beings that [have] conducted [themselves] as they have We lean on the arm of Jehovah, and none else, for our deliverance, and if he dont do it, it will not be done, you may be assured, for there is great thirsting for our blood, in this state; not because we are guilty of any thing: but because they say these men [will] give an account of what has been done to them; the wrongs they have sustaine[ed] if it is known, it [will] ruin the State. So the mob party have sworn, to have our lives, at all hasards, but God will disappoint them we trust. We shall be moved from this [place] at any rate and we are glad of it let what will become of [us] we cannot [get] into a worse hole then this is, we shall not stay here but one night besides this [if that] thank God, we shall never cast a lingering wish after liberty in clay county Mo. we have enough of it to last forever, may God reward fals swearers according to their works, is all I can wish them. My Dear Emma I think of you and the children continualy, if I could want [to] see little Frederick, Joseph, Julia, and Alexander, Joana and old major. And as to yourself if you want to know how much I want to see you, examine your feelings, how much you want to see me, and Judge for [yourself], I would gladly [walk] from here to you barefoot, and bareheaded, and half naked, to see you and think it great pleasure, and never count it toil, but do not think I

am babyish, for I do not feel so, I bare with fortitude all my oppression, so do those that are with me, not one of us have flinched yet, I think you would say it was altogether enough for once, to grattify the malice of hell that I have suffered. I want you [should] not let those litell fellows, forgit me, tell them Father loves them with a perfect love, and he is doing all he can to git away from the mob to come to them, do teach them all you can, that they may have good minds, be tender and kind to them, dont be fractious to them, but listen to their wants, tell them Father says they must be good children [and] mind their mother.[22]

5 April: Hyrum to Mary F. The letter talks about clothing and other items lost. He mentions a man charged with a crime who is placed with them, and a Grinlos, which is probably Sister Grinnals whom he wrote to earlier. The envelope says "Mrs. Mary Smith, Quince, Adams Co. Ilinois 25 cents paid. Post marked April 5, Missouri. A letter with a $20 bill."

Hyrum wrote about Mary's buying a cow, a new milking cow, so the children could have some milk. He told her to keep all his papers in her hands until he returned home. He inquired about specific possessions—his "daule" bags, clothes, etc. and asked if she had them. "If you have I want you should keep them. I have bought some shirts which will last me till I get home."

There seemed to be some question about some of his things being put in a wagon, but no one seemed to know anything about it.

[M]y suppen or camel overcoat I saw it on John William (Verlian). If he has not brought it to you you wait a while to enquire for it and try to hunt it up. Brother John Williams is the man who wore it down here but he was frightened away and carried it off with him. . . . We was yesterday blest with the company of a malifactor and today also. An old man who was taken up for stabbing his neighbor . . . with a trimming chisel who inflicted five deep and dangerous wounds in his body. The prospectus is that he will not get well. If he does not the old man is sure to be hung or go to the penetentiary. It was the act of intoxication. He is very troublesome and noisy. Give my respects to brother and sister Thompson and mother, Grinlas, Father and Mother and all the rest of the family. Give my love to Sarina, Larrina and John and Hiram, Jerusa, Sarah and Joseph, Jr. They are all always present to my mind. . . . [P]ray for me as my duty is well ever pray for you and may God always bless us all and hasten the day of our deliberation and the privilege of seeing each other face to face is the prairs of your husband and friend. Amen. Mary Smith [Signed] Hyrum Smith

Note: Hyrum wrote an incomplete letter to Mary F. dated only 1839, but it was written while he was in the jail. It contained an informative discourse on wisdom and closed with beautiful endearments to Mary. Concerning wisdom, Hyrum said it was about a man put in jail for many years, yet the power of wisdom was there. While men were trying to disgrace him,

> wisdom taught him the knowledge of holy things, lifted him upon height. Why? Because he was patient in tribulation.—All things suffice because of wisdom. . . . Now this is wisdom to understand why these things are so. The spirit shall be with them and deliver them although they are left in bonds, yet he shall deliver them. "The virtuous shall be brought forth in his time and be set on high and that wisdom that hath done this shall give them perpetual glory." All this was the works of that all powerful spirit God's wisdom, even the wisdom of God. And without this, they cannot be saved in the celestial glory. Wisdom shows us that these things are for our salvation spiritually and temporally. Wisdom says this is the way to be made wise that what we do not learn by precepts we may learn by experience. All these things are to make us wise and intelligent that we may be the happy recipient of the highest glory even of that glory that the great luminacy of the heavens is sufficient. The wicked shall come to speedy destruction and have no excuse in the day of judgment but shall have wrought out their own destruction. But God and all his people and all the angels shall be just and holy and shall justly inherit the crowns of celestial glory.
>
> I pray for you, my companion, I will pray for you unceasingly as much as I can. I do realize your sufferings. Try to remember your earthly friend. I am your friend. May God have mercy on us if we keep in remembrance of each other God will remember us and bless us. May the Lord bless children even all is the prayers of your friend and husband.

Further correspondence was written to the prisoners after they left Liberty Jail and was eventually received. The feelings and thoughts are certainly relevant, for they were written thinking the brethren were still in jail.

10 April: Letters from Sidney Rigdon and Alanson Ripley.[23]

11 April: Letters from Don Carlos Smith to Hyrum and Joseph, and a letter from Agnes Smith to Hyrum and Joseph.[24]

Letter from Jacob Stollings to the Prophet.[25]

Letter from Mary F. to Hyrum:

> To Smith, Hyrum (Libery) My dear Husband: I received yesterday a large packet of letters from you which took nearly all my pleasure time to read through the day which I did with mingled

feelings of pleasure and grief. I assure you I had thought it very long before I heard from you your first letter only came to hand a little more than a week ago and this was while Brother Grunson was as I supposed on his way to Libery with a fixed determination never to return without you as I know this to be the case and had sent a message by him. I thought it would be useless for me to write as my letter might be going whilst you were coming homeward but I was not a little disappointed a few days to find him returned without having seen you and bring no intelligence respecting you that was any way satisfactory & now I begin to feel dissatisfied with myself and especially since I read all your letters & cannot but reproach myself with a degree of neglect norwithstanding the hinderances that stood in my way and the flattering prospects that have from time to time to have twice been held out to me respecting you being at home which I hope you will consider as a sufficient apology for such neglect. I am sure if I could have known that you would be in confinement so long I should by no means have omitted to write to you often altho I might have to do it while other slept? as I am now doing not knowing that it will ever come to you but as you request me to write on the receipt of yours I feel disposed to do so even if you should come home before I can finish a letter. The report is now here that you are out of prison, but as so many false reports have been circulated on that subject I know not what to believe. If you are moved according to your expectation in davisse County you are indeed in the midst of a host of ferocious enemys who like gready wolfs are thirsting for your blood. If indeed there was no God I should never expect to see you again in this world but in him is all my trust and I hope and believe that you will be delivered out of their cruel hands and be restored to the society and bosom of your family who greatly desire to see you once more in the flesh. I must here my beloved companion revert? to some remarks you make in your last relative to my having forsaken you which gave me feelings not to be described. I cannot bear the thought of your having any such suspicion. Surely you had none? if so you are yet unacquainted with the principles of my heart what: should I forsake a Friend and a bosom Friend in the time of adversity and affliction when all the sympathy and affection I am capable of feeling is called for to soothe and comfort as far as possible under such circumstances as you are placed in. No: reason, religion, and honor and every feeling of my heart forbids such a though to enter there. How I cannot help asking can things have been represented to you so as to indicate any such thing. surely an enemy must have done this for if you had known the truth and the endeavors and intentions of my heart towards your family from the time you left me to the present moment you would not and I do asure you have had no cause for anxious thoughts or sleepless nights on there account. It has been my desire and aim to do in your absence good by them and for them as in your presence or even more knowing your great care feelings and concerns for our general welfare. How could Brother Rogers say he called on me and received no answer and this is the first word I ever heard of his knowing called upon me. I sent repeatedly for him to come before he left here and was greatly disappointed when I heard that he was gone without my having seen him. Oh Hyrum I am obliged to stop here and take a view of the fagston? so many things crowd up my mind which I should like to tell you but cannot in this way that I long to see you, that I may explain all things to you as I wish to do. As Elder Rigdon told me some time ago that he had given you an account of our situation so I shall skip over many things leave them to be explained when I have the pleasure of seeing you. I will now endeavor to give you some information respecting our present situation and circumstances. I am now through the great mercy of God towards me enjoying good health and fast recovering my strength which is greatly needed after near five months sickness in which have been entirely unable to take care of the household affairs. All the rest of the family are in excellent health except little Sarah. She has a severe cold and cough. She has gone alone for the last month and begins to talk. She calls for baby Joseph. She and all the children are very fond of him. He grows fast and is very strong. He had two teeth when a little more than three months old. You may not think him handsome but to me intelligence seems burn forth in his eyes and countenance. He begins to show signs of a good mind. Which is my estimation of much greater importance than beauty. I think you will be surprised to see Jerusha she has grown very strong and stout but she says she shall sit on Father's knee when he comes. John and Hyrum also grow very fast they often talk of doing great things to the mob for keeping Father away so long. Lovina often expresses a great desire to see you. Sister Grenna? Clarinda . . . she seems much affected when I read what you addressed to them. Clair has behaved herself much better than common ever since. Brother & Sister T are still with us. we all live in a small house in Quincy for which we pay dollars per month. Brother T is in a good situation waiting in the courthouse. I suppose his pay will be good. My means are not yet quite run out. I hope I shall see you before this is the case. I often think of your advice respecting going into the country to take a farm but this appears to me quite impractable. [She then listed the reasons why.] Father says he shall call the waggon his till you come as he redeemed it. He also borrowed the mair which we had left and Brother William has taken and sold her. Brother Miller has settled about 400 miles from here . . . so that we should not know how to go about getting either way over or money. All these things considered I feel discouraged about trying to get into business before you come. I have also mentioned the subject to several of the brethren but they all seem to think you will not be able to attend to farming yourself and if you could it seems uncertain yet when you will be at home so that upon the whole I think we had better decline it. Now my dear husband I must draw to a close once more adjusting to some things contained in yours. My dear you say if you have forsaken me you might write and let me know it be this feelings of a familiar nature I thought if I had not proved to you in the course of the 9 or 10 months I had lived with you that I cared for your own and the welfare of family. I would in further endeavors to do so. . . . I observe a spirit moving through the whole which seems to strengthen attachments to you and if I should again be permitted to enjoy your (company?) I hope to prove to you that I am a never failing friend. . . . My dear husband I have finished my letter and send it off by a brother but as no one knew where you would be, it was sent back to me. I was sorry but am now glad as I have this day received a letter from you dated April 6 and wish to make a few remarks in answer to it. In the first place I would say that your wrapher is safe at home also your saddle bags which were sent home before you left Far West. The brother told me I might bring them with me as you would they expected be here as soon as you were but in this I was disappointed. In the next place I must beg of you to say no more about me having forsaken you or the family. It gives me so much pain of mind that I can hardly bear it. I again tell you that such a thought never entered my heart. Don't my dear be uneasy about any of the children. Little Joseph Jr. he's to near my heart to be neglected but I will take this to heart and I promise you that if this is necessary that your mind may be easy respecting the family that they shall continue to receive all the care and attention I am capable of showing them until your return and afterwards it shall not be lessened. We are all quite well in health at this time excepting brother Thompson who has been so closely confined to writing during the setting of the court that he is now quite layed up. He desires me to give his particular love to you and to say that if he had not been so much engaged he would have written. My sister also with all the family send their sincere love to you and I subscribe myself your most affectionate friend and companion in tribulation. Mary Smith

This correspondence shows the very deep feelings and concerns the brethren had for their families. Joseph emphasized during the first few days at the jail the primary principles of an eternal family unit. He wrote the following in his letter of 16 December, addressed to the Saints in Caldwell county: "Now for a man to consecrate his property and his wife & children to the Lord, is nothing more nor less than to feed the hungry, clothe the naked, visit the widow and the fatherless, the sick, and the afflicted, and do all he can to administer to their relief in their afflictions, and for him and his house to serve the Lord."

As letters were received in the jail, they contained words of consolation regarding the prisoners' families. Don Carlos gave the following report:

> Emma and the children are well; they live three miles from here, and have a tolerably good place. Hyrum's children and mother Grinold's are living at present with father; they are all well. Mary [wife of Hyrum] has not got her health yet, but I think it increases slowly. . . . We are trying to get a house, and to get the family together; we shall do the best we can for them, and that which we consider to be most in accordancd with Hyrum's feelings.

William Smith wrote: "I hope you will be permitted to come to your families before long. Do not worry about them, for they will be taken care of."

These assurances from loved ones and friends were a great source of encouragement to Joseph and the brethren with him. The support was a sustaining part of their experience. Another legacy may very well be the importance of keeping journals, for without theirs, our knowledge of these important occurrences would have been lost.

Chapter 9

REVELATION AND KNOWLEDGE

Joseph was told in his patriarchal blessing, "Thy heart shall meditate great wisdom and comprehend the deep things of God."[1] This prediction literally became a reality. During the eighteen years between 1820 and 1838, Joseph had seen, been visited, or taught by over forty heavenly messengers. These visitations would seem incomprehensible to any who had not had similar experiences. It is staggering even to contemplate the innumerable revelations he received before incarceration at Liberty Jail. Those published in the Doctrine and Covenants number 122.

With all the heavenly communication, Joseph knew what keys he held[2] and knew he would be the instrument in bringing down knowledge that had not yet been revealed to the world. He knew he was more than a recorder or scribe.

As he gained a full comprehension of the doctrines that had been given to him, Joseph became a seasoned prophet. Much of the remarkable transformation took place during the 128 days spent in Liberty Jail. This was the only extensive interval where Joseph had twenty-four hours a day to ponder and meditate on all the glorious doctrines that had been revealed to him.

It was here, in this dreadful dungeon, that everything seemed to come together. In his mind's eye, he beheld the complete, magnificent tapestry of Heavenly Father's plan of salvation as well as the gospel of Jesus Christ in its splendid fullness as described by Moroni fourteen years earlier. Now, Joseph faced the great responsibility and challenge of imparting the knowledge he had been given in words a covenant people could understand. This is the reason why a prophet of God gives enlargements to sacred and supernal concepts. Earlier, Joseph had been told that these very things would transpire.[3]

B. H. Roberts penned some luminous words about Liberty Jail. "It was more temple than prison, so long as the Prophet was there. It was a place of meditation and prayer. A temple . . . is the 'infinite in man seeking the infinite in God.' Where they find each other, there is holy sanctuary—a temple."[4] These words proved true in the concepts of Liberty Jail being "a house of prayer, a house of fasting, a house of faith, a house of learning."[5]

Three years later, Joseph gave the first endowments at his red brick store in Nauvoo. Here, he left a legacy to every worthy soul and started "a house of glory, a house of order, a house of God"[6] by saying, "[A]nd there was nothing made known to these men but what will be made known to all the Saints of the last days, so soon as they are prepared to receive . . . even to the weakest of the Saints . . . knowing assuredly that all these things . . . are always governed by the principle of revelation."[7]

Before Liberty Jail, Oliver Cowdery, Sidney Rigdon, and others often spoke for the Prophet. After leaving Liberty Jail, no one ever spoke for Joseph again. The last six years of his life was a period of eloquent sermons and intriguing and enlightened discourses.[8] Revelations given in Liberty Jail gave prophecy of this knowledge that was about to come:

> What power shall stay the heavens? As well might man stretch forth his puny arm to stop the Missouri River in its decreed course, or to turn it up stream, as to hinder the Almighty from pouring down knowledge from heaven upon the heads of the Latter-day Saints.
>
> A time to come in the which nothing shall be withheld."[9]

In correspondence from Liberty Jail, Joseph instructed the Saints:

> [T]he things of God are of deep import; and time and experience, and careful and ponderous and solemn thoughts can only find them out. Thy mind, O man! if thou wilt lead a soul unto salvation, must stretch as high as the utmost heavens, and search into and contemplate the darkest abyss, and the broad expanse of eternity—thou must commune with God. How much more dignified and noble are the thoughts of God; than the vain imaginations of the human heart. None but fools will trifle with the souls of men. . . . We are called to hold the keys of the mysteries of those things that have been kept hid from the foundation of the world until now.[10]

From all these thoughts, we may be able to understand the soberness that accompanied him as he left the jail.

It has been said that "The key to knowledge (truth) is to learn first of the whole, which is God, then of the parts, which are nature and man."[11] This process was the epitome of Joseph's entire life, as he was a living example of "If thou shalt ask, thou shalt receive revelation upon revelation, knowledge upon knowledge, that thou mayest know the mysteries and peaceable things—that which bringeth joy, that which bringeth life eternal."[12]

In the King Follett discourse, Joseph taught, "Knowledge saves a man; and in the world of the spirits no man can be exalted but by knowledge."

> Hear, O ye heavens, and give ear, O earth, and rejoice ye inhabitants thereof, for the Lord is God . . .
>
> [A]nd [I] delight to honor those who serve me in righteousness and in truth unto the end. . . .
>
> And to them will I reveal all mysteries, yea, all the hidden mysteries of my kingdom from days of old, and, for ages to come, will I make known unto them the good pleasure of my will concerning all things pertaining to my kingdom.
>
> Yea, even the wonders of eternity shall they know, and things to come will I show them.[13]

Another great year for imparting the pinnacle of knowledge was in 1842. Joseph instructed the Saints on the great truths of the spiritual realm in March; and, in April, he gave a great discourse on "The Spirit of God the Spirit of Knowledge" and said, "If it requires the Spirit of God to know the things of God . . . I contend that if one man cannot understand these things but by the spirit of God, ten thousand men cannot; . . . whatever we may think of revelation, that without it we can neither know nor understand anything of God, or the devil."[14]

He gave the endowment for the first time in May. In August, he put to print one of his greatest epistles about "Happiness" in a correspondence to Nancy Rigdon. It contained much about knowledge and one's handling of eternal truths as they become available. "Happiness is the object and design of our existence; and will be the end thereof . . . without first knowing . . . and we cannot expect to know all, or more than we now know unless we comply."[15]

Joseph then gave what some claim is the capstone of the true purpose of the priesthood (September).[16] The wisdom of this work tells of securing mother earth so it will not be wasted. In this beautiful section, given three years after Liberty Jail, we hear about knowledge again—this time acknowledging how far Joseph's mission had progressed:

> which dispensation is now beginning to usher in, that a whole and complete and perfect union, and welding together of dispensations, and keys, and powers, and glories. . . . And not only this, but those things which never have been revealed from the foundation of the world . . . shall be revealed . . . in this, the dispensation of the fullness of times.[17]

Then, Joseph gave a simple description that comes vividly to anyone who has stood on Mount Carmel in Jerusalem and witnessed the dissemination of the dew:"Behold, thy God reigneth! As the dews of Carmel, so shall the knowledge of God descend upon them!"[18]

Revelation and the Holy Ghost are two of the distinguishing elements of true religion. They are the only source of spiritual knowledge. Through this process comes the greatest of doctrines—such as:"This therefore, is the sealing and binding power, and, in one sense of the word, the keys of the kingdom, which consist in the key of knowledge."[19] Also:

> Though the thunders might roll and lightnings flash, and earthquakes bellow, and war gather thick around, yet this hope and knowledge would support the soul in every hour of trial, trouble and tribulation. Thus knowledge through our Lord and Savior Jesus Christ is the grand key that unlocks the glories and mysteries of the kingdom of heaven.[20]

In summary, between 1823-38, 120 sections of the Doctrine and Covenants were received. From 1839-43, eleven sections were received, some of which were letters and instructions from Joseph. From 1839 until his death, Joseph gave over a hundred additional discourses.

Yes, this twenty-one-year span truly manifests his legacy of revelation and knowledge. He wrote:

> God has given to some to hold the keys of revelation and KNOWLEDGE, and wisdom: they become stewards over these gifts: they use these keys to unlock the sacred treasures of eternity, and become acquainted with hidden stores of knowledge, deep mysteries are made plain; secret things are manifested, wonders are exhibited; and the mind, rightly laden with the choice treasures of the heavenly worlds, and the wonderful works of God, feasts upon the delicious food; the soul is filled with joy unspeakable; the heart swells with the love of God; and the bosom yearns with compassion towards all mankind, and especially towards all who are pure in heart.[21]

Joseph said on many occasions that the entire plan of salvation and mysteries of Godliness are available to every worthy Saint. What a challenge Joseph left for each member of the kingdom of God on earth.

Chapter 10

DOCTRINE TO ITS FULLNESS

It is exciting to ponder the declaration about the foundation of the Church made by the Lord in his Preface of the Doctrine and Covenants (Section 1): "And also those to whom these commandments were given, might have power to lay the foundation of this church, and to bring it forth out of obscurity and out of darkness, the only true and *living* church upon the face of the whole earth, with which I, the Lord, am well pleased, speaking unto the church collectively"[1] (italics added). *Living* denotes life, vitality, subsistence, sustenance, expansion, development, and maturity.

"Nothing Shall Be Withheld"

Over the last 166 years, the maturation of every major doctrine Joseph gave bears evidence and testifies of a living church. These major doctrines have developed and will continue to come forth until the dispensation of the fullness is complete. Additional keys have yet to come forth, and, along with them additional knowledge.[2]

We know that Joseph holds the keys of the mysteries that have been sealed and that we have not yet received. The Lord said, "I have given unto him the keys of the mystery of those things which have been sealed, even things which were from the foundation of the world, and the things which shall come from this time until the time of my coming."[3] An example is the sealed portion of the sacred plates returned to Moroni that he has in his care today. Isaiah makes mention of the sealed portion of the Book of Mormon when he refers to "the words which are sealed . . . [that] reveal all things from the foundation

147

of the world unto the end thereof."[4] Moroni was commanded to seal up the writings of the brother of Jared, as they were not to be revealed until men have faith even as the brother of Jared.[5]

The entire plan of salvation or redemption applies to individuals. Joseph explained this principle in his great discourse on happiness: "[W]e cannot keep all the commandments without first knowing them. . . . If we seek first the kingdom of God, all good things will be added. . . . Blessings offered, but rejected, are no longer blessings, but become like the talent hid in the earth."[6]

The Savior talked about the highest blessing, glory, or kingdom of God. The key to obtaining it is to gain an understanding of the doctrines and of all truths given to individuals in our dispensation and to apply them in our lives. "They are they who are priests and kings, who have received of his fullness, and of his glory."[7] Those of a lesser glory are without the fullness. "These are they who receive of his glory, but not of his fullness."[8] Pertaining to this fullness, we are told of the necessity of even the Savior obtaining it. John the Beloved, who knew him so well, explained it as follows: "He was called the Son of God, because he received not of the fullness at the first" but later he "received a fullness of the glory of the Father."[9]

We are encouraged to be participants in this plan. "For if you keep my commandments you shall receive of his fullness, and be glorified in me as I am in the Father."[10] This means the highest degree of the celestial kingdom. "In the celestial glory there are three heavens or degrees; And in order to obtain the highest, a man must enter into this order of the priesthood [meaning the new and everlasting covenant of marriage]; and if he does not, he cannot obtain it."[11]

When Joseph gave the "Lectures on Theology," he listed the priorities of the attributes of God: knowledge first, faith second, justice third, judgment fourth, mercy fifth, and truth sixth.[12] Joseph's summary is interesting: "For where faith is, there will the knowledge of God be also, with all things which pertain thereto—revelations, visions, and dreams, as well as every necessary thing. . . . [H]e that possesses it will through it, obtain all necessary knowledge and wisdom until he shall know God, and the Lord Jesus Christ, whom he has sent—whom to know is eternal life. Amen."[13]

Father Abraham understood the importance of gaining knowledge. He expressed his desire "to be one who possessed great knowledge . . . and to possess a greater knowledge."[14] As we come to understand the far-reaching and eternal aspects of acquiring knowledge and begin to thirst for it, as did Abraham, then we begin to move toward obtaining the fullness. This progression is evidenced when an individual becomes immersed in living and progressing toward the fullness of these beautiful, profound doctrines. The ultimate fulfillment to the individual is his or her love of God and the personal relationship that develops with him or her because of this love.

Development of Four Major Doctrines

To give a full chronology of each doctrine Joseph taught would be a voluminous and overwhelming task. Therefore, only four of the capstone doctrines are included within this work. These doctrines in their fullness depict one of the greatest legacies of Joseph, for we have them as true supernal knowledge vividly unfolding line upon line, precept upon precept.

The first example is the Godhead. To understand and then comply with this doctrine can bring the highest glory to the companion spirits of an eternal union.[15] Other doctrines of this magnitude are (2) the Holy Priesthood, the power and authority of God, (3) ordinances[16] and covenants of Father's plan of salvation, and (4) the eternal family, ultimate glory and fulfillment, even God's work and glory.[17]

A brief listing of discourses, epistles, and writings that Joseph gave on major doctrines following Liberty Jail is given in Appendix D —showing further a capstone of Joseph's legacy. Within every doctrine, as each phase unfolds, the evidence of full and true theology becomes apparent—thereby testifying of a true and living church.

History does show that upon leaving Liberty Jail, Joseph continued month after month to give additional understanding to doctrine just as rapidly as the Saints were ready for it. Joseph testified of this when he said, in 1842, "I have the whole plan of the kingdom before me, and no other person has."[18] Interestingly, at this very time, Joseph gave the Articles of Faith in the Wentworth Letter and published the letter in the *Times and Seasons*.[19] The ninth article states, "We believe all that God has revealed, all that He does now reveal, and we believe that He will yet reveal many great and important things pertaining to the Kingdom of God."

Later, in 1843, after he prefaced his subject by saying, "I am going to take up this subject by virtue of the knowledge of God in me, which I have received from heaven," he then spoke of the three glories, where he mentions Paul's ascent into the third heaven, and of the three principal rounds of Jacob's ladder. He said, "I could explain a hundred fold more than I ever have of the glories of the kingdoms manifested to me in the vision, were I permitted, and were the people prepared to receive them."[20]

Are we ready for the legacy of heavenly knowledge Joseph gave? The measure of personal effect upon each individual who comes in contact with the Lord's pure theology is one of the major purposes of mortality. The importance of the knowledge brought forth by Joseph Smith, Jr. has been beautifully stated by one of the greatest philosophers of our time:

> What are the fundamental ideas which are part of all that he [Joseph Smith] felt, thought, and did? This question is important because the mind of Joseph Smith was shaped by God himself; the thinking . . . which came through him is a prime clue to the nature of the mind of God. And since it is the opportunity of each Latter-day Saint to come to have one mind with God and with all of the holy prophets since the beginning, this question also comes down to what each of us should believe.[21]

The Godhead

Understanding the true nature of the Godhead could well be the most important doctrine Joseph gave us. The Apostle John wrote, "And this is life eternal that they might know thee the only true God, and Jesus Christ whom thou hast sent."[22] "The first principle of the gospel is to know for a certainty the character of God."[23] This knowledge is a prerequisite to eternal life. Joseph Smith taught, "If men do not comprehend the character of God, they do not comprehend themselves. When we understand the character of God, and know how to come to Him, he begins to unfold the heavens to us and to tell us all about it. When we are ready to come to him, he is ready to come to us."[24]

The Father and the Son knew that the philosophies of men had crept into the Godhead theology of Christianity. The Lord told Joseph in the First Vision that "they [the existing churches] were all wrong; and . . . that all their creeds were an abomination in his sight."[25]

The pure understanding of the true character and traits of the Godhead had its genesis in the Sacred Grove when Joseph offered his first prayer. His understanding and knowledge unfolded throughout his life and climaxed just months, even weeks, before he was murdered. Joseph delivered the capstone, the knowledge and procedure of becoming gods, in the King Follett Discourse in March and again in the discourse given in the grove on 16 June 1844, just days before his death.

The First Vision in 1820 made available to all mortals the true concept of God and immediately challenged the false Christian theology of the day. A fourteen-year-old boy saw deity. He knew what he saw, and he knew God knew what he had seen.[26]

What happens to a mortal after such a glorious vision? What would be the feelings: Grandeur? Wonder? Elation? Shock? What happens within the mind, the body, and the soul of an individual who has had such a sacred experience? In his diary of 1832-34, twelve years after the event, Joseph recounts, "I was filled with the Spirit of God and the (Lord) opened the heavens upon me and I saw the Lord and he spake unto me saying, Joseph (my Son), thy sins are forgiven thee."[27] In this first entry, he speaks of the member of the Godhead who gave him instructions. The Anglo-Saxon Christian religion of this time was expounding that there was one God, without a body, manifested in three different ways. The fullness of the character, traits, purposes, and goals of the Godhead was unfolded to the world by Joseph during the ensuing years.

In April of 1829, with nine years of communicating with angelic messengers behind him, Joseph saw the Lord Jesus Christ for the second recorded time.[28] It is fascinating to speculate about the purpose of this visit. Just one month later, the priesthood of God with its true authority was transmitted to the earth for the final time. One year later, in June of 1830, Joseph was given the revelation of Moses 1, which immediately launched him into the translation of the Inspired Version of the Bible. Through the process of restoring the "plain and precious things" to the Bible, Joseph further expanded his understanding. He obtained a greater insight of God's relationship to man, thereby fortifying and solidifying what he knew to be true about the Godhead.

With this enlightenment, Joseph made some additional entries concerning the Savior in the 1837 Book of Mormon. He therefore clarified any misunderstanding about the identity of the Father and the Son by making changes in the earlier translation of 1828-29 and the first edition of 1830.[29] Changes such as these testify of the living church where knowledge comes through a living prophet, precept upon precept, toward its fullness for God's children.

Sidney Rigdon was with Joseph on 16 February 1832 when the Father and the Son appeared to them.[30] The Prophet wept and expressed his thankfulness for a second witness. This revelation, along with Section 84 given seven months later, was the beginning of the knowledge necessary for understanding that mortals can reach godhood and receive all that the Father and Son have.[31]

Subsequent information came in the Lectures on Faith (1834-35) published in the front of the 1835 Doctrine and Covenants. Joseph, in Lecture Five, taught, "There are two personages who constitute the great, matchless, governing and supreme power over all things. . . . They are the Father and the Son—The Holy Spirit being the mind of the Father and Son."[32] This statement certainly brought an expansion of understanding, but a full comprehension of the Holy Ghost was lacking.

In January of 1836, Joseph records his great vision of the celestial kingdom where he saw God the Father, the Son, Father Adam and Abraham, his father and mother, and his brother Alvin. The voice of the Lord said unto him, "All who have died without a knowledge of this gospel, who would have received it . . . shall be heirs to the celestial kingdom of God."[33]

On 3 April, Joseph and Oliver Cowdery saw the Savior again in the Kirtland Temple.[34] It becomes understandable that when Joseph started writing his history on 2 May 1838,[35] he made definitive changes over and above his diary entry six years earlier that stand true and pure today: "I saw two personages"[36]

The Book of Abraham (1835-42) brought to Joseph's mind the precept of the preexistence, the gradation of spirits, and the true kinship between man and God and between Father and Son. It was a period in which Joseph learned one of the greatest, most definitive aspects of the Godhead. Joseph clarified this further in 1841: "[T]hese personages, according to Abraham's record, are called God the first, the Creator; God the second, the Redeemer; and God the third, the witness or Testator."[37]

With this base, Joseph went into confinement for four months and six days in Liberty jail. In the six years following Liberty jail, he expounded on this essential doctrine. In June, two months after leaving the jail, Joseph gave his great instruction on various doctrines that included "the two comforters, the second comforter, and the spirit of revelation."[38] Joseph said, "The first Comforter or Holy Ghost has no other effect than pure intelligence. It is more powerful in expanding the mind, enlightening the understanding, and storing the intellect." This statement was certainly a remembrance of the 128-day incarceration, which was followed by enlightenment on the second comforter, the Lord Jesus Christ.

In January 1841, using a ring as an example, Joseph taught of eternal elements. He said "without form and void" should be read as "empty and desolate." And the word "created" should be "formed," or "organized." In May, Joseph elaborated on the three personages of the Godhead, and in October, he spoke about angels and ministering spirits.

In March 1842, he elaborated on the gift of the Holy Ghost and on the difference between the Holy Ghost and the gift of the Holy Ghost. The next month (April), Joseph gave instructions on spirits. He talked about how to try them, the nature of and how to discern them. He also discussed the Spirit of God and the spirit of knowledge. Then what of the fathers? He covered what "saviors on Mount Zion" means and explained the nature of dwelling with God.

Joseph declared the capstone of our knowledge of the Godhead at the April 1842 conference in Ramus, Illinois, when he stated, "The Father has a body of flesh and bones as tangible as man's; the Son also; but the Holy Ghost has not a body of flesh and bones, but is a personage of Spirit. Were it not so, the Holy Ghost could not dwell in us."[39] This meaningful, glorious explanation is the official doctrinal statement of the Godhead for the Church and for the world.

Joseph simplified this explanation even further when, in 1842, he wrote the "Wentworth Letter" containing the Articles of Faith.[40] The first article of faith is "We believe in God, the Eternal Father, and in His Son, Jesus Christ, and in the Holy Ghost." This true concept of the Godhead has been declared to the world for the last century and a half.

In June 1843, another beautiful discourse on "The Doctrine of Godhead"[41] was given. Joseph included here a statement on the secular Godhead. "The teachers of the day say that the Father is God, the Son is God, and the Holy Ghost is God, and they are all in one body and one God. Jesus prayed that those that the Father had given him out of the world might be made one in them, as they were one [in spirit, in mind, in purpose]. If I were to testify that the Christian world was wrong on this point, my testimony would be true."[42]

Then, on 9 March 1844, just 110 days before his death, in the King Follett Discourse, Joseph discussed how God came to be God, the relationship of God and his posterity, and the power of the Father.[43]

Joseph also included a beautiful dissertation about the third member of the Godhead, stating that the Holy Ghost "is capable of manifesting himself in the form of a man."This enhanced the statement of 1842 that the Holy Ghost does not possess a body of flesh and bone.[44] From the King Follett Discourse, knowledge of paramount importance was given concerning the Holy Ghost:

> All things whatsoever God in His infinite reason has seen fit and proper to reveal to us, while we are dwelling in our mortal state, in regard to our mortal bodies, are revealed to us in the abstract and independent of affinity of this mortal tabernacle. His commandments are revealed to our spirits precisely the same as though we had no bodies at all and those revelations which must of necessity save our spirits will save our bodies.[45]

Interestingly, the subject of Joseph's last-known address, given 16 June 1844 at the meeting in the grove east of the temple, is titled in the *History of the Church*, "The Christian Godhead—Plurality of Gods."[46] Joseph began by reading Revelation 1:6, "And hath made us kings and priests unto God and His Father."

Some of the major doctrinal concepts of these two revealing discourses were, "God himself was once as we are now, and is an exalted man, and sits enthroned in yonder heavens! That is the great secret."[47] During one segment of the beautiful discourse, Joseph said, "I will preach on the plurality of Gods. . . . I have always declared God to be a distinct personage, Jesus Christ a separate and distinct personage from God the Father, and that the Holy Ghost was a distinct personage and a Spirit: and these three constitute three distinct personages and three Gods."[48] They are one in the "new and everlasting covenant,"[49] which they entered into before this world was. That Joseph was close to the Holy Ghost is exemplified over and over again. One example of his long association with "The Testator" comes from his statement, "If you will listen to the first prompting you will get it right nine times out of ten."[50]

The Priesthood Fullness

The most powerful authority on earth is the holy priesthood where a person has the "authority to act in the name of God." This authority began with the restoration of the priesthood to our dispensation of time during the First Vision in 1820. Joseph Smith, Jr., a boy prophet chosen of the Lord, received his first instructions from the Savior.

The priesthood in Church organization had its beginning when John the Baptist conferred the Aaronic Priesthood on Joseph Smith and Oliver Cowdery in May 1829. The keys restored were "of ministering of angels, and of the gospel of repentance, and of baptism by immersion."[51] With these keys and authority of the Aaronic Priesthood, the first members started to preach the gospel and baptize. Peter, James, and John, a month later, conferred the Melchizedek Priesthood upon Joseph Smith, Jr. and Oliver Cowdery and ordained them apostles.[52] Joseph and Oliver now had the authority to organize the Church, confirm individual members, and ordain brethren to all offices within the two priesthoods. The keys given at that time did not contain the fullness of the Melchizedek Priesthood; nor did they contain the sealing power or other vital and necessary keys and ordinances to obtain the fullness. The power to organize and seal families together for eternity was lacking. Also deficient was the ability to grant eternal life unto the faithful. The authority to perform these ordinances was held by Elijah the Prophet, and these sealing keys were not restored until seven years later on 3 April 1836. The power and understanding of the priesthood of God came precept upon precept through Joseph.

Before the Church was organized, converts were baptized for the remission of sins.[53] After the Church was organized, those who had been baptized for a remission of sins were rebaptized into the Church by those having authority to baptize into the Church.

Over the next several years, four of the major offices within the Church unfolded: 1833, the First Presidency; 1834, the office of patriarch of the Church; and 1835, the Quorum of Twelve Apostles and the First Council of Seventy. Six years later, the concept for the fifth council, the Presiding Bishopric, was set in place.

The year of 1836 brought the priesthood keys of sealing up unto eternal life. These keys were restored by Moses, Elias, and Elijah.[54] It was the first time in eighteen hundred years (with the exception of the Book of Mormon time, John the Revelator, the three Nephites, etc.) that the authority necessary to avail each individual the opportunity to reach the measure of his or her creation was available. The magnitude of this event has to be one of the greatest in this dispensation. In our day, it required a holy temple. The Kirtland Temple was the result of the toil, hardship, and sacrifice of the Saints to meet this criterion. These people truly understood the principle that "sacrifice brings forth the blessings of heaven." This holy edifice became the restorative temple of sealing keys in this dispensation. The phenomenal accomplishment of the Saints under such difficult circumstances exemplifies the magnitude of the events that transpired. The Lord was the first to appear. "[L]et the hearts of all my people rejoice, who have, with their might, built this house to my name. For behold, I have accepted this house."[55]

The next to appear was Moses, who held keys of both priesthood powers. His great powers were intrinsic to the gathering of Israel, the leading of the Ten Tribes from the land of the north,[56] and the fullness of the Aaronic Priesthood.[57] Other powers show up in his legacy as a prophet. He gathered the "House of Israel" and conveyed the priesthood upon those appointed. This event equates to the first goal of the Church—missionary work—through gathering the House of Israel to the ordinances, the new and everlasting covenant.[58] It was restored because the world was ready. Watching the Lord's timetable through history is truly fascinating. When his people are ready and have the foundation, his work always unfolds. Moses conferred the powers of the Aaronic Priesthood upon his elder brother Aaron.[59] Inherent to this lesser, preparatory, outward, or temporal priesthood that was restored were the powers within sacred ordinances of the temple.[60] Moses also conferred his keys upon Peter, James, and John on the Mount of Transfiguration in the meridian of time. In our latter day, he was instructed to give these same powers to the Prophet Joseph Smith, Jr. in 1836.

The next to appear in the temple was Elias to restore the gospel of Abraham. What was this gospel? It compares to the second goal of the Church in our dispensation—the moving of an individual toward perfection. These keys enable the priesthood to perform vital and sacred ordinances within the temple. The power or keys restored by Moses are of the Aaronic Priesthood. The gospel of Abraham is another portion or part of the fullness of the Melchizedek Priesthood. The knowledge of this ordinance provides the capability to move past angels and converse with God.[61] The Abrahamic order of the Melchizedek Priesthood also holds the power of eternal marriage,[62] eternal seed,[63] or posterity.[64] It is interesting to review who conferred all of these powers upon Abraham. Was it not Noah?[65] Was Elias Noah?[66] Do we need to be like Abraham and seek for the appointment?[67] The Lord told Joseph we do.[68]

The last heavenly messenger bestowing keys at the Kirtland temple was Elijah the Tishbite, who, as he burst into scripture, sealed the heavens with the proclamation, "there shall not be dew nor rain" for three years.[69] It was Elijah who restored the great sealing power to this dispensation. He brought the keys of sealing up to eternal life, of uniting the eternal unit of husband and wife and children together for eternity.[70] "The keys of the authority to administer in all the ordinances of the Priesthood; and without the authority is given, the ordinances could not be administered."[71] This, of course, was the Restoration that equates to the third goal of the Church—the sealing of families and the welding link.[72] The appearance of these three messengers and the bestowing of their keys in this sequence represent one of the greatest examples of God's house being a house of order.

Joseph received the keys of these three prophets on 6 April 1836. After he was released from Liberty Jail and was once again with the Saints, he started the dynamic unveiling of knowledge and understanding through explanations of the powers and ordinances of these major doctrines, eventually bringing them to the fullness and conveying them to the apostles and others before he was martyred.

This dispersion of intelligence started about two months after his release from Liberty Jail. On 2 June 1839, at Commerce, Illinois, Joseph delivered one of the most informative sermons he ever gave called "The Great Discourse on the Priesthood." This sermon was the genesis of bringing an understanding of priesthood fullness to the world.[73] Interestingly, this discourse was followed a month later, on 2 July, with a priesthood sequel address to the Twelve Apostles. They needed this special instruction. Joseph knew these were the men who eventually must have an understanding of all things concerning the priesthood keys, powers, and authority. He took them back to the beginning, explaining how the priesthood evolved. This discourse revealed a great deal about the priesthood keys Adam held and how he used his priesthood in behalf of his posterity. Joseph taught them, "The Priesthood was first given to Adam; he obtained the First Presidency, and held the keys of it from generation to generation. He obtained it in the Creation, before the world was formed."[74] Further, "this is why Adam blessed his posterity; he wanted to bring them into the presence of God."[75] It is recorded that Adam gathered them together and blessed them.[76] We now can understand that the type of blessing was an endowment. Adam, Eve, and their posterity were very blessed to have the Lord with them at this time.[77]

A great precept was taught in the October 1840 conference as Joseph unveiled another important purpose of the priesthood. This concept proved new to the world, as it is through the priesthood channels that God reveals his word to his people through personal revelation. This additional knowledge was an absolute to the priesthood function of accomplishing all of God's work and glory.[78] Joseph then described it as "the channel through which all knowledge, doctrine, the plan of salvation and every important matter is revealed from heaven . . . is the highest and holiest Priesthood, . . . and all other Priesthoods are *only parts*, ramifications, powers and blessings belonging to the same."[79]

In 1841, the Prophet again reiterated, "All priesthood is Melchizedek, but there are different portions or degree of it. When Moses was on the mount, that portion which brought Moses to speak with God face to face was taken away: but that which brought the ministry of angels remained. All the prophets had the Melchizedek Priesthood and were ordained by God himself."[80]

On 4 May 1842, Joseph administered the endowment to nine men for the first time in this dispensation. All keys of the Aaronic Priesthood part of the endowment were given (those restored by John in 1829[81] and Moses in 1836[82]), and all keys of the Melchizedek (Moses and Elias in 1836) were given. The administration of the endowment for the dispensation of the fullness of times had begun.

On 17 May 1843, Joseph enlarged on priesthood doctrine by teaching the concept that faithful Saints could be sealed up to eternal life.[83]

Then, on 27 August, Joseph repeated two truths previously taught. First, "No man can attain to the joint heirship with Jesus Christ without being administered to by one having the same power and authority of Melchizedek."[84] The second truth again expounded was titled the

"Three Grand Orders."[85] In this sermon, Joseph stated that the Melchizedek Priesthood "is a perfect law of theocracy . . . to give laws to the people, administering endless lives to the sons and daughters of Adam."[86] This statement fully explains the oath and covenant of the priesthood and how it is accomplished. The sons and daughters of God can become joint heirs with God only by receiving the fullness of priesthood ordinances and in no other way.[87] Joseph further taught, "The power of the Melchizedek Priesthood is to have the power of 'endless lives'; for the everlasting covenant cannot be broken." This knowledge witnessed that the oath and covenant is eternal. Only the individual can sever it through transgression. Once the recipient puts his life back in compliance to Father's will, the ordinances are not readministered but are restored by one with authority to do so.

On this same date, Joseph began to reveal the different and many powers that are in the keys Elijah restored. First, he explained that these keys were inherent with "The anointing and sealing [that] is to be called, elected and made sure."[88] Joseph said it is "the key of the revelations, ordinances, oracles, powers and endowments, the fullness of the Melchizedek Priesthood and the kingdom of God on the earth; and to receive, obtain, and perform all the ordinances belonging to the kingdom of God."[89]

On 20 January 1844, he spoke again about the mission of Elijah, but he substituted a word used by that prophet. *Turn* should be *bind*—hence again the power to seal the living and the dead was included within Elijah's keys. Two months later, on 10 March 1844, Joseph taught that the keys from Elijah had the powers of the priesthood to turn individuals over to the buffeting of Satan.[90]

There are keys of the Holy Priesthood that must still be restored—for example, the keys of translation that existed during the time of Enoch[91] (probably held by him) and used by the Savior at Bountiful with the Three Nephites.[92] In 3 Nephi 28, Mormon gives a beautiful review of what transpires in the translation process. Another example is that the keys of resurrection must still be restored.[93]

Ordinances and Covenants to Their Fullness

In 1831, the Lord told Joseph, "Verily I say unto you, blessed are you for receiving mine everlasting covenant, even the fulness of my gospel, sent forth unto the children of men, that they might have life and be made partakers of the glories which are to be revealed in the last days, as it was written by the prophets and apostles in days of old."[94] The new and everlasting covenant containing all covenants, ordinances, and even the fullness of the gospel had been restored to the earth. Now, the great challenge that lay before Joseph was making it all available to the Saints through authoritative administration in a proper place.

The laws and commandments, the statutes, and the judgments that come from God constitute ordinances. When the Saints promise to keep all the commandments and statutes, they are covenanting to "walk in all the ordinances of the Lord."[95]

Much information was given to Joseph concerning ordinances at the beginning of the Restoration. In June of 1831, he was told by the Lord that ordinances are the "pattern in all things." Accomplishment of sacred things comes "if [one] obeys my ordinances."[96] Four months later, the revelation that has become "the Lord's preface to the doctrines, covenants, and commandments given in this dispensation."[97] The reason for the door's being shut on five virgins within the kingdom was plainly described to Joseph. "For they have strayed from mine ordinances, and have broken mine everlasting covenant."[98]

Ten months later, in September 1832, a beautiful clarifying statement on ordinances followed: "Therefore in the ordinances thereof [the greater priesthood], the power of godliness is manifest."[99] In June 1833, he was told how and where: "Yea, verily I say unto you, I gave unto you a commandment that you should "build a house, in the which house I design to endow those whom I have chosen with power from on high."[100] One year later, the Lord told Joseph concerning the elders of the Church, "For behold, I have prepared a great endowment and blessing to be poured out upon them, inasmuch as they are faithful and continue in humility before me."[101]

In the theology of the kingdom of God, a covenant is the free, conscientious binding of a person to Father, Son, and Holy Ghost and to an eternal partner and an eternal family. The only way a person can love God with all his or her heart, might, mind, and strength is through the laws and the ordinances of the new and everlasting covenant.[102] The two words "new" and "everlasting" are descriptive in meaning. Each covenant entered into by an individual is new, and it is everlasting to that individual.

Moroni's visits to the young prophet did much to lay the foundation of understanding ordinances and covenants. As Joseph translated the title page written by the hand of Mormon, the three purposes of the Book of Mormon were revealed. The title page must have had a great impact upon him in the ensuing months of translating. The Prophet found it to be a book of covenants and knowledge of ordinances. In 2 Nephi 9, Jacob gives an excellent example of one of the purposes of the book of Isaiah. Having just read two chapters of Isaiah to a gathering of the people of Nephi, Jacob went on to explain, "And now, my beloved brethren, I have read these things that ye might know concerning the covenants of the Lord that he has covenanted with all the house of Israel." [103]

Following a moving sermon King Benjamin gave to his people about covenants, they responded with, "And we are willing to enter into a covenant with our God to do his will, and to be obedient to his commandments in all things that he shall command us, all the remainder of our days." King Benjamin replied:

> Ye have spoken the words that I desired; and the covenant which ye have made is a righteous covenant. . . .
>
> There is no other name given whereby salvation cometh; therefore, I would that ye should take upon you the name of Christ, all you that have entered into the covenant with God that ye should be obedient unto the end of your lives.
>
> And it shall come to pass that whosoever doeth this shall be found at the right hand of God, for he shall know the name by which he is called; for he shall be called by the name of Christ. [104]

In his ministry to the Nephites at Bountiful, Jesus talked about other sheep. In this discourse, he covered the past, present, and future of all the fragments of the "covenant people." The past were the covenant people of Palestine. Christ was with the "covenant people" of the Americas at this time, and he spoke of the Ten Tribes that would return. [105] The Savior then talked about the covenant entered into first with Father Abraham and then later with Isaac and Jacob. This scripture identifies the fulfillment of the new and everlasting covenant made by Creator, Redeemer, and Testator before this earth was ever created: "And then will I gather them in from the four quarters of the earth and then will I fulfil the covenant which the Father hath made unto all the people of the house of Israel." [106]

After speaking of ordinances, the next verse refers, as it does so many times in the Book of Mormon, to the three members of the

Godhead.[107] These references serve as a reminder to us that the perfect unity of the Godhead is founded in the new and everlasting covenant. They are always one in and through this great covenant. It took Joseph until 1841 to put into print a descriptive reference of how the members of the Godhead are one. He said this covenant was an everlasting covenant that "was made between three personages before the organization of this earth."[108]

The translation of the Bible must have solidified Joseph's understanding of covenants. The covenants are the golden thread of the Old Testament. Crucial information is provided in the Old Testament for those who have entered into the new and everlasting covenant. It helps them to understand the significance of the covenant and explains God's dealings with the children of Israel—the blessings or curses promised as they were obedient or disobedient to the conditions of the covenant.

As Joseph translated the Bible, he came to understand that "covenant" means testament. (See specifically the Joseph Smith Translation, Genesis 9.) Genesis 17 was corrected to read:

> And I will make my covenant between me and thee, and I will multiply thee exceedingly.
>
> And it came to pass, that Abram fell on his face, and called upon the name of the Lord.
>
> And God talked with him, saying, My people have gone astray from my precepts, and have not kept mine ordinances, which I gave unto their fathers;
>
> And they have not observed mine anointing, and the burial, or baptism wherewith I commanded them.[109]

In January 1834, Joseph asked some searching questions. "We all admit that the Gospel has ordinances, and if so, had it not always ordinances, and were not its ordinances always the same?"[110] And, "If in any other name was it the Gospel? And if it was the Gospel, and that preached in the name of Christ, had it any ordinances? If not, was it the Gospel? And if it had ordinances what were they?"[111]

The Prophet wrote a long epistle (three sections) to the elders of the Church in September 1835. In this letter, he used the term *everlasting covenant* "and used every influence and argument that lay in my power to get those who believed in the everlasting covenant . . . having a zeal not according to knowledge, and not understanding the pure principles of the doctrine of the Church." He closed the epistle, "In the bonds of the new and everlasting covenant, Joseph Smith, Jun."[112]

About 3 p.m. on Thursday, 21 January 1836, while the brethren were attending a session of the School of the Prophets in the Kirtland Temple, the first washing and anointing took place.[113]

Following the Liberty Jail experience, the Prophet taught with greater discernment concerning ordinances and covenants, line upon line and precept upon precept, as shown below:

14 May 1840: "A Blessing to the Covenant People"[114]

August: "New and Everlasting Covenant"[115]

5 October: "Ordinances Always The Same"[116] and "All Ordinances Restored"[117] (both given at October Conference, 1840)

At this same conference, Joseph taught this beautiful truth: "Michael . . . was the first and father of all, not only by progeny, but the first to hold the spiritual blessings, to whom was made known the plan of ordinances for the salvation of his posterity unto the end, and to whom Christ was first revealed."[118]

19 October 1840: "The Temple"

15 January 1841: "The Temple and the Gathering of Saints"[119]

19 January: "But I command you, all ye my saints, to build a house unto me; and I grant unto you a sufficient time to build a house unto me, and during this time your baptisms shall be acceptable unto me. . . . [A]nd if you do not these things at the end of the appointment, ye shall be rejected as a church, with your dead, saith the Lord your God."[120]

The revelatory knowledge was then given:

> For verily I say unto you, that after you have had sufficient time to build a house to me, wherein the ordinance of baptizing for the dead belongeth, and for which the same was instituted from before the foundation of the world, your baptisms for your dead cannot be acceptable unto me.
>
> For therein are the keys of the holy priesthood ordained, that you may receive honor and glory. . . .
>
> And again, verily I say unto you, How shall your washings be acceptable unto me, except ye perform them in a house which you have built to my name?
>
> For, for this cause, I commanded Moses that he should build a tabernacle, that they should bear it with them in the wilderness,

and to build a house in the land of promise, that those ordinances might be revealed which had been hid before the world was.

Therefore, verily I say unto you, that your anointings, and your washings, and your baptisms for the dead . . . and for the glory, honor, and endowment of all her municipals, are ordained by the ordinance of my holy house, which my people are always commanded to build unto my holy name.

And verily I say unto you, Let this house be built unto my name, that I may reveal mine ordinances therein unto my people;

For I deign to reveal unto my church things which have been kept hid from before the foundation of the world, things that pertain to the dispensation of the fulness of times,

And I will show unto my servant Joseph all things pertaining to this house, and the priesthood thereof, and the place whereon it shall be built.[121]

March and April 1842: The Book of Abraham was published for the first time in the *Times and Seasons*, "The Lord's Chosen People."

May: Joseph talked about the "The Temple—All Things to be Gathered in One,"[122] and on 4 May, he administered the first endowments.[123]

22 January 1843: It was revealed that "All the ordinances, systems, and administrations on the earth are of no use to the children of men, unless they are ordained and authorized of God; for nothing will save a man but a legal administrator; for none others will be acknowledged either by God or angels."[124]

16 and 17 May: "In the celestial glory there are three heavens or degrees; And in order to obtain the highest, a man must enter into this order of the priesthood; And if he does not, he cannot obtain it. He may enter into the other, but that is the end of his kingdom; he cannot have an increase."[125]

11 June: Joseph stressed the purpose of the temple:

The main object was to build unto the Lord a house whereby He could reveal unto His people the ordinances of His house and the glories of His kingdom, and teach the people the way of salvation; for there are certain ordinances and principles that, when they are taught and practiced, must be done in a place or house built for that purpose. . . .

If a man gets a fullness of the priesthood of God he has to get it in the same way that Jesus Christ obtained it, and that was by keeping all the commandments and obeying all the ordinances of the house of the Lord.[126]

August 1843: Joseph spoke on "Prophet, Priest, and King," which denotes some of the most sacred and holy ordinances.[127] At this time, he gave the "Mission of Elijah," which was most enlightening, as it tied together the sealing ordinances. In the discourse, Joseph described the importance of Elijah's mission: "How shall God come to the rescue of this generation? He will send Elijah the Prophet. . . . Elijah shall reveal the covenants to *seal* the hearts of the fathers to the children, and the children to the fathers. The anointing and sealing is to be called, elected and made sure"[128] (italics added). Notice that where the word *turn* was used by Malachi[129] and in the Doctrine and Covenants,[130] here Joseph has changed *turn* to read *seal*. Joseph's diary reads "anointing and sealing, called elected and made sure."

A discourse was given explaining the ultimate efficacy of the covenant of eternal marriage:

> Four destroying angels holding power over the four quarters of the earth until the servants of God are sealed in their foreheads, which signifies sealing the blessings upon their heads, meaning the everlasting covenant, thereby making their calling and election sure. When a seal is put upon the father and mother, it secures their posterity, so that they cannot be lost, but will be saved by virtue of the covenant of their father and mother.[131]

16 May: Joseph spoke about the ordinances of "More Sure Word of Prophecy"[132] and "Calling and Election Made Sure."[133]

11 June: Joseph taught that the principles of the gospel never change. "Ordinances instituted in the heavens before the foundation of the world, in the priesthood, for the salvation of men, are not to be altered or changed. All must be saved on the same principles."[134]

June 1843: Joseph talked on the subject of "Purpose of Gathering Israel."[135]

> What was the object of gathering the Jews, or the people of God in any age of the world? The main object was to build unto the Lord a house whereby He could reveal unto His people the ordinances of His house and the glories of His kingdom, and teach the people the way of salvation; for there are certain ordinances and principles that, when they are taught and practiced, must be done in a place or house built for that purpose."

Further, "All men who become heirs of God and joint heirs with Jesus Christ will have to receive the fullness of the ordinances of his kingdom; and those who will not receive all the ordinances will come short of the fullness of that glory, if they do not lose the whole."

11 June: Joseph taught the purpose of gathering in relation to the temple:

> These things are revealed in the most holy places in a temple prepared for that purpose. Why gather the people together in this place? For the same purpose that Jesus wanted to gather the Jews—to receive ordinances, the blessings, and glories that God has in store for His Saints. I will now ask this assembly and all the Saints if you will now build this house and receive the ordinances and blessings which God has in store for you; or will you not build unto the Lord this house, and let Him pass by and bestow these blessings upon another people? I pause for a reply.[136]

9 July: "Necessity of Ordinances"[137]

August: "The Mission of Elijah"[138]

28 September 1843: As the first fulfillment of eternal mates (one flesh)[139] in our dispensation, Joseph and Emma received all the fruits of the Restoration, as they were given the ordinance of washing and were anointed to the fullness of the priesthood.[140]

October 1843: Joseph said:

> The organization of the spiritual and heavenly worlds, and of spiritual and heavenly beings, was agreeable to the most perfect order and harmony: their limits and bounds were fixed irrevocably, and voluntarily subscribed to in their heavenly estate by themselves, and were by our first parents subscribed to upon the earth. Hence the importance of embracing and subscribing to the principles of eternal truth by all men upon the earth that expect eternal life. I assure the Saints that truth, in reference to these matters, can and may be known through the revelations of God in the way of His ordinances, and in answer to prayer.[141]

8 October: On this day, the ordinance of the fullness was administered to Hyrum and Mary F. Smith. It seems only fitting that this dedicated couple was the second couple to receive this ordinance in this dispensation.[142] During the month and through November, other couples received these sacred ordinances. In December, Joseph administered these ordinances to the first group of Saints.[143]

20 January 1844: Joseph said:

> The question is frequently asked, "Can we not be saved without going through with all those ordinances?" I would answer, No, not the fulness of salvation. Jesus said, There are many mansions in my Father's house, and I will go and prepare a place for you. *House* here named should have been translated kingdom; and any person who is exalted to the highest mansion has to abide a celestial law, and the whole law too.

But there has been a great difficulty in getting anything into the heads of this generation. It has been like splitting hemlock knots with a corn-dodger for a wedge, and a pumpkin for a beetle. Even the Saints are slow to understand.[144]

21 January: The "Sealing Power"[145] and "All Ordinances Necessary"[146]

7 March: "The Worthy to Receive Endowments"[147]

10 March: "Discourse on Elias and Elijah and Messiah,"[148] "Fullness of Ordinance Living and Dead,"[149] "Sealing on Earth and in Heaven,"[150] and "Sealing Power of Elijah Is as Follows"[151]

7 April: "King Follett Discourse"

April: Joseph taught:

The declaration this morning is, that as soon as the Temple and baptismal font are prepared, we calculate to give the Elders of Israel their washings and anointings, and attend to those last and more impressive ordinances, without which we cannot obtain celestial thrones. But there must be a holy place prepared for that purpose. There was a proclamation made during the time that the foundation of the Temple was laid to that effect, and there are provisions made until the work is completed, so that men may receive their endowments and be made kings and priests unto the Most High God, having nothing to do with temporal things, but their whole time will be taken up with things pertaining to the house of God. There must, however, be a place built expressly for that purpose, and for men to be baptized for their dead. It must be built in this central place; for every man who wishes to save his father, mother, brothers, sisters and friends, must go through all the ordinances for each one of them separately, the same as for himself, from baptism to ordination, washing and anointings, and receive all the keys and powers of the Priesthood, the same as for himself.[152]

April: Joseph taught:

The Lord has an established law in relation to the matter; there must be a particular spot for the salvation of our dead. I verily believe there will be a place, and hence men who want to save their dead can come and bring their families, do their work by being baptized and attending to the other ordinances for their dead, and then may go back again to live and wait till they go to receive their reward.[153]

April: Joseph said:

I am going on in my progress for eternal life. It is not only necessary that you should be baptized for your dead, but you will have to go through all the ordinances for them, the same as you have gone through to save yourselves. There will be 144,000

167

saviors on Mount Zion, and with them an innumerable host that no man can number. Oh! I beseech you to go forward, go forward and make your calling and your election sure.[154]

April: "In regard to the law of the Priesthood, there should be a place where all nations shall come up from time to time to receive their endowments. . . . A man may act as proxy for his own relatives; the ordinances of the Gospel which were laid out before the foundations of the world have thus been fulfilled."[155]

16 June: Joseph said, "I learned a testimony concerning Abraham, and he reasoned concerning the God of Heaven." Joseph went on to declare the immense learning that took place while he was translating the papyri.[156]

Our dispensation is truly a dispensation of all ordinances for the living and dead. To remember and keep the covenants is a standing obligation resting upon the Lord's people.

But a person cannot keep a covenant before it is made, and a calling in the priesthood cannot be magnified until it is received. The covenant is the contract that sets forth the terms and conditions by obedience to which eternal life may be won. The covenants and vows are the channels of divine power to the eternal patriarchal order. The highest manifestation of integrity is exhibited by those who conform their conduct to the terms of those gospel covenants and promises they have made. The covenants or channels are the divine key and the justification for finding the Saints, gathering the Saints, and perfecting the Saints on both sides of the veil—the very reason why we build temples.

The ordinances of the temple are known as the mysteries of godliness and are among the most sacred of the plan of salvation. One of the duties of the apostles is to be stewards of the mysteries of God.[157] A few of the scriptures that speak of this sacredness are Hebrews 5:12, Alma 12:9-11, and D&C 63:64.

Eternal Marriage and Families

Eternal marriage and families are the foundation of all the eternities and the very essence of God's "work and glory." An understanding of this principle was impressed upon the soul of Joseph Smith, Jr., in the earliest stage of his ministry. His first tutor, Moroni, revealed to him the supernal role of marriage and the eternal consequence of it. (See Chapter 2.)

Just months later, Joseph started the experience of spiritually reading, correcting, inserting, and making additions to both the Old and New Testament. His understanding of eternal marriage was greatly expanded during this period. This knowledge included what God told Adam and Eve even before they were placed in the Garden of Eden. He told them "Therefore shall a man leave his father and his mother, and shall cleave unto his wife: and they shall be one flesh. Wherefore they are no more twain, but one flesh."[158] Their marriage was an eternal relationship having been solemnized by God himself.[159] During his ministry, Christ further declared, "What therefore God hath joined together, let no man put asunder."[160]

While working in the Old Testament, the Lord's answers to Joseph's questions concerning Abraham-Sarah and Isaac-Rebecca were paramount for his obtaining a eternal aspect of eternal marriage.[161] As Joseph brought the Old Testament to a close, he became the first in our dispensation to understand what the prophet Malachi was really telling us when he referred to the subject of "roots and branches".[162]

Joseph came to know that those who are wicked and will not come unto Christ and partake of his ordinances will be burned at his coming. Thus they will lose their roots backward (progenitors) and their branches forward (descendants). This same statement is quoted by the Savior as his ministry with the Nephites at Bountiful drew to a close.[163] From the mouth of two witnesses truth is established.

While translating the New Testament, Matthew 22 and/or parallels, further understanding came to him concerning Christ's reply to the Sadduces: "For in the resurrection they neither marry, nor are given in marriage, but *are as the angels of God in heaven*." (Italics added)[164]

Also during this time frame, Joseph was instructed by the Lord to get himself to Ohio where he would give him the "law."[165] In Ohio, the Lord gave him the "Law," a part of which was "Thou shalt love thy wife with all thy heart, and shalt cleave unto her and none else."[166]

In translating the New Testament, Joseph made a change in John 5:29. "And shall come forth; they who have done good, in the resurrection of the just; they who have done evil, in the resurrection of the unjust." This correction opened up the entire Section 76 of the Doctrine and Covenants, which followed a year later. The petition of Joseph to know more about these changes brought forth one of the most beautiful visions ever given him. In it, many of the requirements for gaining the highest glories afforded in the plan of salvation were listed.[167]

The first written instruction on the sanctity of marriage came in March 1831.[168] The Church had many converts from the Shakers religion, and this revelation was an answer to the Shakers' communal society based on the "female principle":

> And again, verily I say unto you, that whoso forbiddeth to marry is not ordained of God, for marriage is ordained of God unto man.
>
> Wherefore, it is lawful that he should have one wife, and they twain shall be one flesh, and all this that the earth might answer the end of its creation;
>
> And that it might be filled with the measure of man, according to his creation before the world was made.[169]

In one brief passage, the concepts of a premortal existence, creation of the earth, marriage, and procreation were woven together. The design of God started to unfold.[170]

The physical evidence of these principles, "one flesh" and "measure of man, according to his creation," can be seen in almost all correspondence to and from the jail. Examples are found in the letters written by Bishop Edward Partridge and Don Carlos. Both letters secure the brethren in the jail with the best assurance concerning their wives. Almost half of Edward's letter gives each brother news of his wife and family.[171]

A general assembly of the Church was called on 17 August 1835 to approve the Book of Doctrine and Covenants. According to Church history, the assembly was called "to take into consideration the labors of a committee appointed by a general assembly of the Church on the 24th of September, 1834 for the purpose of arranging the items of the doctrine of Jesus Christ for the government of the Church."[172]

The "Article on Marriage" for secular marriage was not presented for a sustaining vote by W. W. Phelps as a revelation but only as an expression of belief to the general assembly.[173] This procedure was designed to put down rumors that certain Saints were teaching and living principles that were not sanctioned by Joseph and certainly without divine authority. Members of the committee all signed the preface to the Doctrine and Covenants on 17 February 1835.[174] All members of the Quorum of Twelve Apostles signed the testimony to the Doctrine and Covenants.[175]

On 24 November 1835, Joseph performed his first temporal marriage (Elijah had not restored the sealing power at that time) between Newel Knight and Lydia Goldthwaite.[176] As part of his comments during the marriage ceremony, Joseph said that "marriage was an institution of heaven, instituted in the garden of Eden; that it was necessary it should be solemnized by the authority of the everlasting Priesthood."[177]

A form of marriage certificate for secular marriage was used and signed by Joseph on 19 January 1836.[178]

Joseph Smith taught that Elijah restored the power to seal families together for eternity (see Chapter 2), which was culminated in a revelation on 6 September 1842 that explained why the earth would be smitten with a curse without the restoration of the sealing power. "It is sufficient to know [that the earth would be smitten] . . . unless there is a welding link of some kind or other between the fathers and the children. . . . For we without them cannot be made perfect; neither can they without us be made perfect."[179] Thus, in the great foundation for marriage, the family, the welding link was performed.

On 28 September 1842, Joseph and Emma were sealed in the new and everlasting covenant of marriage by the power and authority restored in this last dispensation through the prophet himself. With a complete understanding of this essential ordinance, this sealing was administered to a number of faithful Saints. In the history of the Church, this was the beginning of eternal relationships between husbands and wives and parents and children. Because of the controversy on this subject and the bitter persecution it brought, Joseph was only able to approach privately those whom he believed were worthy to receive it and who were capable of living the higher law of marriage. At this time, only those who had been proven true and faithful received the ordinance of eternal marriage.

On Wednesday, 12 July 1843, Joseph finally consented to record in the presence of his brother Hyrum and William Clayton the revelation he had received on the marriage covenant. [180] Hyrum recognized the magnitude of this doctrine (which is recorded in Section 132 of the Doctrine and Covenants) and the impact it would have not only on the Saints, but upon the whole world. Concerned about the reprisal, he asked Joseph to use the Urim and Thummin whereby there could be no doubt in the minds of the faithful Saints as to the validity of this profound revelation. Joseph, who had been acquainted with this doctrine since 1831, told his brother Hyrum, "he need not to, for he knew the revelation perfectly from beginning to end."[181]

This revelation was later shown to the High Council. Many of those who saw it recorded this historic event in their journals; however, the revelation was not made public until 1852 after the Church had migrated to Utah and was free from mobs and persecution.

A review of this sacred revelation by those who have partaken of the new and everlasting covenant would be most rewarding as it would refresh the memory of eternal truths and covenants received in the House of the Lord. The first twenty verses discuss the eternal nature of marriage and how godhood is achieved. The next twelve verses deal with the beauty of this covenant ending with a meaningful description of "seed." The Lord then gives a declaration to all the recipients of this covenant, "Go ye, therefore and do the works of Abraham..."

In a revelation given on the 16th and 17th of May 1843, the word "celestial glory" is described. "In the celestial glory there are three heavens or degrees; and in order to obtain the highest, a man must enter into the fullness of the priesthood [meaning the new and everlasting covenant of marriage] and if he does not, he cannot obtain it. He may enter into the other, but that is the end of his kingdom; he cannot have an increase."[182]

Joseph gave an insightful and revealing discourse on eternal family relations in August, 1843. [183]

On 28 September 1843, one year after their sealing, Joseph Smith, Jr. and Emma Hale Smith were the first in this dispensation to receive their second annointings which are necessary to achieve the fullness of one's creation. [184]

At a meeting of the Nauvoo City Council on 8 June 1844, just 19 days before his death, Joseph declared, "...men in this life must marry in view of eternity, otherwise they must be as angels, or be single in heaven."[185] The Prophet of God had verified one last time the doctrine of celestial marriage. This great eternal truth along with all the others would be sealed by his blood a few days later.

In every dispensation of Father's children, all keys and ordinances pertaining to the everlasting covenant of marriage were restored by the power and authority of God the Father and his Son Jesus Christ. The importance of these eternal ordinances have always been essential to man's exaltation.

God's type of marriage, glory, or exaltation has, is, and always will be associated with an eternal unit of husband and wife and continuing seed.

Joseph's comprehension for the imparting of this beautiful ordinance to worthy Saints throughout the world could very well be considered the greatest blessing to mankind given through his legacy.

It is only fitting that Joseph and his eternal love and joy, Emma, received all the blessings that had been revealed to Joseph during their sojourn on earth together. Their calling and election is sure. As Adam and Eve were the prototype for all who followed them, so Joseph and Emma are the great prototype for all in this last dispensation. They have left us a legacy worthy of sacrifice and endurance with a promise of everlasting life.

Chapter 11

LIVING ORACLES/
APOSTLES OF THE LORD

Webster defines an oracle as "one who serves a deity, especially as a medium for prophecies."[1] Among Joseph's great legacies was the restoration of living oracles.[2] This restoration was not an easy task. The modern apostles of this dispensation,[3] including Oliver Cowdery, suffered great tribulation as they were tried and tested by the Lord "to prove them herewith." Joseph was directed by the Lord as to what the tests would be. Of those who were close to the Prophet, two were faithful in every and all trials and remained steadfast no matter how great the cost.[4] Four could not withstand the refiner's fire and left the Church.[5] Four left and came back.[6] William Smith left, came back, and then left again. Even Parley P. Pratt talks of his apostasy experiences.[7] On 28 May 1843, Joseph said, "Of the Twelve Apostles chosen in Kirtland, and ordained under the hands of Oliver Cowdery, David Whitmer and myself, there have been but two but what have lifted their heel against me—namely Brigham Young and Heber C. Kimball."[8]

Among those who were faithful, or who left briefly and returned, twelve were chosen to be the first living oracles of modern times. They received all "heavenly powers" within The Church of Jesus Christ of Latter-day Saints and were revered by the members of the Church. They were then, and continue to the present, to be the constant receptacles of divine revelation from God to his Church. Today, there are fifteen prophets, seers, and revelators who have that sacred mandate.

The living oracles/apostles of our dispensation went through the same supernal experiences as did the living oracles/apostles in the meridian of time. These individuals are the receptacles of revelation for the Savior's kingdom on earth today[9] as the Judean apostles were for their dispensation and the Nephite disciples for their time.[10]

A comparison of Christ's original apostles in the meridian of time with the first apostles of this dispensation is very revealing. Christ called his apostles.[11] He ordained them[12] and conferred upon them the Melchizedek Priesthood.[13]

This same Melchizedek Priesthood was given to the latter-day apostles by Joseph Smith, Jr. and the Three Witnesses, as they were instructed by the Lord. In 1829, the Lord, speaking to Oliver Cowdery and David Whitmer said, "[F]or you are called even with that same calling with which he [Paul] was called."[14] Concerning the twelve chosen by the Savior in the latter days, Jesus stated, "Yea, even twelve; and the Twelve shall be my disciples, and they shall take upon them my name; and the Twelve are they who shall desire to take upon them my name with full purpose of heart."[15]

Joseph and Oliver Cowdery were ordained apostles in June of 1829[16] and were enlightened about their ordination by Peter, James, and John.[17] Other apostles were ordained 14 February 1835 under the hands of the Three Witnesses: Oliver Cowdery, David Whitmer, and Martin Harris. Each subsequent apostle received the Apostolic authority at his ordination on various dates.

In March 1835, a published revelation stated that the Quorum of the Twelve Apostles was equal in "authority and power" to the organized First Presidency.[18]

To the Judean apostles, while at Caesarean Philippi, Christ promised additional authority. Peter was told he would receive the sealing power. It was not bestowed at that time, as the sealing power was not on the earth. The glorious restoration by Elijah was yet to take place on the Mount of Transfiguration.[19]

Joseph Smith shared his insight concerning this great event when he related how Christ, while on Mt. Hermon or Tabor, received the fullness of the priesthood, including the keys of the sealing power. Joseph also spoke of Peter, James, and John and their receiving the keys of the sealing power from Elijah[20] while transfigured on the mount.[21]

On 3 April 1836, Joseph received from Elijah "the key of the revelations, ordinances, oracles, powers and endowments of the fullness of the Melchizedek Priesthood and of the kingdom of God on the earth; and to receive, obtain, and perform all the ordinations belonging to the kingdom of God."[22] These were the very same powers Elijah bestowed on Peter, James, and John. This is the authority that seals families together—thus providing the welding link for roots and branches to be recorded in the "Book of Life."

On 4 May 1842,[23] Joseph Smith bestowed the knowledge and powers of the Aaronic and Melchizedek endowment on nine faithful men, three of whom were apostles—Brigham Young, Heber C. Kimball, and Willard Richards.[24] With these ordinances, Joseph "instituted the ancient order of things for the first time."[25] The following day, 5 May,[26] Joseph and Hyrum received this endowment from these men, the same communicated to them the previous day.[27] Joseph said, "With all the ordinances in place for the dispensation of the fullness of the Priesthood in the last days, all the power of earth and hell can never prevail against it."[28] The remaining apostles were endowed during subsequent months as they returned from their missions.

It was during the North Galilean ministry that the Savior gave verbally to all the Twelve Apostles power to seal and loose on earth and in heaven.[29] In the last week of the Savior's ministry, he washed the feet of his apostles, making the apostles clean every whit.[30] This washing was in preparation for giving them the fullness of the priesthood.[31] The Savior then taught the apostles about the Second Comforter and the Holy Spirit of Promise, which would teach them all things and give them peace.[32] The last ordination was given to the apostles when Christ anointed and ordained them to the fullness of the priesthood, making them kings and priests.[33] With the fullness came the sealing power of the priesthood, which he had previously discussed with them.[34] Jesus then revealed to his apostles that he must leave them for the Holy Spirit to come and seal them up to eternal life and give them the power of God. This was fulfilled on the Day of Pentecost.[35] Peter said that he, James, and John also received a more sure word of prophecy, which made their calling and election sure.[36] Further enlightenment came from John the Beloved when he related that he and others had been made "kings and priests unto our God."[37] They had received the holy anointing,[38] which sealed them up unto eternal life[39] and which bestowed upon them the blessings of the Second Comforter. This declaration came from Christ's own lips.[40] The same blessings were bestowed upon the Nephite disciples.[41]

The sequence of events was the same in our dispensation. In May 1843,[42] Joseph met with the brethren who had previously been endowed and bestowed upon them this higher endowment "and the holy priesthood which he administered unto us,"[43] which included the fullness of the sealing power stated in Isaiah 22:22, Matthew 16:19, D&C 124:93, 132:7, and Helaman 10:4-10.[44] Referring to these events, Joseph said, "Have we not learned the Priesthood after the order of Melchizedek, which includes both Prophets, Priests and Kings."[45]

Joseph further instructed the apostles, "Those holding the fullness of the Melchizedek Priesthood are kings and priests of the Most High God, holding the keys of power and blessings. . . . The anointing and sealing is to be called, elected and [the election] made sure."[46] That the blessing of calling and election is available to all was reiterated by both the Apostle Peter of old and Ezra Taft Benson of our day. They both gave great discourses admonishing all to push forward and make one's calling and election sure.[47]

It was during the Council of Fifty meetings that the Prophet Joseph passed on to the Twelve the fullness of all the keys.[48] Concerning this event, Elder Orson Hyde wrote that "in the latter part of the month of March" 1844, Joseph and his brother Hyrum appointed the Twelve to lead the Church and passed on to them all the keys that Joseph held. "This appointment was made, and confirmed by the holy anointing under the hands of Joseph and Hyrum." Since the Twelve had already received their endowment (including the fullness of the priesthood) between May 1842 and February 1844, the "endowments" referred to here apparently meant the endowment of keys that Joseph had received from holy angels but that had not yet been passed to the Twelve. These keys were such as those received from Raphael, Moses, Elias, and Elijah.[49] The keys of translation (with which individuals are translated and taken into heaven) may have been passed to Joseph from Elijah. All these events certainly fulfilled what Joseph talked about in the Lectures on Faith. After quoting parts of the Savior's intercessory prayer, Joseph said concerning the Twelve, "He had given them the glory that the Father had given him that they might be one; or in other words to make them one."[50]

On about 26 March 1844, just before his death, Joseph called together the Twelve Apostles and others who comprised the Council of Fifty and committed unto them the responsibility of carrying forth the work of the kingdom of God on earth, thereby clearing his own "skirts." Benjamin F. Johnson, a member of this council, recorded the meeting in these words:

> At one of the last meetings of the Council of Fifty after all had been completed and the keys of power committed and in the presence of the Quorum of the Twelve and others who were encircled around him, he [Joseph] arose, gave a review of his life and sufferings, and of the testimonies he had borne, and said that the Lord had now accepted his labors and sacrifices, and did not require him longer to carry the responsibilities and burden and bearing of this kingdom. Turning to those around him, including the Twelve, he said, "and in the name of the Lord Jesus Christ I now place it upon my brethren of this council, and I shake my skirts clear of all responsibility from this time forth."[51]

In this meeting on 26 March 1844, Wilford Woodruff stated that Joseph said:

> Brethren, I have had sorrow of heart and anguish of soul from fear that my life might be taken from the earth while the keys of the Kingdom of God and of this dispensation rested upon my head alone, but, thanks be unto the great Eloheim, the God of Israel, I have been permitted to seal all the keys, powers, and Priesthood upon the heads of my brethren, the Twelve Apostles, that have ever been sealed upon my head by any Prophet, Apostle, or Messenger of Life and Salvation, and now I am free. I now say unto you, the Twelve Apostles, that I now roll off the responsibility and the work of the Church and Kingdom of God upon your shoulders, and now you must round up your shoulders and bear off this Kingdom. We have had a charge given us by our prophet, and that charge we intend to honor and magnify. It was given in March last [1844]. He [Joseph] said, "let no man take your crown, and though you should have to walk right into death, fear not, neither be dismayed. You have to die but once." To us were committed the keys of the Kingdom, and every gift, key and power, that Joseph ever had, confirmed upon our heads by an anointing.[52]

These same keys are now vested in the First Presidency and the Twelve today. Although each apostle holds these keys, it is the President and Prophet who can activate them through assignments.

These living oracles were and always have been under the mandate to take the gospel to the world. It is apparent the modern-day apostles have done just that.[53] It certainly fulfills the admonition of the Savior to the original Twelve, as it so appropriately fits the living oracles of today. "It hath gone forth in a firm decree, by the will of the Father, that mine apostles, the twelve which were with me in my ministry at Jerusalem, shall stand at my right hand, . . .being clothed with robes of righteousness, with crowns upon their heads, in glory even as I am."[54] The challenge for the members of the Church is to stand as true Saints of the kingdom and sustain them.[55]

Today, the legacy of the modern-day apostles fulfills the Lord's statement that his gospel will remain pure and undefiled until he comes:[56] "Verily I say unto you, the keys of this kingdom shall never be taken from you [Joseph], while thou art in the world, neither in the world to come; Nevertheless, through you shall the oracles be given to another, yea, even unto the church."[57] The tremendous responsibility of the living oracles/apostles is eloquently but simply stated by the Apostle Paul who said, "Let a man so account of us, [apostles] as of the ministers of Christ, and stewards of the mysteries of God."[58] It is interesting what Hyrum said so appropriately about this statement. Just three months before he and his brother were killed, Hyrum said, "For when God commands men to teach such principles the saints will receive them. For the mysteries of God are not given to all men; and unto those to whom they are given they are placed under restrictions to impart only such as God will command them."[59]

The imagery of watchman is fitting for those fifteen men who have been called by the Lord as prophets, seers, and revelators and who have been sustained as such by the body of the Church. These men have been anointed of the Savior and serve as his special witnesses. It has been so designated by the Lord in the various dispensations of time. These witnesses are found in the Old Testament, the Book of Mormon, and the Doctrine and Covenants and are identified as those who are to watch over Christ's Church.

> The term watch helps to define their roles which, in part, are: to be attentive to trends, drifts, and conditions within and without the Church; to be vigilant and alert to dangers from the archenemy, Satan; to guard, tend, heed, and warn as in the following scripture passages: (Ezekiel 33:1-7, Mosiah 15:28-29, D&C 101:45). These men are of varying backgrounds, abilities, and temperaments. Their individual stories are unique to themselves, but in some things they are alike. Each has been trained, tested, and tempered over many years. Each has a sure witness that Jesus is the Christ, the Son of the living God. And each is committed for life to be obedient to His will—no retirement because of illness, infirmity, or personal burden. They simply carry on.[60]

In this way, the Lord has perfect control. One prophet/president of the Church said, "God knows all things, the end from the beginning, and no man becomes President of The Church of Jesus Christ by accident, nor remains there by chance, nor is called home by happenstance."[61]

Chapter 12

PASSING
THE MANTLE

The succession of authority and power within Christ's kingdom on earth has always been orderly and under the Lord's direct supervision. In July 1837, the Lord revealed, "For unto you, the Twelve, and those, the First Presidency, who are appointed with you to be your counselors and your leaders, is the power of this priesthood given, for the last days and for the last time, in the which is the dispensation of the fullness of times."[1]

Since opposition is found in all things, the plan of redemption involves people on both sides of truth. In the early days of the Church, enemies of the Church were numerous and powerful. In the minds of many of the Saints, there was a lack of conclusive direction as to where the mantle of authority rested. Much of this inconclusiveness was caused by the times in which the Saints were living. During this period, communications were difficult, published directives were scarce, and correspondence was slow. It sometimes took months and even years before all fragments of the Saints were aware of callings, ordinances, assignments, etc.

In the Nauvoo era, Joseph conferred upon the Twelve many sacred things preparatory for their future role as leaders, and the majority of the Saints knew nothing about such matters. The few tried-and-tested leaders and faithful, close associates who knew the full workings of the Lord proved to be Joseph's foundation of strength. They were the ones with whom he shared the beautiful, sacred doctrines that had been revealed, and they were the ones to first receive the ordinances. By the time of his death, the fullness of knowledge, power, and authority had been passed on and was in place for the transition of leadership.

Following Joseph's death on 27 June 1844, many claims of succession quickly came into play. A few are listed briefly:

Sidney Rigdon based his claim to the presidency or "Guardian of the Church" on the fact that he had been the first counselor to the Prophet.

William Smith was sustained to be the presiding patriarch of the Church at the October conference in 1844. He was ordained to that position by the apostles on 24 May 1845. By 27 June 1845, William insisted that he was president of the Church by virtue of his patriarchal office.

James J. Strang, Lyman Wight, and **Alpheus Cutler** advanced the claims of private appointment, each attracting fewer adherents than their predecessor.

James J. Strang claimed Joseph Smith had written a lengthy letter dated 18 June 1844 that officially appointed him as Joseph's successor.

Lyman Wight said that Joseph Smith in 1834 had ordained him to the office of "Benamey" in the presence of an angel.

Alpheus Cutler was the last man who claimed a right of succession on the basis of a secret ordination by the Prophet.

Many years later, succession through lineage was the claim used to put Joseph Smith III in the leadership role of the Reorganized Church.

Scriptures proclaim the fate of those who reject the Lord's anointed oracles. The account of Gamaliel and Theudas is found in Acts 5. Here, two witnesses, one a modern doctor of the law and the other of the past, relate vivid results when divine authority is rejected. Always, they are "brought to naught" or "will come to naught."[2] History has borne this out in the foregoing examples where each apostate group has come to naught.

The Twelve are the Lord's. They are his friends.[3] It is interesting that in our dispensation, the Lord established the foundation of the Twelve before he did the First Presidency, but after he called a prophet of God. In June 1829, the Prophet Joseph Smith received the first definitive revealed word concerning the apostles. In this revelation, we are told concerning the highest office of the Lord's priesthood that they (his apostles) have the same calling as Paul of old. They are given power to take the gospel to the Jews and Gentiles. These truths are so important that the Lord repeated them in March 1835[4] and again in September 1842.[5] With these revelations, the structural foundation of Christ's church for the millennial reign was revealed and recorded in the Doctrine and Covenants.

The 28 March 1835 revelation was published and stated that the Quorum of the Twelve Apostles was equal in "authority and power" to the organized First Presidency.[6] This revelation provided a scriptural basis for the succession claim of the apostles but was far less important as a proof-text of succession than the actual ecclesiastical, economic, and political powers Joseph Smith had conferred upon the Quorum of the Twelve Apostles from 1841 to 1844.

The first major action came while the First Presidency[7] was in Liberty Jail. The extermination order of Governor Boggs necessitated moving twelve thousand saints out of Missouri. From Liberty Jail, the First Presidency wrote a letter to Brigham Young and Heber C. Kimball giving them instructions concerning the leadership of the Church. "Inasmuch as we are in prison, for a little season, it needs be, the management of the affairs of the Church devolves on you, that is the twelve." A footnote to this letter from Joseph, Sidney, and Hyrum directs them to "Appoint the oldest of these of the Twelve, who were first appointed, to be the president of your quorum."[8]

Under the direction of Brigham and the Twelve, the Saints left Missouri. The Twelve were later responsible for the settling of the Saints in and around Nauvoo. They administered the finances of the Church in concert with Joseph Smith as trustee-in-trust and helped administer the first baptisms for the dead. The Twelve became Joseph's foundation for the doctrinal developments of Nauvoo: the administration of the endowment, the performances of plural marriages, the initial preparations for the movement into the American West, and the organization of the Council of Fifty.[9]

During the dedication ceremony for the Kirtland Temple on 27 March 1836, Joseph Smith asked the congregation "to acknowledge" the apostles as "Prophets and Seers and special witnesses to all the nations of the earth." Even this designation, however, was limited to the Twelve's jurisdiction outside the ecclesiastical stakes of the Church.[10]

In the spring of 1844, from a statement made by the Prophet, he knew that only those who held the fullness of the priesthood held legitimate power to govern the Church. He said:

> There is something going to happen. I don't know what it is, but the Lord bids me to hasten, and give you your endowment before the temple is finished. He conducted us through every ordinance of the holy priesthood, and when he had gone through with all the ordinances he rejoiced very much, and said, "now if they kill me you have got all the keys, and all the ordinances, and you can confer them upon others."[11]

With the death of the Prophet Joseph Smith, the First Presidency was no longer operative. The actual passing of the mantle took place under the Lord's direction and moved to the Twelve when Joseph took his last breath. The administrative events started a week after the Prophet was killed when Parley P. Pratt and George A. Smith, who had just returned to Nauvoo, conferred with John Taylor and Willard Richards about choosing a guardian or president and trustee of the church. They extended an invitation to Sidney Rigdon to meet with them on Sunday, 4 August 1844, at 8 a.m. After accepting the invitation, Sidney didn't come. Instead, he met with William Marks and a few other brethren and made plans to have himself presented to the Saints as "guardian" of the Church. The regular Sunday morning service held at 10 a.m. was conducted by William Marks, president of the stake in Nauvoo. Sidney Rigdon mentioned here for the first time that he had a vision that a guardian should be appointed to lead the Church. At the close of the meeting, President Marks announced that there would be a special meeting on Thursday, 8 August.

Brigham Young and several other members of the Quorum of the Twelve arrived in Nauvoo on 6 August. The next morning, 7 August, the quorum members in town met at the home of John Taylor, who was still convalescing. At 4 p.m., they met with the Nauvoo high council and others.

On 8 August, during the scheduled morning session, Sidney talked from a wagon for about an hour and a half. President Young then dismissed the meeting and gave an appointment for the brethren to meet at 2 p.m. A majority of the Quorum of Twelve Apostles (seven) assembled: Brigham Young, Heber C. Kimball, Parley P. Pratt, Orson Pratt, Willard Richards, Wilford Woodruff, and George A. Smith. Five were not present: John Taylor was confined to his home still recovering from the wounds received at Carthage Jail; Orson Hyde, John E. Page, and William Smith had not yet arrived; and Lyman Wight was still in the East.

It was at this meeting while Brigham Young was speaking that a transformation of the apostle occurred in voice, person, and manner.[12] He seemed to be the personification of Joseph Smith. George Q. Cannon said of this event:

> If Joseph had arisen from the dead and again spoken in their hearing, the effect could not have been more startling than it was to the many present at that meeting. It was the voice of Joseph himself: and not only was it the voice of Joseph which was heard, but it seemed in the eyes of the people as if it were the very person of Joseph which stood before them. A more wonderful and miraculous event than was wrought that day in the presence of that congregation we never heard of. The Lord gave his people a testimony that left no room for doubt as to who was the man chosen to lead them.[13]

Brigham Young boldly declared to the Saints:

> Here are the Apostles, the Bible, the Book of Mormon, the Doctrine and Covenants—they are written on the tablet of my heart. If the church want the Twelve to stand as the head, the First Presidency of the Church, and at the head of this kingdom in all the world, stand next to Joseph, walk up into their calling, and hold the keys of this kingdom, every man, every woman, every quorum is now put in order, and you are now the sole controllers of it. All that are in favor of this, in all the congregation of the saints, manifest it by holding up the right hand. (The vote was unanimous.) If there are any of the contrary mind, every man and every woman who does not want the Twelve to preside, lift up your hands in like manner. (No hands up.)[14]

Wilford Woodruff said concerning succession:

> There is a feeling—it was so in the days of Joseph Smith—that he was not the man to lead the Church. Even his bosom friends, men with whom he saw the angels of God, Oliver Cowdery and others, considered him a fallen prophet and thought they ought to lead the Church. There were other men who thought they should be appointed to that office. But the God of heaven manifested to you, and to me, and to all men, who were in Nauvoo upon whom the mantle had fallen. Brigham Young took his place, and led the Church and kingdom of God up to the day of his death.[15]

In 1835,[16] the Lord gave instructions to Joseph concerning the First Presidency as the supreme governing body of the Church with the president holding all priesthood keys of this dispensation. Upon the death of the President of the Church, the First Presidency is dissolved. All the keys, powers, and authority of the Church pass to the Quorum of the Twelve Apostles. When a man is ordained to the apostleship, the keys of the mantle are all conferred upon the individual; hence, each apostle holds the sacred keys and can exercise any one of them when designated by the First Presidency. The Twelve Apostles have intuitively within them an equality as a quorum equal in authority and power to the First Presidency. This principle is called the "apostolic succession." It follows under this principle that each apostle, so set apart, received the inherent power and authority to preside over the Church and direct all its affairs when those keys are activated by the full Quorum of Twelve Apostles. This is done only at the death of the President, and the presidency is reorganized within the full Quorum of Twelve Apostles. Thus, the very important principle of seniority was established in the beginning. Since Joseph's death and followed by Brigham Young, every president's call with the full support of the Quorum of Twelve Apostles has come through this system of apostolic succession.[17]

Brigham Young[18] was not a self-appointed leader of the Church. He was the mouthpiece by virtue of his ordination. When the Prophet was martyred, the responsibility of leading the Church fell upon the Twelve Apostles. Brigham Young was the president of the Twelve and, as such, had the responsibility of presiding. On many occasions, Brigham declared that he was an apostle of Jesus Christ and Joseph Smith[19] and that he was president of the Church by virtue of his position as senior apostle.

Revelation brought the mantle. Concerning what Joseph taught Brigham and the other living oracles, Brigham said, "This is the key of knowledge that I have today, that I did hearken to the words of Joseph, and treasured them up in my heart, laid them away, asking my Father in the name of his Son Jesus to bring them to my mind when needed. I treasured up the things of God, and this is the key that I hold today."[20] The passing of the mantle in 1844 established the procedures and principles that have been followed with the death of each president.[21]

Chapter 13

PROPHECIES

Much has been written on the prophecies of Joseph Smith, Jr. Following the glorious first vision, the heavens were opened and revelation became a reality once more. From that spring day in 1820 to the day of martyrdom, revelation upon revelation flowed through the man chosen to open the last dispensation. Joseph not only received revelation for the Church but also prophesied abundantly to individuals. A small sampling of some of his prophecies follows.

One of the most vivid had to do with the growth of the Church. The great revelation on "Key to Restoration" given in July of 1832 revealed that "Missouri is the land of promise, and the place for the city of Zion . . . and a spot for the temple is lying westward."[1] In September of that same year, the Lord told Joseph, "Go ye into all the world; and unto whatsoever place ye cannot go ye shall send, that the testimony may go from you into all the world unto every creature."[2]

The following year, in April of 1834, Joseph told a group of priesthood holders:

> I want to say to you before the Lord, that you know no more concerning the destiny of this Church and Kingdom than a babe upon its mother's lap. You don't comprehend it. It is only a little handful of Priesthood you see here tonight, but this Church will fill North and South America—it will fill the world. It will fill the Rocky Mountains. There will be tens of thousands of Latter-day Saints who will gather in the Rocky Mountains and there they will open the door for the establishing of the Gospel among the Lamanites.[3]

Statistics of 1997 showed 4,712,000 members in the U.S.A., with 3,104,000 in the Rocky Mountains. Outside the U.S.A. were 4,630,000, with 1,052,000 in Central America and 1,948,000 in South America.

A prophecy of safety was given to the captive Mormon leaders in Missouri on 3 November 1838 as they journeyed toward Independence. Joseph said: "Be of Good cheer, brethren; the word of the Lord came to me last night that our lives should be given us, and that whatever we may suffer during this our captivity, not one of our lives shall be taken."[4] Elder Parley P. Pratt, one of the prisoners, said, "Of this prophecy I testify in the name of the Lord . . . [that] its fulfillment and the miraculous escape of each one of us is too notorious to need my testimony."[5] No life was lost in any of the imprisonments among Church members in Missouri.

Another prophecy concerning safety was given to Orrin Porter Rockwell by the Prophet during the nine-month period Porter spent in Missouri jails. "I prophesied, in the name of the Lord Jesus Christ, that Orrin Porter Rockwell would get away honorably from the Missourians."[6] After nearly a year in Missouri jails, he was finally acquitted and made his way home to Illinois. On Christmas day 1843, Porter arrived at the Mansion House in Nauvoo. After hearing a recounting of the trials endured by this faithful friend, Joseph put his arm around Porter's shoulder and said, "I prophesy, in the name of the Lord, that you—Orrin Porter Rockwell—so long as ye shall remain loyal and true to thy faith need fear no enemy. Cut not thy hair and no bullet or blade can harm thee!"[7] Porter embraced this prophecy and abided by it. With one exception, he wore his hair unshorn for the rest of his life, and his enemies were unable to harm him.

Joseph's prophecy concerning the Civil War is available to all members of the Church (see D&C 87). While a prisoner in Liberty Jail, Joseph enlarged upon that prophecy. It seems from a number of such incidents that when a prophet of God receives a revelation, much more is seen in vision by the prophet than is written. In December 1838 or January 1839, the Prophet's attorney, Alexander Doniphan, had the sheriff bring Joseph to his office in Liberty for consultation. While Joseph was with Mr. Doniphan, a man came in to pay the firm of Doniphan & Baldwin for legal services. He offered a deed to property in Jackson County as payment. Doniphan told him that he would have to consult with his partner, James Baldwin, who was not there at the time, before taking it. After the man left, Joseph counseled him:

> Doniphan, I advise you not to take that Jackson county land in payment of the debt. God's wrath hangs over Jackson county. God's people have been ruthlessly driven from it, and you will live to see the day when it will be visited by fire and sword. The Lord of Hosts will sweep it with the besom of destruction. The fields and farms and houses will be destroyed, and *only the chimneys will be left* to mark the desolation[8] (italics added).

Years later, in 1902, A. Saxey reported he saw the land (Jackson County) when his regiment went south in 1862 to comply with "Order No. 11." He went back in 1864 and reported, "I went down the Blue river, we found houses, barns, outbuildings, nearly all burned down, and *nothing left standing but the chimneys* which had, according to the fashion of the time, been built on the outside of the buildings"[9] (italics added).

In January or February of 1842, another exciting prophecy on missionary work was given when Joseph wrote the famous document called "The Wentworth Letter." In this correspondence to Mr. Wentworth, Joseph gave a brief, early history of the Church followed by four pages of Missouri history and concluded with:

> Many sickened and died, in consequence of the cold, and hardships they had to endure; many wives were left widows, and children orphans, and destitute. It would take more time than is alloted me here to describe the injustice, the wrongs, the murders, the bloodshed, the theft, misery and woe that has been caused by the barbarous, inhuman, and lawless, proceedings of the state of Missouri.

The following beautiful prophecy then followed:

> Our missionaries are going forth to different nations: the standard of truth has been erected. No unhallowed hand can stop the work from progressing; persecutions may assemble, calumny may defame, but the truth of God will go forth boldly, nobly and independent until it has penetrated every continent, visited every clime, swept every country, and sounded in every ear until the purposes of God shall be accomplished and the great Jehovah shall say "the work is done."[10]

There are today approximately sixty thousand missionaries laboring in 330 missions throughout the world. Missionary training centers number sixteen.

An example of God's giving efficacy to the words spoken by his prophets is found in a prophecy given to Stephen A. Douglas. Judge

Douglas, the "little giant," as he was known in the Congress of the United States, ordered Joseph dismissed from custody after Boggs had Joseph arrested in Illinois. Joseph and party went to visit Judge Douglas at their earliest opportunity. An account of their meeting was recorded in the journal of William Clayton under the date of 18 May 1843:

> Dined with Judge Stephen A. Douglas, who is presiding at court. After dinner Judge Douglas requested President Joseph to give him a history of the Missouri persecution, which he did in a very minute manner for about three hours. The Judge listened with the greatest attention, and then spoke warmly in depreciation of Governor Boggs and the authorities in Missouri, who had taken part in the extermination, and said that any people that would do as the mobs of Missouri had done ought to be brought to judgment.

> President Smith, in concluding his remarks, said . . . "I prophesy in the name of the Lord God of Israel, you will aspire to the presidency of the United States; and if you ever turn your hand against me or the Latter-day Saints, you will feel the weight of the hand of the Almighty upon you; and you will live to see and know that I have testified the truth to you; for the conversation of this day will stick to you through life." He appeared very friendly, and acknowledged the truth and propriety of President Smith's remarks.

Fourteen years after the interview containing the prophecy here under discussion, and about a year after the prophecy had been published in the *Deseret News*, Mr. Douglas was called upon to deliver a speech in Springfield, the capital of Illinois. His speech was delivered on 12 June 1857 and was published in the *Missouri Republican* on 18 June 1857. It was a time of much excitement throughout the country concerning the Mormon Church in Utah. Crimes of the most repulsive nature—murders, robberies, rebellion, and high treason—were falsely charged against its leaders. It was well known that Mr. Douglas had been on terms of intimate friendship with the Prophet Joseph Smith and was well acquainted with the other Church leaders. He was, therefore, looked upon as one competent to speak upon the "Mormon Question" and was invited to do so in the speech to which reference is made. Mr. Douglas responded to the request. He grouped the charges against the Mormons, which were then passing current, in the following manner:

> First, that nine-tenths of the inhabitants are aliens by birth who have refused to become naturalized, or to take the oath of allegiance, or do any other act recognizing the government of

the United States as the paramount authority in the territory [Utah]. Second, that the inhabitants, whether native or alien born, known as Mormons (and they constitute the whole people of the territory) are bound by horrible oaths, and terrible penalties, to recognize and maintain the authority of Brigham Young, and the government of which he is head, as paramount to that of the States, in civil as well as in religious affairs; and they will in due time, and under the direction of their leaders, use all means in their power to subvert the government of the United States and resist its authority. Third, that the Mormon government, with Brigham Young at its head, is now forming alliances with Indian tribes in Utah and adjoining territories—stimulating the Indians to acts of hostility—and organizing bands of his own followers under the name of Danites or destroying angels, to prosecute a system of robbery and murders upon American citizens who support the authority of the United States, and denounce the infamous and disgusting practices and institutions of the Mormon government.

Stephen A. Douglas did aspire to the presidency of the United States and was nominated for that office by the Democratic convention held in Charleston on 23 June 1860. When in the convention he was declared the regular nominee of the Democratic party, "The whole body rose to its feet, hats were waved in the air and many tossed aloft; shouts, screams, and yells and every boisterous mode of expressing approbation and unanimity, were resorted to."

As Mr Douglas aspired to the presidency, no man in the history of American politics had more reason to hope for success. The political party of which he was the recognized leader, in the preceding presidential election, had polled 174 electoral votes, as against 122 cast by the other two parties that opposed it; and a popular vote of 1,838,169, as against 1,215,798 for the two parties opposing. But before the election took place, his popularity drastically declined, and Mr. Abraham Lincoln, candidate of the Republican party, was triumphantly elected. He received 180 electoral votes; Mr. Breckinridge received 72 electoral votes; Mr. Bell 39; and Mr. Douglas 12. "By a plurality count of the popular vote, Mr. Lincoln carried 18 states."

"Twenty days less than one year after his nomination by the Charleston convention, while yet in the prime of manhood—forty-eight years of age—Mr. Douglas died, at his home in Chicago, a disappointed, not to say heartbroken, man."[11]

A prophecy concerning the Book of Mormon was given by Joseph on Sunday, 28 November 1841:

> I spent the day in the council with the Twelve Apostles at the house of President Young, conversing with them upon a variety of subjects. I told the brethren that the Book of Mormon was the most correct of any book on earth, and the keystone of our religion, and a man would get nearer to God by abiding by its precepts, than by any other book.[12]

The testimony of fourteen additional prophets and a few million members bears witness to the truthfulness of this prophecy. Over 81 million copies of the Book of Mormon have been distributed throughout the world, and it has been published in eighty-eight languages. The Bible (the other witness of Jesus Christ) is the only book in the world that has more copies published each year than the Book of Mormon.

The prophecy of the perfecting of the "Saints" through ordinances was depicted in Joseph's awesome historic comment on 4 May 1842:

> I spent the day in the upper part of the store, that is my private office, in council with General James Adams of Springfield, Patriarch Hyrum Smith, Bishops Newel K. Whitney and George Miller, and President Brigham Young and Elders Heber C. Kimball and Willard Richards, instructing them in the principles and order of the Priesthood, attending to washings, anointings, endowments and the communication of keys pertaining to the Aaronic Priesthood, setting forth the order pertaining to the Ancient of Days, and all those plans and principles by which any one is enabled to secure the fullness of those blessings which have been prepared for the Church of the First Born, and come up and abide in the presence of the Eloheim in the eternal worlds. In this council was instituted the ancient order of things for the first time in these last days. And the communications I made to this council were of things spiritual, and to be received only by the spiritual minded: and there was nothing made known to these men but what will be made known to all the Saints of the last days, so soon as they are prepared to receive, and a proper place is prepared to communicate them, even to the weakest of the Saints; therefore let the Saints be diligent in building the Temple, and all houses which they have been, or shall hereafter be, commanded of God to build; and wait their time with patience in all meekness, faith, perseverance unto the end, knowing assuredly that all these things referred to in this council are always governed by the principle of revelation.[13]

This prophecy has been and continues to be fulfilled on an ongoing basis. In regards to temples, as of September 1997, there are fifty-two functioning temples, and another forty-six new temples have been announced and are in various phases of construction. Today hundreds of millions of microfilms containing genealogy are stored in the Granite Mountain vault. The information on these records is available to all people on the earth. (Other prophecies are found in Chapters 4 and 5.)

The test of a prophet was stated by Jeremiah, "[W]hen the word of the Prophet shall come to pass, then shall the prophet be known, that the Lord hath truly sent him."[14] The test for membership was given by Moses, "The Lord thy God will raise up unto thee a Prophet from the midst of thee, of thy brethren, like unto me; unto him ye shall hearken."[15] The prophetic legacy of Joseph Smith, Jr. was and is for our time but will and does stretch into the eternities.

Chapter 14

CONCLUSION

J oseph Smith, Jr. could well be appraised by the crown of his own legacy—the priesthood with its ordinances that can lead to exaltation; the Book of Mormon, the keystone of our religion; the temples where both sides of the veil come together; and the knowledge that the Lord promised Joseph in the dungeon at Liberty Jail that "has not been revealed since the world was until now." All those things that were restored is the legacy of the Prophet Joseph Smith, Jr.

Future readers of the Book of Mormon were told by Moroni to "remember how merciful the Lord hath been unto the children of men from the creation of Adam even down until the time that ye shall receive these things and ponder it in your hearts,"[1] that time being 1830 through the hand of Joseph. In the fulfillment of this promise, Joseph would have to be declared its champion testator. Heavenly messengers from every period of time had conversed with the Prophet, and it was in Liberty Jail that Joseph "pondered it" in his heart. His legacy leaves no doubt that "by the power of the Holy Ghost," Joseph came to "know the truth of all things." It could be said that in the midst of affliction, Liberty Jail was the point of expansion of Joseph's very soul. He, the strongest of the faithful on earth at that time, was tried and tested and found sufficient. Grace for grace, this prophet of the fullness emerged from the fourteen-by-fourteen-foot dungeon worthy to receive the promise, "[I]f you are faithful you shall receive the fulness of the record of John."[2]

Since the first vision 168 years ago, members of the Church have enjoyed the fruits of Joseph's labors. As a result of this noble and valiant prophet, millions of people have gained a testimony (by the power of the Holy Ghost) of the truths he restored. The Church has grown and expanded to all the earth. Members today certainly should have a more sure knowledge and firm understanding of the gospel than any previous group of Saints.

Joseph declared, "It is not the will of the Lord that I should live, and I must give you, here in this upper room, all those glorious plans and principles whereby men are entitled to the fullness of the priesthood."[3] With all that has been given, if the Saints do not keep the covenants and labor to move the kingdom forward, their condemnation will be great. Where much has been given, much is expected.

The Prophet's pronouncement about Zion may best summarize a large part of his supernal mission. He said on Monday, 2 May 1842:

> The building up of Zion is a cause that has interested the people of God in every age; it is a theme upon which prophets, priests and kings have dwelt with peculiar delight; they have looked forward with joyful anticipation to the day in which we live; and fired with heavenly and joyful anticipations they have sung and written and prophesied of this our day but they died without the sight; we are the favored people that God has made choice of to bring about the Latter-day glory; it is left for us to see, participate in and help to roll forward the Latter-day glory, "the dispensation of the fullness of times, when God will gather together all things that are in heaven, and all things that are upon the earth, even in one," when the Saints of God will be gathered in one from every nation, and kindred, and people, and tongue, when the Jews will be gathered together into one, the wicked will also be gathered together to be destroyed, as spoken of by the prophets; the Spirit of God will also dwell with His people, and be withdrawn from the rest of the nations, and all things whether in heaven or on earth will be in one, even in Christ. The heavenly Priesthood will unite with the earthly, to bring about those great purposes and whilst we are thus united in the one common cause, to roll forth the kingdom of God, the heavenly Priesthood are not idle spectators, the Spirit of God will be showered down from above, and it will dwell in our midst. The blessings of the Most High will rest upon our tabernacles, and our name will be handed down to future ages; our children will rise up and call us blessed; and generations yet unborn will dwell with peculiar delight upon the scenes that we have passed through, the privations that we have endured; the untiring zeal that we have manifested; the all but insurmountable difficulties

that we have overcome in laying the foundation of a work that brought about the glory and blessing which they will realize; a work that God and angels have contemplated with delight for generations past; that fired the souls of the ancient patriarchs and prophets; a work that is destined to bring about the destruction of the powers of darkness, the renovation of the earth, the glory of God, and the salvation of the human family.[4]

On 8 March 1844 from Nauvoo, Joseph wrote a friendly hint to Missouri revealing that his time in Missouri and its important role never left his mind. After giving a recap of the treatment of the Saints there, in relationship to the laws of the land, he said, "For is it not written, the tree is known by its fruit?" He then called them to repentance and closed with a most eloquent summary of gospel principles:

Finally, if honor dignifies an honest people; if virtue exalts a community; if wisdom guides great men; if principle governs intelligent beings; if humanity spreads comfort among the needy; and if religion affords consolation by showing that charity is the first, best and sweetest token of perfect love: then, O ye good people of Missouri, like the woman in scripture who had lost one of her ten pieces of silver, arise, search diligently till you find the lost piece, and then make a feast and call in your friends for joy.[5]

President George Q. Cannon said of Joseph:

There was no end scarcely, in many respects, to the knowledge that he received. He was visited constantly by angels . . . and these various angels, the heads of dispensations, having also ministered unto him . . . he had vision after vision in order that his mind might be fully saturated with a knowledge of the things of God, and that he might comprehend the great and holy calling that God has bestowed upon him. In this respect he stands unique.[6]

To the question posed to him, "Who are you?" Joseph made this profound statement: "Noah came before the flood. I came before the fire."[7]

The legacy of Joseph continues through prophets today as they exercise the keys and authority that came through him.

Nephi, toward the end of his life, wrote, "And now I, Nephi, cannot say more; the Spirit stoppeth mine utterance, and I am left to mourn because of the unbelief, and the wickedness, and the ignorance, and the stiffneckedness of men; for they will not search knowledge, nor understand great knowledge, when it is given unto them in plainness, even as plain as word can be."[8]

We have been given more knowledge in this dispensation than any other time in the history of the world. Are we searching for it and enlarging our ability to live the gospel in its fullness? The Church is a "progressive" church, and major doctrines do unfold chronologically. The following quotes may increase our understanding of this truism: President Charles W. Penrose said, "[T]he church of Christ is progressive, that is, it advances in the knowledge of the truth. As fast as its members are prepared for additional light, through the practice of principles already revealed, new manifestations are given, for the growth of all who will receive the truths unfolded towards the fullness of the stature of Jesus Christ."[9]

President Joseph F. Smith expressed it this way:

> The Church has been organized according to the pattern which God gave in the days of our Savior and His Disciples, only I think the organization has been perfected to a greater extent, perhaps, in this dispensation than in the days of Jesus and His disciples. All that was given to them has been conferred upon us, and, as greater things are to be accomplished, we may look for still greater perfection in the organization of the Church, as well as for greater things in other directions.[10]

Joseph's legacy takes us back to the Angel Moroni literally. The angelic ministry of Moroni was seen by John the Beloved in his revelation: "And I saw another angel fly in the midst of heaven having the everlasting gospel to preach unto them that dwell on the earth." He now flies through the midst of heaven with all the eternal blessings to every nation, kindred, tongue, and people."[11] This legacy is literally the fulfillment of the great prophecy the Lord gave to Habakkuk: "For the earth shall be filled with the knowledge of the glory of the Lord, as the waters cover the sea."[12]

At the end of the introduction to his book, *A New Witness for the Articles of Faith*, Elder Bruce R. McConkie said, "And we testify— hear it, O ye heavens, and give ear, Oh earth—that Joseph Smith was called of God to restore the gospel, to establish anew the church and kingdom of God on Earth, and to send the message of salvation to all men."[13]

JAIL CALENDAR—128 DAYS

Visits, Letters, Events

There are many accounts of various people visiting Liberty Jail that are not included on the calendar because the date of the visit could not be determined. Examples are Orin Porter Rockwell, Amos Rees, Wm. T. Wood, and Jacob Shoemaker (Shumaker). (See Appendix B.)

Some visited numerous times.[1]

December 1838

1: Joseph, Hyrum, Sidney, Lyman, Caleb, and Alexander entered the jail and began their confinement.[2] Joseph wrote to Emma (see Chapter 8).

8: Emma Smith and Phebe Rigdon arrived with their sons, Joseph III and John, and stayed overnight at Liberty.[3] There is conflict between stories.[4]

9: Wives left Liberty.

10: Lyman's wife with four boys arrived at the jail and stayed for two nights in Liberty.[5] Lyman's son Orange was one of the sons.[6]

11: The youngest Wight boy was blessed.[7]

12: Lyman's family left Liberty.[8]

13: Alexander McRae's wife Eunice and two small sons arrived and stayed in Liberty for two days.[9]

14: Isaac Morley, Reynolds Cahoon, W. M. Allred, Mr. Harris, and other gentlemen of Clay County visited.[10]

15: The McRae family left Liberty.[11]

16: Letter—Joseph wrote to the Church.[12]

17: Alexander Doniphan and Mr. N. West visited.[13]

20: Emma Smith with son Joseph Smith III, Caleb Baldwin's wife Nancy, and Mrs. Reynolds Cahoon visited and remained in Liberty until the 22nd.[14]

21: Wm. Clark and Attorneys Doniphan and Burnett visited.[15]

22: Bp. Benjamin Covey (later of the Twelfth Ward of Salt Lake) brought each prisoner a pair of boots. He was helped by a son-in-law, Eathan Barrows.[16] Deacon Covey and Mr. Rase visited the jail.[17]

23: Joseph turned thirty-three years of age.

25: Christmas day: Howard Evert, a Disciple preacher, visited them.[18]

30: Mr. Thompson from Ray County visited.[19]

31: Their thoughts exemplify the meager "celebration".[20] "Thus in their gloomy prison house, cheered only by occasional visits from friends and the comfort of the Holy Spirit, they beheld the eventful year 1838 pass away. Its closing hours found them deprived of liberty, their families robbed and destitute, their brethren scattered and driven from their once pleasant, happy homes by a ruthless mob—and all this for the testimony they bore, that Jesus was the Christ, his gospel true, and his promised blessings sure."[21]

January 1839

1: Joseph's comment on New Year's Day 1839.[22]

3: Mrs. Phebe Rigdon, Harriet Wight, and two daughters visited.[23]

5: Lyman Cowdrey visited.[24]

8: Attorney Burnett and Judge Joel Turnham visited.[25]

9: Attorneys A. Doniphan and Burnett visited.[26]

10: Alexander's wife Eunice visited.[27]

11: Mr. Moore, James Sloan, and his wife and daughter visited.[28]

12: Mr. Bennett visited.[29]

13: Mrs. Fowler, Mrs. Sloan, daughter Jane, Messrs. Morey, Hedlock and Lawyer Burnett visited.[30]

16:     Bp. E. Partridge, Messrs. Barlow, Gordon, and Burnett visited.[31] Bishop Partridge took a bill to the Senate to provide for investigation of late disturbances.[32] Heber C. Kimball's journal shows a letter to B. Young and himself from the First Presidency (J. Smith, S. Rigdon, H. Smith) dated this date.[33] (See Chapter 8.)

17:     Messrs. Barlow, Sloan, and Burnett visited.[34]

18:     General Hughes visited.[35]

19:     Mrs. Sloan and daughter visited.[36]

20:     Mrs. Fowler and Mrs. Blevin visited.[37]

21:     Emma Smith, Joseph III, G. W. Robinson, Don Carlos Smith, and John Daley visited. Joseph gave his son a blessing.[38] It was probably this date that the singing took place if brother Erastas Snow sang the two songs, "The Massacre at the River Basin" and "Mobbers of Missouri."[39] The only other date mentioning Erastus Snow is 7 February. Hyrum inferred that Alexander McRae was the vocalist.

22:     Writ was served on prisoners. Taken to courthouse where a trial was set for the 25th.[40]

23:     Bp. E. Partridge, Don C. Smith, A. Ripley, and Mr. Morley visited.[41]

24:     Joseph wrote a letter to the Missouri Legislature.[42] Mr. Samuels visited.[43]

25:     Trial began in Liberty; Judge Turnham presided.

26:     Trial continued; then adjourned until Monday, 28 December.[44] Mr. Samuels and Mr. Bird visited.

27:     Mrs. Wight and Mrs. Baldwin visited.[45] Emanuel Masters Murphy visited. (See Chapter 7.)

28:     Major Dorothy visited. Trial continued with new evidence that was all in by noon.[46]

29:     Mary Fielding Smith and her sister Mercy Thompson came so Hyrum could administer to and bless his ten-week-old son. He gave him the name of Joseph Fielding Smith.[47] The trial continued with A. Doniphan giving defense, followed by Sidney and then Joseph. In the afternoon, Hyrum, Lyman, and Caleb testified.[48] Note: Mercy Thompson wrote in 1894 that the visit was in February.[49]

30:     Messrs. Newberry, Baldwin, and Samuels visited.[50] Trial ended; Sidney to bail; others refused bail.[51]

February 1839

Note: Heber C. Kimball, Mr. Huntington, and his daughter Percindia Buell visited on 3 February.[52] This reference puts her and H. C. Kimball at the jail on the same day. Kimball was there on other days, one being 15 March. She was there on 14 March and PHB with note to legislature who is the unknown in the *History of the Church* may have been she.

1 or 2: Judge Joel Turnham visited.[53]

3: H. C. Kimball, Brigham Young, and George A. Smith visited.[54] They brought clean clothes to the prisoners. George Smith wrote: "Priveledge to be locked up with them even if it was only for an hour." This visit seemed to be an apostolic calling in organizing the exodus from Missouri. Lyman Wight wrote of an escape attempt.[55]

5: Sidney Rigdon liberated from the jail. Joseph's history says the 25th, but that would have been a long time following the trial.[56] (See Chapter 8.)

7: Escape attempt.[57] Alexander McRae's letter of 9 October 1854 and RLDS HC 2:316 both give references to A. Ripley, D. Holman, W. Barlow, Wm. Huntington Jr., E. Snow, and C. Daniels as the brethren who came to visit. Court records that brought charges show Samuel Tillery, lawful deputy jailer, listing six brethren with charges. These records do not mention C. Daniels but list Jonathon Tilatson. Five were tried, excluding Tilatson. (See Exhibit 6.1 in Chapter 6.)

8-13: Four of the five visitors were held in the jail, except Erastus Snow, until they paid bail of $150 each. They were released on the 13th.

9: Hyrum turned thirty-nine years of age.

25: Determined to Escape.[58] Note: Heber C. Kimball and Alanson Ripley were in Liberty almost weekly importuning the judges. Judge Hughes was one of the judges.[59]

March 1839

Sometime in the first week of March, David W. Rogers brought Isaac Galland's letter to the Prophet.[60]

1: Started working on escape by breach with augers, but handles gave out before the task was completed.[61] Note: Mr. Gorden brought information from the legislature.[62]

3: Escape attempt continues. Lyman Wight's letter.[63]

4: Escape foiled.[64]

5: Letters from Bishop Edward Partridge.[65]

6: Don Carlos and Wm. Smith both wrote letters to Joseph and others.[66]

7: Letter to Joseph from Emma this date.[67] Received on 19th.[68]

14: Joseph B. Noble and Alanson Ripley visited and Sister Buel tried to visit with Fredrick G. Williams.[69] Partial letter of Hyrum to wife Mary, no date.

15: Letters of Petition to Judge Tumpkins, Missouri Supreme Court.[70] Joseph appeared before Abraham Shafer, a justice of the peace.[71] Petitions taken by Ripley and H. C. Kimball plus letter to Presendia Huntington Buell.[72]

16: Letter from Hyrum to "Mary my dear companion."[73] Letter from Hyrum to Sister Grinnals. (See Exhibit 8.2 in Chapter 8.)

17: Hyrum says jailer found auger handle this day.

18: Hyrum's letter of 19 March to Mary said all things calm.[74] Received letter from Bishop Partridge brought by Brother Rogers. Lyman's says Elder Kimball and Turley started on mission to see governor.[75]

19: Hyrum wrote wife Mary and delivered through hand of Brother Rogers.[76] Joseph received 7 March letter from Emma[77] and letters from brothers Don Carlos and William and Bishop Partridge, which he felt necessitated an immediate answer.

20: The Epistle to the Church through Edward Partridge was begun.[78] Hyrum wrote wife Mary again since Brother Rogers came back and said he would not be back for two weeks. This is the letter in which he speaks of tears. The original letter has tear stains on it.[79]

21: Epistle to the Church continues. Joseph wrote Emma.

22: Epistle to Church continues. Letter to Isaac Galland. Brother Ripley visited and took the letters.

23: Epistle to Church continues. Hyrum wrote his wife Mary, and mentioned the attorneys visited them this day.[80]

25: Epistle to the Church finished. It was sent to Emma because Joseph wished her to be the first to see it.[81] Brother Horace Cowan put in jail for debt.[82] Discrepancy here on Kimball and Turley visit.[83]

28: Hyrum's letter of this date mentions attorneys visited.

30: Hyrum's letter of this date to wife Mary. Brother Turley and H. C. Kimball returned. Missed seeing governor but saw three supreme court judges.[84] Brother Horace Cowin put in jail for three days because of consequences of mob.[85]

31: Hyrum's letter of this date mentions A. Ripley called in evening and the expectancy of their leaving the jail on 6 April.[86]

Note: H. C. Kimball and Theodore Turley visited occasionally to talk through the grate.[87] Hyrum mentions Jane Bleven and daughter many times, handing cakes through the grates. O. Porter Rockwell visited many times.[88]

April 1839

1: Horace Corwin released this day.[89]

2: Brother John Dawson came to the grate with letter from Jacob Scott. The brethren started a reply.[90]

3: Brother Dawson (Dorson) and Sister Walton were abused by the jailer but came in. "An Apistle was written to Sister Walton and put in her own hand. The letter wrote to Jacob Scot was put in to the hands of brother Dorson." "An old man by the name of McCord put in to the Jail for stabbing a man with a Chisel."[91]

4: Joseph wrote Emma a three-page letter. Brother Marcomb came but was not allowed in. Brother Huntington came but could not go in or speak to the prisoners.[92] Kimball and Turley spoke through the grate of the dungeon.[93]

6: On this very special day for Christendom and the Church, the prisoners left Liberty Jail. Various individual comments were recorded on this date.[94]

8: The prisoners arrived about a mile from Gallatin, Missouri.[95]

9:      Trial commenced. Brother Markham brought $100 from Brother Kimball. Judge Morin brought change of venue.[96]

10:     Trial continued. Letter from Sidney Rigdon and Alanson Ripley to prisoners.[97]

11:     Letter from Don Carlos and Agnes Smith to Joseph and Hyrum.[98]

12:     Jacob Stollings and Isaac Galland wrote to Joseph.[99]

15:     Left Gallatin Jail for Boone County. Sheriff Wm. Morgan and four guards.[100]

16:     Escape from guards.[101]

21:     Alexander McRae left the group.

22:     Arrived at Quincy, Illinois.

Appendix B

VISITORS AND DATES

Wives:

Nancy Baldwin, 20 December and 27 January.

Eunice F. McRae, 13 December with two sons and 10 January.

Phebe Rigdon, 8 December with son, 3 January, and 5 February.

Emma Smith, 8 December with child, 20 December with child, and 21 January with child.

Mary F. Smith, 29 Jan with baby.

Harriet Wight, 10 December with four sons, 11 December baby was blessed, 3 January with two daughters, and 25 January.

Attorneys:

Peter H. Burnett, 21 December, 8, 9, 13, 16, and 17 January.

Alexander W. Doniphan, 17 and 21 December and 9 January.

J. A. Gordon, 16 January and 1 March.

Andrew S. Hughes, 18 January.

Amos Rees.

James S. Rollins.

Joel Turnham, 8 January and 1 or 2 February.

William T. Wood.

Females:

Mrs. Jane Bleven, 20 January.

Bleven, Daughter, 20 January.

Buell, Percindel Huntington; 14 March and once with Heber C. Kimball and once with Fredrick G. Williams.

Mrs. Fowler, 20 January.

Mercy Thompson, 19 January with baby.

Mrs. Sloan, 11, 13, and 19 January.

Jane Sloan, daughter, 11, 13, and 19 January.

Walton and sister, 3 April.

Males:

Wm. Allred, 14 December.

Mr. Baldwin, 30 January.

Mr. Barlow, 16, 17 January and 7 February.

Eathan Barrows, 22 December.

Mr. Bennett, 12 January.

Mr. Bird, 26 January.

Reynolds Cahoon, 14 and 20 December.

Mr. Clark, 21 December.

Benjamin Covey, 22 December.

Lyman Cowdry, 5 December.

John Daley, 21 January.

C. Daniels, 7 February.

John Dawson, 2 and 3 April.

Major Dorothy, 28 January.

Howard Evert, 25 December.

Mr. Harris, 14 December.

Mr. Hedloch, 13 January.

D. Holman, 7 February.

Wm. Huntington Jr., 7 February.

Heber C. Kimball, 3 February, 15 25, or 30 March

Mr. Marcomb, 4 April.

Joseph McRae, 13 December, as a baby with a brother.

Mr. Moore, 11 January.

Mr. Morey, 13 January.

Isaac Morley, 14 December and 23 January.

Emanuel Masters Murphy, 27 January and 7 February.

Mr. Newberry, 30 January.

Joseph B. Noble, 14 March.

John Outhouse, 7 February.

Alanson Ripley, 23 January, 7 February, 14, 22, and 32 March.

G. W. Robinson, 21 January.

David W. Rogers, after 28 February but before 15 March.

Mr. Rose, 22 December.

Mr. Samuels, 26 and 30 January.

James Sloan, 11 and 17 January.

Don Carlos Smith, 21 and 23 January.

George A. Smith, 3 February.

Joseph Smith III, 20 December.

Joseph Fielding Smith baby, 29 January.

Erastus Snow, 7 February.

Mr. Thompson, 30 December.

Theodore Turley, 15 and 25 March and other times.

Orange L. Wight, 10 December, 3 January, and possibly others.

Wight baby, Loami Limhi 10 December, was blessed 11 December.

Fredrick G. Williams, 14 March.

N. West, 17 December.

Brigham Young, 3 February.

Others Known to Visit but Date Not Known:

Porter O. Rockwell (Dean C. Jessee "Walls, Grates and Screeking Iron doors: The Prison Experience of Mormon Leaders in Missouri, 1838-1839," 26 and various letters mention Porter and Jacob Shoemaker [Shumaker].) (See Chapter 8.)

Other Prisoners Incarcerated During This Time:

Horace Cowin (Cowan), 30 March—for debt.

Mr. McCord, 3 April—attempted murder (chisel).

Appendix C

FORMER PRISONERS
FOR CHRIST

The words *prison* and *hell* have the same roots. For the dead, we are told by Isaiah that Jehovah/Jesus Christ is the keeper of the gate:"I the Lord have called thee in righteousness, and will hold thine hand, and will keep thee, and give thee for a covenant of the people, for a light of the Gentiles; to open the blind eyes, to bring out the prisoners from the prison, and them that sit in darkness out of the prison house."[1]

It is true that the Lord is also the keeper of the gate for the living. This role was proven to be the case for Joseph of Egypt, Jeremiah, the two Johns, Peter, the apostles, Paul, Abinadi, Alma, Ammon, Amulek, Nephi, and Lehi. To enumerate all the disciples of Christ who have suffered incarceration is a difficult task. Over thirty are listed. By reviewing former prisoners and pondering them, we may have an improved idea of the depth of faith and sacrifice the brethren at Richmond, Liberty, and Carthage had and were willing to endure.

Of these, probably the most interesting and germane to Liberty Jail is Joseph of Egypt.[2] His experiences in Egypt paralleled those of Joseph Smith's in Missouri. The scriptures say that although it will be Joseph's descendants who are primarily the Lord's choice to carry the gospel, it will be the knowledge of Joseph Smith that provides the foundation for understanding the doctrine.

Joseph was sold into Egypt at seventeen.[3] He was there seventeen years before he became the Pharaoh's overseer at thirty years of age.[4] We know he was in jail for a season (three months and possibly much longer).[5] We also know that he was in a dungeon without good clothes or personal-hygiene facilities.[6] "Whose feet they hurt with fetters: he was laid in iron."[7] This kind of suffering was identical to Joseph's at both Richmond and Liberty. Then, the great similarity becomes evident: "[T]he word of the Lord tried him."[8]

Another parallel to Joseph's incarceration is Jeremiah, who was also in a dungeon for an extended period of time. The experiences of his personal treatment and of the food and water were very similar.[9] The Book of Mormon gives some interesting insights on these experiences where Jeremiah is used to emphasize that when a prophet of God is rejected, the "Spirit of Lord ceaseth to strive with them [the people]."[10] This was certainly the case with the Gentiles in the state of Missouri, as was so testified by Joseph.

Following is a partial list and references of other prisoners of the past:

John the Baptist: Matthew 4:12, 14:3, and John 3:24.

Our Lord Jesus Christ: Isaiah 53:8 (Mosiah 14:8).

The Savior's apostles: Acts 5:18-20, 8:3, 16:26, and 22:4.

Peter: Acts 12:4-5.

Paul and Silas: Acts 16:25-26, 2 Corinthians 11:23, Ephesians 3:1, 4:1, and Philemon 1:1.

Abinadi: Mosiah 12:16-18, 17:5-7, and 21:23.

Ammon, Amaleki, Helem, and Hem: Mosiah 7:7.

Amulek: Alma 14:22.

The striking similarities with Joseph Smith in the above instances are the physical afflictions they both suffered[11] along with the great supplications to the Lord. In Alma's case, "How long shall we suffer these great afflictions, O Lord?"[12]

Aaron, Muloki, and Ammon: Alma 20:3.

Nephi and Lehi: Helaman 5:21.

The Three Nephites: 3 Nephi 28:19.

Appendix D

DOCTRINAL EXPANSION 1839-1844

Joseph Smith, Jr. said, "I advise all to go on to perfection and to search deeper and deeper into the mysteries of Godliness. As for myself, it has always been my province to dig up hidden mysteries, new things, for my hearers."

He also said, "And the communications I made to this council were of things spiritual, and to be received only by the spiritual minded: and there was nothing made known to these men but what will be made known to all the Saints of the last days."

And he said, "The organization of the spiritual and heavenly worlds, and of spiritual and heavenly beings, was agreeable to the most perfect order and harmony: their limits and bounds were fixed irrevocably, and voluntarily subscribed to in their heavenly estate by themselves, and were by our first parents subscribed to upon the earth."[1]

From such statements, we can see the importance of embracing and subscribing to principles of eternal truth by ALL men and women who expect eternal life. Concerning this very subject, the letter of 20-25 March sent from the jail contained the revelations received and collaborating information. We are told about

> a time when nothing shall be withheld, when all the glories of earth and heaven, time and eternity shall be manifest. . . . If there be bounds set to the heavens, the seas, the dry land, they shall be manifest, as well as the various revolutions of the sun, moon, and planets; and a full development of all the glorious laws by which they are governed shall be revealed in the "dispensation of the fullness of time" according to that which was ordained in the midst of the council of heaven in the presence of the eternal God, before this world was.[2]

215

To see the fulfillment of such prophetic statements, we need only to look at the inventions that immediately began to come forth in the subsequent forty years (see Appendix E) and on into the present where secular knowledge is said to be doubling every ten years.

The doctrinal maturation of the Prophet Joseph Smith following his Liberty Jail experiences is truly amazing. Following is a post Liberty Jail subject and chronological listing of the major sermons and epistles of the Prophet by general subject area.

The Godhead

1839	June	"Two Comforters" and "The Second Comforter"[3]
1841	May	"The Three Personages"[4]
1842	March	"The Wentworth Letter"[5]
		"Difference Between the Holy Ghost and Gift of Holy Ghost"[6]
	April	"The Spirit of God"[7]
	June	"The Gift of the Holy Ghost" and "Things of God Only Known by the Spirit of God"[8]
	December	"The Rule of Christ in the Millennium"[9]
1843	February	"The Sign of the Son of Man"[10]
	June	"The Doctrine of Godhead"[11]
1844	March	"How God Came to Become God"[12]
	April	"King Follett"[13] (The Capstone)
	June	"Kings and Priests unto God and His Father"[14]

Spiritual Knowledge

1839	March	"Revelation on Eternal Truth"[15]
	June	"Resurrection and Election" and "The Spirit of Revelation"
	July	"Mortal Existence, Intelligence, Truth, and Light,"[16] "The Spirit of Man,"[17] "Revelation,"[18] and "Spirit Angels"[19]
1841	October	"Angels and Ministering Spirits[20]

1842	April	"Satan—False Spirits in the Church"
	May	"How to Detect Spirits"[21]
	June	"Gifts of the Spirit" and "Diversity of Gifts and Gifts of Prophecy"
1843	May	"Spirit and Matter"
	October	"Angels and Spirits"[22]
1844	March	"Eternal Duration of Matter"[23] "Universal Resurrection"[24]
	April	Spiritual Birth—Spirit Elements[25] "King Follett Discourse"[26] (his greatest on spirits)
	May	"Universal Resurrection"[27]
	June	Mortal Existence, Intelligence, Truth, and Light[28]

Priesthood and Church Government

1839	June	"The Priesthood"[29]
	July	"Apostles of the Lord" and "Priesthood Keys and Father Adam" (the Prophet's address to the Twelve)[30]
1840	May	"Duties of Seventies Under the Twelve"[31]
	October	"Priesthood and Doctrine of Translation"[32] "Adam and Keys of Presidency"[33] "Elijah and the Authority of Ordinances"[34] "Epistle to the Twelve"[35]
1841	January	"Different Degrees of Melchizedek Priesthood"[36]
	April	"The Order of Priesthood in Temple Building"[37]
	August	"Priesthood Responsibilities"[38] and "The Twelve Next to the First Presidency"[39]
1842	March	"Fifth Article of Faith"[40]
	April	"Discerning Spirits by Power of Priesthood"[41]

		"The Gift held by the Prophets"[42]
		"The Father and the Everlasting Priesthood"[43]
		"Instructions Through the Priesthood"[44]
	May	"Keys of the Kingdom"[45]
		"Keys of Ministry Held by Twelve Apostles"[46]
		"Highest Order of Priesthood Revealed"[47]
	July	"The Government of God"[48]
1843	January	"The Kingdom of God, The Aaronic Priesthood, The Kingdom and Its Fruits"[49]
	June	"How to Get the Fullness of the Piesthood"[50]
	August	"Keys of Endless Life and How Acquired"[51]
		"Priesthood Is a Perfect Law of Theology"[52]
	October	"Keys of Plural Marriage"[53]
1844	January	"The Sealing Power of the Priesthood"[54]
	February	Council of Fifty—The Political Kingdom of God[55]
	April	"King Follett Discourse"[56]

Eternal Progression

1839	June	"Resurrection and Election" and "The spirit of Revelation"
	April	"Spiritual Birth—Spirit Eements"[57]
1841	May	"The Doctrine of Agency" and "The Doctrine of Election"[58]
	April	"Spiritual Birth—Spirit Elements"[59]
1842	March	"The Prophet's Sermon on Life and Death; the Resurrection and Salvation of Children"[60]
	April	Great Discourse on "Spirits"[61]
		"Men are Saved Through Obedience to Knowledge"[62]

		"Plan of Salvation"[63]
	September	"Saints Come Through Tribulation"[64]
1843	April	"The Resurrection"[65]
	May	"No Salvation Without a Tabernacle" and "Calling and Election"[66]
		"Importance of the Eternity of the Marriage Covenant" and "Celestial Glory"[67]
	June	"The World of Spirits"[68]
	July	"Kingdom of Heaven"[70]
	August	"Discourse on Priesthood"[71]
	October	"Angels and Spirits" and "How Salvation Is Acquired"[72]
1844	April	Eternal Spirits Through Intelligent-Spirit Elements[73]
	June	"Eternal Glories"[74]

The New and Everlasting Covenant

1839	June	The great discourse on the priesthood[75]
1840	May	"A Blessing to the Covenant People"[76]
	August	"New and Everlasting Covenant"[77]
1843	May	"More Sure Word of Prophecy"[78]
		"Calling and Election Made Sure"[79]
	October	"Two Seals of Marriage"[80]
1844	January	"Sealing Power in the Priesthood"[81]
	April	"King Follett Discourse"
	June	Father Abraham[82]

Temple Ordinances for the Living—"The Endowment"

1840	October	"Ordinances Always the Same"[83]
		"All Ordinances Restored"[84]
		"The Temple"[85]
1841	January	"The Temple and the Gathering"[86]
		"Pertaining to the House of the Lord and Priesthood Thereof"[87]

1842	March	Book of Abraham "The Lord's Chosen People"[88]
	April	"The Church and the Temple"[89]
	May	"The Temple—All Things to Be Gathered in One"[90]
		First endowment administered[91]
1843	January	"Divine Authority Necessary to Make Ordinances Valid"[92]
	May	"Sealed up unto Eternal Life"[93]
	June	"Purpose of Gathering Israel"[94] and "All Ordinance Must Be Received"[95]
	July	"Necessity of Ordinances"[96]
		"Eternity of Marriage Covenant"[97]
		"Ordained for Man by the Council of Heaven"[98]
		"Prophet, Priest and King"[99]
	August	"The Mission of Elijah"[100]
	December	Joseph administered to the first group the ordinances of the fullness[101]
1844	January	"All Ordinances Necessary"[102]
		"Sealing Power"[103]
	March	"The Worthy to Receive Endowments"[104]
		"Discourse on Elias and Elijah and Messiah"[105]
		"Fullness of Ordinance Living and Dead"[106]
		"Sealing on Earth and in Heaven"[107]
		"Sealing Power of Elijah Is As Follows"[108]
	April	"King Follett Discourse," "Obtaining Celestial Thrones," the "Ultimate Potential of Human Beings"[109]
	May	"The Paramount Need for a Temple"[110]

Endowments were given in the Joseph Smith Store on 4 May and 28 September 1842 and on 5 November 1843. They were given in the Mansion House on 29 October 1843. Records show that other temple ordinances were performed during Joseph's lifetime at his store, the "Old House" or "Old Homestead," the Mansion House, and the Brigham Young Home.[111]

Eternal Families

1842	April	"Salvation of Human Family"[112]
	September	"A Welding Link Between Fathers and Children."[113]
1843	May	"The Eternity of the Marriage Covenant and Celestial Glory"[114]
	July	D&C 132
	August	"Keys of Endless Life and How Acquired"[115]
		"Eternal Family Relations"[116]
	October	"Keys of Plural Marriage"[117]
		"Instructions Respecting Plurality of Wives"[118]
	April	"The King Follett Discourse"[119]

Salvation for the Dead

1823		Moroni's first visit started it
1836		The First Vision on this subject was received[120]
1840	August	"Doctrine of Baptism for Dead"[121]
	October	"Mission of Elijah"[122]
		"Baptism for Dead"[123]
1841	January	"Baptism for Dead to be Done in Temple"[124]
	October	"Baptism for the Dead"[125] and "Salvation for the Dead"[126]
1842	March	Performed great number of baptisms for the dead[127]

		"Sermon on Baptism for the Dead"[128]
	April	"Baptism for the Dead" and "Christ to Spirits in Prison"[129]
1843	June	"Salvation of Dead"[130]
	August	"The Mission of Elijah"[131]
1844	January	"The Sending of Elijah"[132]
	March	"Mission of Elijah to Prepare the Way"[133]
	April	Greatest discourse on this subject: "King Follett"
	May	"Resurrection of the Dead"[134]

Discourses and Prophecy

1841	May	"Discourse on Gospel Principles,"[135] which included "Doctrine of Agency" and "Doctrine of Election"
	November	"Perfection of the Book of Mormon"[136]
1842	Spring	"Joseph Smith gave approval for printing the "Articles of Faith"
	August	"Prophecy on Rocky Mountains"[137]
1843	May	Stephen A. Douglas Prophecy[138]
1844	April	King Follett Discourse; some of the eternal truths found in the discourse:[139]

1. Grand Council in Heaven
2. Plurality of Gods
3. Origin of the Doctrine of the Plurality of Gods
4. Men Can Become Gods
5. Nature of the Creator
6. Sons of Perdition
7. Personal Identity with God and Savior
8. The Doctrine of Preexistence
9. The Creation

	June 16	Joseph's last address
		Enlargement on plurality of Gods

Appendix E

SECULAR KNOWLEDGE
AFTER 1837

During Joseph Smith's incarceration of the winter of 1838-39, part of the revelations given included the following: "God shall give unto you knowledge by His Holy Spirit . . . that has not been revealed since the world was until now."[1]

The knowledge given Joseph included both spiritual and physical[2] truths. The concepts of light, astronomy, and time-relativity from the Book of Abraham, Doctrine and Covenants, and Book of Mormon and the great discourses of the last six years of his life are well documented.[3] That a great surge of knowledge spread over the earth is also documented.

Secular history shows that all aspects of man's communal living had not really changed in five thousand years. There was no system of free enterprise because the individual independence, law, industry, and technical knowledge was not there. Hundreds of inventions and advancements had come forth that had set the foundation. It was not until the middle 1800s that the knowledge and productivity developed to change the living structure of the world. These changes quickly followed Joseph's incarceration, bringing forth that which was necessary to accomplish mighty changes. The changes have been going on ever since.

Following 1838-39 came the great blessings. A partial list for the forty-year period following 1838 is given below:[4]

Inventions:

1839   Daguerreotype (photography), electric telegraph, electrotype process (first printing by electricity), electric motor, iron blast furnace, and vulcanized rubber

1840   Lithographs (wireless transition) and electroplating, fertilizer, and germ theory

1841   General anesthesia

1843   Typewriter

1844   Gas engine, cylinder printing press, and local anesthetic

1845   Giant telescope and hydraulic crane

1846   Sewing machine

1849   Internal combustion engine

1850   Synthetic oil, ophthalmology, and refrigerator

1851   Aviation, aerodynamic steel, wood pulp, and mechanical lift

1852   Gyroscope

1855   Celluloid

1856   Pasteurization and microphone

1857   Phonautograph

1858   Aerial photograph

1859   Steam engine, evolution "On the Origin of Species" from work of 1831-36, and rifle

1860   Debasscope cutting machine for patterns and automobile

1861   Thermometer and colored photography

1862   Photosynthesis and machine gun

1863   Sphygmomanometer

1864   Radio

1865   Genetics and lock

1869   DNA and fingerprinting

1877   Phonograph

1879   Filament lamp

Events:

1838   April 23: The first transatlantic steamship service began, although scheduled for service, was not established until 1840

1840   January: Wilkes expedition discovered the Antarctic continent

1851   August 12: Isaac Singer was granted a patent for his sewing machine; he set up business in Boston with $40 capital

1855   February 17: Congress authorized construction of a telegraph line from the Mississippi River to the Pacific

1859   August 27: The first oil well in the United States was drilled near Titusville, Pennsylvania

1863   April 14: A continuous-roll printing press was patented, the first press to print both sides of a sheet

1866   July 27: The first permanent transatlantic cable between the United States and Great Britain was completed

1869   November 17: The Suez Canal, linking the Mediterranean Sea and the Red Sea, was opened

1870   July 24: The first railroad car from the Pacific Coast reached New York City, opening the way for transcontinental train service

1876   March 7: The patent was issued for Alexander Graham Bell's telephone

1878   December 1: The first telephone was installed in the White House

1879   October 21: Thomas Edison tested an electric incandescent light bulb in Menlo Park, New Jersey, that burned for 13 1/2 hours, marking the beginning of a new era of electric lighting

NOTES

(See Bibliography for full citations)

Introduction

1. Doctrine and Covenants 110:11-15 (hereafter D&C). These messengers brought the keys of power for the mission of the Father through Jesus Christ. They are interlocking and inseparable (Moses 1:39). The three goals given by President Spencer W. Kimball at the October 1981 General Conference were first established and declared by the Prophet Joseph Smith: (1) To proclaim the gospel to the world to bring God's children to the ordinances of the temple, (2) To perfect the saints through the ordinances of the House of the Lord, and (3) To redeem the dead through the vicarious ordinances of the temple.

2. Truman G. Madsen, *Joseph Smith the Prophet*, see Endnote 12, 168.

3. Church Educational System, *Church History in the Fullness of Times*, 303-04. The original source is the Nauvoo Temple registry.

4. D&C 57:1-3.

5. G. Homer Durham, "Joseph Smith and the Political World," Eighth Annual Joseph Smith Memorial Sermon, Logan LDS Institute of Religion, 3 December 1950.

6. 3 Nephi 26:6.

7. Joseph Smith, *Teachings of the Prophet Joseph Smith*, p. 350, 6 April 1844; hereafter TPJS.

8. Joseph Smith, *History of the Church of Jesus Christ of Latter-day Saints*, 1:252-53; hereafter HC.

9. TPJS, 361.

10.   Orson F. Whitney, *Life of Heber C. Kimball*, 322.

11.   HC 1:252-53.

12.   Edward W. Tullidge, *Life of the Prophet Joseph*, 827 pages. Liberty Jail incidences mentioned twice, two paragraphs.

      Harry M. Beardsley, *Joseph Smith and His Mormon Empire*, 465 pages. Liberty Jail not mentioned.

      Fawn M. Brodie, *No Man Knows My History*, 518 pages. Liberty Jail not mentioned.

      John A. Widtsoe, *Joseph Smith: Seeker After Truth Prophet of God*, 359 pages. Liberty Jail mentioned in chronology highlights.

      George Q. Cannon, *Life of Joseph Smith the Prophet*, 541 pages. One page on incidences at Liberty Jail.

      Hyrum L. Andrus, *Joseph Smith, the Man and the Seer*, 140 pages. Liberty Jail mentioned once only in reference to a letter.

      B. H. Roberts, *The Missouri Persecutions*, 333 pages. Liberty Jail mentioned in only one paragraph.

      William Edwin Berrett, *The Restored Church*, 490 pages. Liberty Jail mentioned in one paragraph.

      John J. Stewart, *Joseph Smith the Mormon Prophet*, 235 pages. Three sentences concerning incidences at Liberty.

      Donna Hill, *Joseph Smith The First Mormon*, 527 pages. About four pages comprising a chapter, but mixes events at Richmond Jail with Liberty.

      Alvin Dyer, *Refiner's Fire*, 344 pages. A chapter with 13 pages on Liberty Jail with a picture.

      Madsen, *Joseph Smith the Prophet*, 126 pages. Two paragraphs on the Liberty Jail.

      Susan Evans McCloud, *Joseph Smith: A Photo Biography*, 157 pages. Three pages on the Liberty Jail and a picture.

13.   Smith. *The Papers of Joseph Smith Vol. 2, Journal 1832-1842*, 301 and 317.

14.   Jerry Johnston, *Liberty Jail may not be Contradiction*, 10 October 1990.

15.   D&C 121:26, 28; Transcript of the original letter in Joseph Smith, *The Personal Writings of Joseph Smith*, 397.

16. *Journal of Discourses,* JohnTaylor, 7 December 1879,Vol. 21, p. 160; hereafter JD.

17. HC 6:346.

Chapter 1: The Foundation of a Prophet

1. Ephesians 1:10; D&C 27:13.

2. George A. Smith, *Memoirs of George A. Smith,* 2, cited in Anderson, *Joseph Smith's New England Heritage,* 112; HC 2:443.

3. President JohnTaylor said, "It is a dispensation in which all other dispensations are merged or concentrated. It embraces and embodies all the other dispensations that have existed upon the earth wherein God communicated himself to the human family." JD 21:94.

4. D&C 130:2.

5. 2 Nephi 2:27; 10:23; D&C 29:35-36; 37:4.

6. 1 Nephi 1:1; 2 Nephi 25:26; D&C 68:25; Moses 6:58.

7. D&C 101:43; 130:21; Moses 5:11 (one of the few recorded doctrines taught by Mother Eve).

8. Mosiah 2:17; D&C 4:2.

9. HC 4:190.

10. Patriarchal Blessings, 1:3-4.

11. Ibid.

12. Ibid.

13. Lucy M. Smith, *History of Joseph Smith by His Mother Lucy Mack Smith,* Chapter 15.

14. Church Education System, *Church History in the Fullness of Times,* 341-43.

15. John Smith, Journal.

16. Patriarchal Blessings, 1:3-4.

17. Alma 13:3.

18. *Times and Seasons,* Vol. 3, No. 23, 1 October 1842, 928-29.

19. *Messenger and Advocate,* Vol. 1 (October 1834), 16.

20. Joseph Smith-History 1:17; hereafter JS-H

21. *History of Joseph Smith by Himself,* p. 3, spelling, punctuation, and capitalization standardized, in Smith, *The Personal Writings of Joseph Smith,* 6.

22. JS-H 1:25.

23. HC 6:364.

24. JS-H 1:29.

25. JS-H 1:30, 33.

26. JS-H 1:36-41. Joseph tells of five scriptures that Moroni quoted: part of Malachi 3; all of Malachi 4; Isaiah 11; Joel 2:28-31; and Acts 3:22-23. Joseph then said of Moroni, "He quoted many other passages of scripture and offered many explanations." From Oliver Cowdery's account, we obtain information about some of these scriptures: Psalms 107:7; 146:10; Isaiah 1:7, 23, 25-26; 45:19; Deuteronomy 32:23-24, 43; Jeremiah 16:16; 30:18; 31:6, 27-28, 32-33; 50:3-5; Matthew 20:16; Acts 2:20; 11:16; Revelation 6:12; and parts of Psalms 100; 144; Isaiah 2; 4; and Matthew 24. *Messenger and Advocate,* Vol. 1, No. 7, Kirtland, Ohio, 1835. Letter VI to W. W. Phelps, 108-112.

27. JS-H 1:37-39.

28. D&C 2:3.

29. See Chapter 2, Reference 7.

30. See Note 26.

31. *Messenger and Advocate,* October 1834, 15.

32. Ibid.

33. D&C 13.

34. D&C 21:1-2.

35. D&C 27:12-13.

36. D&C 35:17-18.

37. D&C 109:15.

38. D&C 110:11.

39. D&C 110:12.

40. HC 5:1.

41. D&C 115:19.

42. Smith, *History of Joseph by His Mother Lucy Mack Smith,* 90.

43. TPSJ, 324.

44. HC 1:252-53.

45. Danel W. Bachman, "Even the Faith of Elijah", 213, from Joseph Fielding McConkie, *His Name Shall Be Joseph,* 153-84.

46. Hugh W. Nibley *Nibley on the Timely and the Timeless,* Vol. 1, 234.

47. Paul H. Dunn, *Improvement Era,* June 1970, 72.

48. Parley P. Pratt. *Autobiography of Parley P. Pratt,* 31-32.

Chapter 2: The Messengers of the Fullness

1. 1 Nephi 9:6.

2. Malachi 3:Heading.

3. 2 Nephi 32:3.

4. Moroni 7:31.

5. Matthew 11:10; Mark 1:2.

6. 3 Nephi 24:Heading.

7. The Prophet Joseph's two great discourses, which are noted for knowledge concerning God, 7 April 1844 and 16 June 1844, used the word *Eloheim* as plural, meaning *Gods* or *Council of Gods.* At the turn of the century, it was clarified as *Father* when James Talmage, in his work *Jesus the Christ,* page 38, first stated, "Elohim, as understood and used in the restored Church of Jesus Christ, is the name-title of God the Eternal Father." The First Presidency and The Twelve, in their 30 June 1916 doctrinal exposition entitled "The Father and the Son," referenced Elder Talmage as to their usage of *Elohim* as *Father.*

8. H. Donl Peterson, "Moroni: Joseph Smith's Tutor," 22-29, from *Messenger and Advocate,* Kirtland Ohio, April 1835, 112.

9. D&C 7 since Joseph was translating a parchment of John and hidden up by himself; HC 1:35-36.

10. D&C 7.

11. D&C 77.

12. D&C 74.

13. D&C 27:10.

14. Abraham 3:22.

15. D&C 128:21.

16. HC 3:386.

17. D&C 2:3.

18. Abraham 1:2.

19. JS-H 1:17, 31.

20. 3 Nephi 17:15-16.

21. Pearl of Great Price following Joseph Smith-History, page 59.

22. JS-H 1:31-32.

23. Joseph Smith, *Lectures on Faith*, Lecture Seven, Item 3, 61.

24. Smith, *Lectures on Faith*, Lecture Seven, Item 4, 61.

25. D&C 121:26-28.

26. D&C 128:21.

27. JD 21:94.

28. See Chapter 1, Note.

29. Peterson, "Moroni: Joseph Smith's Tutor," 22-29.

30. D&C 27:5; JS-H 1:27-54.

31. D&C 27:5.

32. HC 4:537; George Q. Cannon, in JD 13:47; John Taylor, in JD 17:374; 21:94.

33. Smith, *History of Joseph by his Mother Lucy Mack Smith*, 100-101.

34. JS-H 1:59.

35. HC 1:21-22.

36. D&C 6:37.

37. Peterson, "Moroni: Joseph Smith's Tutor," 22-29.

38. Ether 5:2.

39. Ether 5:3.

40. Ether 5:4.

41. Peterson, "Moroni: Joseph Smith's Tutor," 22-29.

42. HC 1:40-41 ftnt.

43. D&C 128:20.

44. D&C 27:12.

45. D&C 81:2; 128:20.

46. D&C 21.

47. D&C 27:1.

48. See Bible Dictionary on Elias and the great discourse Joseph gave on "Elias," HC 6:249.

49. D&C 27:13.

50. D&C 27:14.

51. D&C 76:12, 14, 21, 23.

52. Abraham H. Cannon Journal, 25 August 1880.

53. D&C 107:41-57.

54. D&C 137.

55. D&C 137:7.

56. D&C 137:10.

57. D&C 137:5.

58. D&C 132:20, 37.

59. D&C 132:30.

60. D&C 132:29-50; Abraham 2:6-11.

61. D&C 132:29, 37.

62. HC 2:381.

63. D&C 27:12.

64. D&C 29:12.

65. 1 Corinthians 4:1.

66. HC 2:383.

67. D&C 110:1.

68. D&C 110:8.

69. D&C 110:11.

70. D&C 110:12.

71. D&C 107:52.

72. D&C 107:52.

73. Malachi 4:1.

74. Revelation 7:1-3; D&C 77:9; 110:12.

75. Richard Ware, "The Holy Priesthood, A History and Doctrine of the Priesthood as Taught by Joseph Smith and His Successors and as Contained in Latter-Day Saint Scripture."

76. Joseph Fielding Smith, *Doctrines of Salvation*, 127.

77. Luke 1:19.

78. D&C 128:21.

79. Malachi 4:5-6.

80. *Contributor*, Vol. 4, 53.

81. D&C 110:13-16.

82. *Contributor*, Vol. 4, 54.

83. D&C 110:16.

84. HC 3:388.

85. Bruce R. McConkie, "This Final Glorious Gospel Dispensation," 23.

86. Oliver B. Huntington Diary, Part 2, 214, BYU Library.

87. Moses 4:26; 1 Nephi 5:11.

88. Moses 5:11.

89. JD 18:325; HC 3:388.

90. D&C 107:42-43.

91. D&C 38:4.

92. D&C 107:57.

93. D&C 128:21.

94. D&C 128:21; Bruce R. McConkie, *Mormon Doctrine*, 618.

95. Genesis 5:21-27.

96. D&C 107:50, 52, 53; Moses 8:1-3.

97. JD 25:304.

98. Matthew 8:11.

99. Genesis 28:1-4, 12-22.

100. D&C 132:37.

101. D&C 27:10.

102. Smith, *Lectures on Faith*, Lecture 2, Item 56, 23.

103. TPJS, 180.

104. JD 17:374.

105. 3 Nephi 26:3.

106. 3 Nephi 28:10.

107. 3 Nephi 28:7.

108. Mormon 3:19.

109. HC 2:79-80 (1904 edition); Andrew Jenson, *The Historical Record*, 581.

110. Smith, *Doctrines of Salvation*, 238; Heber C. Kimball Journal, 4 June 1834.

111. 1 Nephi 10:4-5.

112. D&C 128:21.

Chapter 3: Joseph's Legacy of Scriptures

1. D&C 24:1.

2. D&C 21:1.

3. Mosiah 8:15-16.

4. Mosiah 8:13; 28:16.

5. Mosiah 8:15-18.

6. JS-H 1:50.

7. JS-H 1:52.

8. JS-H 1:53.

9. JS-H 1:54.

10. JS-H 1:59.

11. Smith, *History of Joseph Smith by His Mother Lucy Mack Smith*, 119-23.

12. D&C 3:4-10.

13. Smith, *History of Joseph Smith by His Mother Lucy Mack Smith*, 135.

14. D&C 10:10.

15. HC 2:170.

16. JS-H 1:67.

17. *Messenger and Advocate*, October 1834, 14.

18. HC 1:58.

19. HC 1:71.

20. HC 4:461; Book of Mormon, Introduction.

21. D&C 20:9-12.

22. D&C 20:17-19.

23. Alma 41:13.

24. Alma 41:14.

25. D&C 124:89.

26. D&C 35:18.

27. D&C 45:60.

28. HC 1:324.

29. Moses 1:40-41.

30. 1 Nephi 13:26.

31. 1 Nephi 13:23-29, 38-40.

32. Robert J. Matthews, "What Is the Book of Moses?" 24-25.

33. Melvin R. Brooks, *LDS Reference Encyclopedia*, 108-10.

34. 2 Nephi 31:21.

35. 3 Nephi 11:31-32.

36. HC 2:235-36, 348-51.

37. *Times and Seasons*, Vol. 3, No. 9, 1 March 1842, 703.

38. D&C 110:12.

39. Genesis 12:2.

40. 1 Nephi 15:18.

41. John 8:39.

42. D&C 132:32.

43. 1 Nephi 13.34.

Chapter 4: Jail Participants

1. Annaleone D. Patton, *California Mormons by Sail and Trail*, 127.

2. HC 6:78.

3. HC 7:512.

4. Smith, *The Personal Writings of Joseph Smith*, 425; Joseph Smith, Letter to Emma, 4 April 1839.

5. McCloud, *Joseph Smith: A Photo Biography*, 91.

6. Cannon, *Life of Joseph Smith the Prophet*, 289.

7. Ibid., 290.

8. Andrew Jenson, *Autobiography of Andrew Jenson*, Vols. 7 and 8, 18 September 1888, 667.

9. Smith, *History of Joseph Smith by His Mother Lucy Mack Smith*, 248.

10. Letter of 20 March 1839, Liberty Jail, HC 3:290; Dean C. Jessee, "Walls, Grates and Screeking Iron doors: The Prison Experience of Mormon Leaders in Missouri, 1838-1839," *The Missouri Historical Review*, 28.

11. Garcia N. Jones, *Emma's Glory and Sacrifice*, 82.

12. Joseph Fielding Smith, *Church History and Modern Revelation*, 1:57.

13. Pearson H. Corbett, *Hyrum Smith—Patriarch*, 194.

14. D&C 124:91.

15. Joseph Smith, *The Words of Joseph Smith*, 232-33; HC 6:288.

16. HC 2:522.

17. O. J. P. Widtsoe, *The Utah Genealogical and Historical Magazine*, April 1911, 1.

18. D&C 124:15.

19. Dean C. Jessee, "Walls, Grates and Screeking Iron Doors", 27.

20. Ibid., 29.

21. HC 3:374.

22. Matthew 11:11.

23. Joseph A. McRae and Eunice H. McRae, *Historical Facts Regarding the Liberty and Carthage Jails*.

24. History written by Regina McRae.

25. Jenson, *Autobiography of Andrew Jenson*, Vols. 7 and 8, 18 September 1888, 620.

26. Ibid.; Preston Nibley, *Stalwarts of Mormonism*, 10-102; David F. McRae, "Sketch of the Life of Alexander McRae."

27. *Deseret Evening News*, 11 December 1906; Nibley, *Stalwarts of Mormonism*, 100-102; Annie W. Burns Record of Marriage Bonds in Henry County, Kentucky, gives the date as 11-2-1824, but this is questionable.

28. Jenson, Autobiography of Andrew Jenson, 18 September 1888, 1:620.

29. Andrus, *Joseph Smith, the Man and the Seer,* 50, as taken from HC 3:259.

30. Joseph Smith, III. *Joseph Smith III and the Restoration,* 13.

31. Linda King Newell and Valeen Tippetts Avery, *Mormon Enigma Emma Hale Smith,* 78.

32. McRae, *Historical Facts Regarding the Liberty and Carthage Jails*

33. Rosa V. Black, *Under Granger Skies,* 186-87.

34. LDS Eleventh Ward Record, Salt Lake City.

35. History written by Regina McRae.

36. McRae, *Historical Facts Regarding the Liberty and Carthage Jails,* 47.

37. Statement of Zina McRae Irving, 15 March 1966.

38. Church Education System, *Church History in the Fullness of Times,* 188.

39. HC 2:88 ftnt.

40. HC 2:305.

41. Dyer, *Refiner's Fire,* 204.

42. HC 3:315.

43. Church Education System, *Church History in the Fullness of Times,* 188.

44. HC 7:435.

45. History of Lyman Wight, *Millennial Star,* 1865, 4.

46. HC 3:448.

47. HC 7:212, cited in Madsen, *Joseph Smith the Prophet,* 174 ftnt 3.

48. Letter to Wilford Woodruff, 24 August 1857, LDS Historical Department.

49. Ronald G. Watt, "A Dialogue Between Wilford Woodruff and Lyman Wight," *BYU Studies* 17 (Autumn 1976), 108-13.

50. Wilford Woodruff to Lyman Wight, 1 July 1857, Historical Department Letterbooks.

51. Wight to Woodruff, 24 August 1857, Woodruff Collection.

52. Woodruff to Wight, 30 June 1858, Historical Department Letterbooks.

53. Kathryn S. Gilbert et al., *The Life of Caleb Baldwin*, 1.

54. Ibid.

55. Ibid.

56. Ibid.

57. Ibid., 2.

58. Ibid., 4.

59. HC 1:120.

60. D&C 37:2.

61. F. Mark McKiernan, *The Voice of One Crying in the Wilderness: Sidney Rigdon, Religious Reformer*, 98.

62. *Times and Seasons*, Vol. 4, No. 18, 1 August 1843, 277.

63. McKiernan, *The Voice of One Crying in the Wilderness: Sidney Rigdon, Religious Reformer,* 98; *Daily Missouri Republican* (St. Louis), 14 February 1839.

64. McKiernan, *The Voice of One Crying in the Wilderness: Sidney Rigdon, Religious Reformer,* 98.

65. Richard S. Van Wagoner, *Sidney Rigdon: A Portrait of Religious*, 254.

66. McKiernan, *The Voice of One Crying in the Wilderness: Sidney Rigdon, Religious Reformer,* 99; Van Wagoner, *Sidney Rigdon: A Portrait of Religious,* 255.

67. D&C 25:3.

68. D&C 25:5.

69. Emma Smith, Letter to Joseph, March 1839, spelling and grammar modernized.

70. Smith, *The Personal Writings of Joseph Smith*, 361.

71. HC 5:107.

72. Andrew Ehat, List of ordinances prior to Nauvoo Temple; D. Michael Quinn, *The Mormon Hierarchy Origins of Power*, 495-96.

73. Corbett, *Hyrum Smith—Patriarch*, 155-58.

74. Dyer, *Refiner's Fire*, 288.

75. Mercy Fielding Thompson, "Letter to My Posterity."

76. Corbett, *Hyrum Smith—Patriarch*, 155-58.

77. McRae, *Historical Facts Regarding the Liberty and Carthage Jails*, 45.

78. Gordon Irving, "Alexander and Eunice McRae," 2; Endowment House Sealings, Book E, 169.

79. McRae, *Historical Facts Regarding the Liberty and Carthage Jails*, 3; history written by Regina McRae.

80. McRae, *Historical Facts Regarding the Liberty and Carthage Jails*, back fly leaf.

81. Ibid., 6; Joseph A. McRae, Letter, 7 March 1939; N. B. Lundwall, 109-10.

82. N.B. Lundwall, *Joseph A. and Eunice H. McRae*, 55.

83. Susan Ward Easton, *Membership of the Church of Jesus Christ of Latter-Day Saints, 1830-1848*, 30:450.

84. Gilbert, *Histories of Caleb Baldwin by Family Members*, p. 1.

85. Ibid., 4.

86. T. R. Turk, "Lyman Wight Texas Community," 23.

87. Ibid., 23-24.

88. McKiernan, *The Voice of One Crying in the Wilderness: Sidney Rigdon, Religious Reformer,* 16.

89. Ibid., 17.

90. Ibid.

91. Van Wagoner, *Sidney Rigdon: A Portrait of Religious,* 211.

92. Ibid., 17.

93. Ibid., 35-36; John Jaques, "Life and Labors of Sidney Rigdon," *Improvement Era* 3 (1899-1900), 100.

94. Van Wagoner, *Sidney Rigdon: A Portrait of Religious,* 17.

95. Ibid, 255.

96. Rollin J. Britton, "Early Days on the Grand River and the Mormon War," 14 *Missouri Historical Review*, 1920, 95.

97. Gregory P. Maynard, "Alexander William Doniphan, the Forgotten Man from Missouri," 7; Record Book 2, Clay County, Missouri Circuit Court, Liberty, 213.

98. HC 1:425.

99. Maynard, "Alexander William Doniphan, the Forgotten Man from Missouri, 37.

100. Patton, *California Mormons by Sail and Trail,* 126.

101. Ibid., 127.

102. Hill, *Joseph Smith The First Mormon,* 245; Peter H. Burnett *Recollections and Opinions of an Old Pioneer,* 39-40.

103. Burnett, *Recollections and Opinions of an Old Pioneer,* 53.

104. Patton, *California Mormons by Sail and Trail,* 127-28, from Burnett, *Recollections and Opinions of an Old Pioneer.*

105. *History of Clay and Platte Counties, Missouri,* 126.

106. Ibid., 128.

107. Burnett, *Recollections and Opinions of an Old Pioneer.*

108. R. Kenneth Elliott, "The Rhetoric of Alexander Doniphan," 14 *The Trail Guide,* December 1969, No. 4.

109. Evelyn Petty, "History of Clay County," *Liberty Tribune,* 27 April 1973.

110. Quinn, *The Mormon Hierarchy Origins of Power,* 100-101.

111. Ibid., 2.

112. Pearl Wilcox, "Clay County—A Haven for the Exiled," Part IV, Clay County Museum, Liberty, Missouri, 1.

113. Jessee, "Walls, Grates and Screeking Iron Doors," 26, from Smith, "Memoirs of George A. Smith," 123-25 Ms.

114. Burnett, *Recollections and Opinions of an Old Pioneer,* 64.

115. Ibid.

116. Berrett, *The Restored Church,* 147; Burnett, *Recollections and Opinions of an Old Pioneer,* 53-54; and court documents in authors' possession.

117. Burnett, *Recollections and Opinions of an Old Pioneer,* 54.

118. Clay County Census, Clay County Archives, Liberty, Missouri.

119. Burnett, *Recollections and Opinions of an Old Pioneer,* 65; and copies of original court transcripts in authors' possession.

120. *History of Clay and Platte Counties, Missouri,* 135.

121. Clark V. Johnson, ed., *Mormon Redress Petitions Documents of the 1833-1838 Missouri Conflict*, 16:93.

122. Burnett, *Recollections and Opinions of an Old Pioneer*, 55.

123. Clay County History, p. 2, Clay County Archives, Liberty, Missouri.

124. *History of Clay and Platte Counties, Missouri*, 126.

125. HC 1:424-25.

126. *History of Clay and Platte Counties, Missouri*, 2.

127. Cannon, *Life of Joseph Smith the Prophet*, 293.

128. *History of Daviess County*, 206.

129. Johnson, *Mormon Redress Petitions Documents*, 16:36.

130. *Sun Liberty Edition*, 5 February 1986, 2; *Historical Review of Clay County Sheriffs, 1822-1986*.

131. *History of Clay and Platte Counties, Missouri*, 146.

132. Probate Records, Clay County Archives, Liberty, Missouri.

133. Newell, *Mormon Enigma Emma Hale Smith*, 78.

134. *History of Clay and Platte Counties, Missouri*, 221.

135. Copy of oaths found on microfilm at the Clay County Archives, Liberty, Missouri.

136. *History of Clay and Platte Counties, Missouri*, 115.

137. Clay County History, p. 2, Clay County Archives, Liberty, Missouri.

138. Johnson, *Mormon Redress Petitions Documents*, 16:36.

139. Ibid., 16:664.

140. Gilbert, *Histories of Caleb Baldwin by Family members*.

141. Johnson, *Mormon Redress Petitions Documents*, 16:636.

Chapter 5: Liberty Jail

1. *An Illustrated Historical Atlas of Clay County Missouri*, page 24, lists two posts of Francois Chauteaus (north and south of the river), also Andrew Woods, Curtis and Eley, and Grandlouis Bertholet.

2. Edward Stevenson, "Reminiscence of Joseph, the Prophet," 34.

3. *An Illustrated Historical Atlas of Clay County Missouri*, 123; Stevenson, "Reminiscence of Joseph, the Prophet," 41-42.

4. Wilcox, "Clay County—A Haven for the Exiled," 2.

5. These parts were removed by Robert Steele Withers, as confirmed by a letter written on 5 November 1957, witnessed and notarized on 6 November 1957, County of Clay, State of Missouri.

6. Wilcox, "Clay County—A Haven for the Exiled," 2.

7. Ibid.

8. This part was removed by Robert Steele Withers, as confirmed by a letter written on 5 November 1957, witnessed and notarized on 6 November 1957, County of Clay, State of Missouri.

9. The question of blankets is seen from Joseph's writing Emma asking for one and the story of her plight. Madsen, *Joseph Smith the Prophet*, 56.

10. Psalms 107:15-20.

11. D&C 121:3.

12. Jenson, *The Historical Record*, January 1888, 455.

13. Ibid., 257.

14. Habakkuk 2:14.

15. B.H. Roberts, *Comprehensive History of the Church*, 1:526.

16. HC 3:293.

17. Cannon, *Life of Joseph Smith the Prophet*, 292.

18. HC 3:244; Joseph Smith, III and Heman C. Smith, *History of the Church of Jesus Christ of Latter-day Saints*, 2:309; hereafter RLDS.

19. HC 3:245; RLDS 2:310.

20. HC 3:257.

21. In his letter, Brother McRae says 7 February. He then tells why they did not go that night. Court records show that the jail break attempt was on the 7th. See copies of original charges. Therefore, the night Brother McRae is referring to would be the 6th.

22. HC 3:257.

23. HC 3:258.

24. Cannon, *Life of Joseph Smith the Prophet*, 295.

25. HC: 3:258.

26. HC 3:258.

27. HC 3:257.

28. HC 3:258.

29. D&C 98:12-14.

30. TPJS, 149-50.

31. Smith, *The Personal Writings of Joseph Smith*, 397.

32. Ibid., 387.

33. D&C 121:45-46.

34. Gerry Avant, "Collector Finds Rare Book, Autographed Statement by Prophet," *Church News*, 23 June 1985, 10.

35. Cannon, *Life of Joseph Smith the Prophet*, 297.

36. McRae, *Historical Facts Regarding the Liberty and Carthage Jails*, 258.

37. HC 3: 259.

38. HC 3:259.

39. HC 3:374.

40. N. B. Lundwall, *The Fate of the Persecutors of the Prophet Joseph Smith*, 108-109, from Andrew Jenson and Edward Stevenson, *Infancy of the Church*, 25-27.

41. HC 3: 259.

42. HC 3:259.

43. HC 3:259.

Chapter 6: Jail Breaks

1. HC 3:257.

2. HC 3:372.

3. Cannon, *Life of Joseph Smith the Prophet*, 293.

4. HC 3:292.

5. HC 3:257.

6. HC 3:257-58.

7. Alexander McRae's letter of 9 October 1854 found in HC 3:257 and RLDS 2:316.

8. Cannon, *Life of Joseph Smith the Prophet*, 295.

9. HC 3:264.

10. March 1 is the date recorded in RLDS history by Lyman Wight as when the escape attempt started; RLDS 2:317.

11. Hyrum Smith, Letter to wife Mary, 16 March 1839; Harold Schindler, *Orrin Porter Rockwell: Man of God Son of Thunder*, 64.

12. Hyrum Smith, Letter to wife Mary, 16 March 1839.

13. HC 3:292.

14. Hyrum Smith, Letter to wife Mary, 16 March 1839.

15. HC 3:292.

Chapter 7: People and Spiritual Attributes

1. Berrett, *The Restored Church*, 146.

2. HC 3:184.

3. HC 3:283-84.

4. Daniel 2:44-45.

5. Smith. *The Papers of Joseph Smith Vol. 2*,, 298-99 ftnt; HC 3:167.

6. HC 3:167, Richmond, Missouri, 24 October 1838.

7. Woodruff to Wight, 30 June 1858, Historical Department Letterbooks.

8. HC 4:162-63.

9. HC 4:163-64.

10. HC 7:152-53.

11. *Millennial Star*, Vol. 36, 808, 809; HC 3:215 ftnt.

12. HC 3:287.

13. HC 3:288.

14. HC 3:313.

15. HC 3:288.

16. HC 3:289.

17. HC 3:329-330.

18. D&C 135.3.

Chapter 8: Correspondence and the Gaol (Jail)

1. Smith, *The Personal Writings of Joseph Smith*, 374-83.

2. HC 3:226-33.

3. HC 3:226.

4. HC 3:227; Cannon, *Life of Joseph Smith the Prophet*, 291; Smith, *The Personal Writings of Joseph Smith*, 375.

5. Heber C. Kimball's journal, 16 January 1839.

6. Moses 1:39.

7. HC 3:247, 249.

8. HC 3:265-67.

9. Johnson, *Mormon Redress Petitions Documents*, 16:41-44.

10. HC 3:277-81.

11. HC 3:282; Johnson, *Mormon Redress Petitions Documents*, 36-37.

12. HC 3:282; Johnson, *Mormon Redress Petitions Documents*, 38-39.

13. HC 3:282; Johnson, *Mormon Redress Petitions Documents*, 45-46.

14. HC 3:282; Johnson, *Mormon Redress Petitions Documents*, 46-48.

15. HC 3:285-86; Smith, *The Personal Writings of Joseph Smith*, 386-87.

16. Hyrum Smith, Letter to wife Mary, 16 March 1839.

17. HC 3:272-73.

18. HC 3:273-74.

19. HC 3:274.

20. *Times and Seasons*, Vol. 1, No. 9, July 1840, 99-104, 131-34; HC 3:289-305.

21. Joseph Smith, Letter to Emma, 4 April 1839; transcript and copy of this letter in Smith, *The Personal Writings of Joseph Smith*, 425-30.

22. For a copy of full text transcription and original, see Smith, *The Personal Writings of Joseph Smith*, 425-30.

23. HC 3:310-13.

24. HC 3:313-14.

25. HC 3:316-17.

Chapter 9: Revelation and Knowledge

1.   Patriarchal Blessings,Vol. 1, 3-4; Neal A. Maxwell, *But for a Small Moment*, 7.

2.   A few of these powers are described in D&C 28:2, 7; 35:17-18; 84:19-20; 90:1-16; 107:18-19; and 115:19.

3.   Sidney B. Sperry, *Doctrine and Covenants Compendium*, 39, as cited in the *Far West Record*, 8 November 1831 Conference, Portage County, Ohio.

4.   HC 3:526.

5.   D&C 109:8.

6.   Ibid.

7.   HC 5:1.

8.   A great witness of this is the compilation by Andrew F. Ehat and Lyndon W. Cook in Smith, *The Words of Joseph Smith*. Their work begins on 27 June 1839, just two and one-half months after Joseph's release from Liberty Jail.

9.   D&C 121:33, 28.

10. TPJS, 137.

11. Chauncey C. Riddle, "As a Prophet Thinketh in His Heart So Is He: The Mind of Joseph Smith," 272, found in Black *Joseph Smith The Prophet, The Man*, 17.

12. D&C 42:61.

13. D&C 76:1-8.

14. TPJS, 205.

15. HC 5:134-36; TPJS, 255-56.

16. D&C 128.

17. D&C 128:18.

18. D&C 128:19.

19. D&C 128:14.

20. HC 5:388-89.

21. Orson Pratt, *The Seer*, 297-98.

Chapter 10: Doctrine to Its Fullness

1. D&C 1:30.

2. Spencer W. Kimball specifically mentions the keys of resurrection. Conference Report, April 1977, 69; JD 15:137.

3. D&C 35:18.

4. 2 Nephi 27:10.

5. Ether 4:4-7.

6. HC 5:134-36.

7. D&C 76:56.

8. D&C 76:76.

9. D&C 93:16.

10. D&C 93:14, 16, 20.

11. D&C 131:1-3.

12. Smith, *Lectures on Faith*, Lecture 4, Items 4-10, 41-42.

13. Smith, *Lectures on Faith*, Lecture 7, Item 20, 68.

14. Abraham 1:2.

15. John 17:3.

16. D&C 84:20.

17. Moses 1:39.

18. HC 5:139.

19. *Times and Seasons*, Vol. 3, No. 19, 1 March 1842, 706-10.

20. HC 5:402.

21. Chauncey C. Riddle, "As a Prophet Thinketh in His Heart, So Is He: The Mind of Joseph Smith, found in Black, *Joseph Smith The Prophet, The Man,* 261.

22. John 17:37.

23. HC 6:305.

24. Thomas D. Cottle, "Priesthood and Temple Chronology."

25. JS-H 1:19.

26. JS-H 1:25.

27. Joseph Smith's Diary (1832-34), page 3, lines 16-19.

28. D&C 6:37.

29. 1 Nephi 3:58 (the son of); 1 Nephi 3:62 (son of the); 1 Nephi 3:86 (the son of); and 1 Nephi 3:193 (the son of). These changes were made by Joseph for clarification.

30. D&C 76:23.

31. D&C 76:58; 84:38.

32. Smith, *Lectures of Faith*, Lecture 5, Items 1 and 2, 48.

33. D&C 137:7.

34. D&C 110:2.

35. HC 1:2 ftnt.

36. JS-H 1:17.

37. TPJS, 190.

38. TPJS, 149-51.

39. D&C 130:22.

40. *Improvement Era*, February 1964, 96-97, 114-18.

41. HC 5:423-27.

42. TPJS, 311.

43. TPJS, 343-55.

44. D&C 130:22.

45. *Ensign*, May 1971, 15.

46. HC 6:473.

47. King Follett Discourse, see HC 6:305 and TPJS, 345.

48. HC 1:474.

49. TPJS, 190.

50. Diary of Charles L. Walker, p. 902, as cited in Madsen, *Joseph Smith the Prophet*, 103.

51. D&C 13. John the Baptist outlined the keys he was restoring because he knew other keys of this priesthood would be restored later.

52. D&C 20:2; 27:12.

53. McConkie, *Mormon Doctrine*, 71.

54. D&C 110:11-13.

55. D&C 110:6-7.

56. D&C 110:11.

57. Exodus 40:13-14; D&C 110:11.

58. TPJS, 190.

59. Exodus 28:1-4; D&C 84:18, 26-27.

60. Exodus 4:1-8, 15-17; Deuteronomy 6:8; 13:1.

61. D&C 84:19-22; Facsimile No. 2, Book of Abraham.

62. D&C 131:1-4; 132:26, 29.

63. Genesis 15:5; Hebrews 11:8-12; D&C 132:30-32.

64. Genesis 12:3; 3 Nephi 20:25.

65. Smith, *Doctrines of Salvation*, 3:127, "This Elias was a prophet who lived in the days of Abraham and who held the keys of that dispensation. He came and bestowed the gifts and the blessings that were pronounced upon Abraham's head"; Abraham 1:3.

66. See Chapter 2, "The Messengers of the Fullness," under Noah.

67. Abraham 1:4.

68. D&C 132:32.

69. 1 Kings 17:1.

70. Isaiah 22:22; Matthew 18:18; Revelation 3:7-12; D&C 124:93; 132:46.

71. TPJS, 172.

72. D&C 128:17-18.

73. TPJS, 322-23; *The Contributor*, Vol. 3, No. 2, 92-95.

74. HC 3:385-87; TPJS, 157, 169 where Joseph goes over this again, explaining that "every man holding the Presidency of his dispensation, and one man holding the Presidency of them all, even Adam; and Adam receiving his presidency and authority from the Lord."

75. HC 3:383-92; TPJS, 159.

76. Moses 5:12; D&C 107:53.

77. HC 3:388.

78. Moses 1:39.

79. TPJS, 166-67.

80. TPJS, 180-81.

81. D&C 13:1.

82. D&C 110:11.

83. HC 5:392;TPJS, 301.

84. HC 5:554-56; Joseph Smith Diary, 27 August 1843.

85. Ware, "The Holy Priesthood," part 1, p. 3 ftnt 4 says: "TPJS, pp. 322-323. The original source documentation for Joseph's discourse on the three orders, as found in TPJS is the Joseph Smith Diary kept by Willard Richards. Willard Richards recorded the three orders as being (1) 'King of Shiloam,' (2) 'Priesthood, Patriarchal,' and (3) 'priesthood of Aaron' and the 'Levitical.' In addition, there were three other individuals who kept minutes of this discourse: Franklin D. Richards, James Burgess, and Levi Richards. Franklin D. Richards listed the priesthoods as (1) 'Levitical,' (2) 'Abraham's Patriarchal power,' and (3) 'That of Melchizedek.' James Burgess gave them as 'the priesthood of Aaron, Abraham, and Melchizedek.' Levi Richards recorded them as 'the priesthood Aaronic, Patriarchal, and Melchizedek.'" (Smith, *The Words of Joseph Smith*, 243-48, 301-302, misspellings in original).

86. HC 5:554-56;TPJS, 322.

87. D&C 84:32-42.

88. TPJS, 323.

89. TPJS, 337.

90. HC 6:183-85, 273;TPJS, 338.

91. HC 4:209.

92. 3 Nephi 28.

93. Spencer W. Kimball specifically mentions the keys of resurrection. Conference Report, April 1977, 69; JD 15:137.

94. D&C 66:2.

95. D&C 136:2-4.

96. D&C 52:14-16.

97. D&C Chapter 1: Heading.

98. D&C 1:15; Isaiah 24:5.

99.   D&C 84:20.

100. D&C 95:8.

101. 22 June 1834, D&C 105:12.

102. Chauncey C. Riddle, "As a Prophet Thinketh in His Heart So Is He:The Mind of Joseph Smith," 271, found in Black, *Joseph Smith The Prophet, The Man,* 17.

103. 2 Nephi 9:1.

104. Mosiah 5:5-6, 8-9.

105. 3 Nephi 16:1-4.

106. 3 Nephi 16:5.

107. 3 Nephi 16:6.

108. TPJS, 190.

109. JST Genesis 17:3-5.

110. TPJS, 59.

111. TPJS, 60.

112. HC 2:255, 259.

113. HC 2:379.

114. TPJS, 163.

115. TPJS, 190.

116. TPJS, 168.

117. TPJS, 173.

118. TPJS, 167.

119. TPJS, 182.

120. D&C 124:31-32.

121. D&C 124:33-42.

122. TPJS, 230-31.

123. HC 5:1.

124. TPJS, 274.

125. D&C 131:1-4.

126. TPJS, 308.

127. TPJS, 322-23.

128. TPJS, 323.

129. Malachi 4:6. This is the last verse of the Old Testament.

130. D&C 2.

131. TPJS, 321.

132. HC 5:391-92.

133. HC 5:387, 401.

134. TPJS, 308.

135. HC 5:423-27; Smith, *The Words of Joseph Smith*, 215.

136. HC 5:423-27.

137. TPJS, 314; HC 5:498-500.

138. *Contributor* 4:52-55.

139. Genesis 2:24.

140. Smith, *The Words of Joseph Smith*, 294, 303; Quinn, *The Mormon Hierarchy Origins of Power*, 640.

141. TPJS, 325.

142. Ware, "The Holy Priesthood," Part 5, 5-6.

143. Andrew F. Ehat, "Joseph Smith's Introduction of Temple Ordinances and the 1844 Mormon Succession Question."

144. TPJS, 331.

145. HC 6:183.

146. HC 6:183-85.

147. TPJS, 333.

148. HC 6:249-54.

149. HC 6:363.

150. TPJS, 338.

151. TPJS, 340.

152. TPJS, 362-63.

153. TPJS, 363.

154. TPJS, 366.

155. TPJS, 367.

156. TPJS, 373.

157. 1 Corinthians 4:1.

158. Genesis 2:24.

159. Moses 3:23-24.

160. Matthew 19:4-6.

161. Genesis 16:1, 3; 24:4, 67; 29:4, 9.

162. Malachi 4:1.

163. 3 Nephi 15:1

164. Matthew 22:30.

165. D&C 38:32.

166. D&C 42:22.

167. D&C 76:50-70.

168. HC 1:167-69; D&C 49.

169. D&C 49:15-17.

170. Danel W. Bachman, "New Light on an Old Hypothesis: The Ohio Origins of the Revelation on Eternal Marriage," *Journal of Mormon History*, Vol. 5.

171. See Chapter 7 or HC 3:272-77.

172. HC 2:243.

173. HC 2:246 ftnt.

174. HC 2:251.

175. HC 2:245.

176. HC 2:320.

177. HC 2:320.

178. HC 2:377.

179. D&C 128:18; HC 5:148-53.

180. D&C 132. For an in-depth discussion on the history of this revelation, see Bachman, "New Light on an Old Hypothesis", Vol. 5.

181. HC 5:xxxii.

182. D&C 131:1-4.

183. TPJS, 321.

184. Smith, *The Words of Joseph Smith*, 294, 303; Quinn, *The Mormon Hierarchy Origins of Power*, 640.

185. Danel W. Bachman, "The Eternity of the Marriage Relationship," 212. The minutes of this very important meeting were published in the *Nauvoo Neighbor*, 19 June 1844.

Chapter 11: Living Oracles/Apostles of the Lord

1. *Webster's II New Riverside Dictionary*, 494.

2. 2 Samuel 16:23; 1 Peter 4:11. "Living oracles" have always directed the kingdom of God on earth. His "living oracles" direct it today. There have been ninety-two apostles of the Lord Jesus Christ called in this dispensation. The current fifteen have been set apart and ordained with all keys to be sustained as prophets, seers, and revelators for the Church. The President of the Church is such because all keys have been activated and are inherent within him.

3. To the apostles from Jesus Christ, "Unto whom I have committed the keys of my kingdom, and a dispensation of the gospel for the last times; and for the fullness of times, in the which I will gather together in one all things, both which are in heaven, and which are on earth" (D&C 27:13).

4. David W. Patten, Brigham Young, and Heber C. Kimball. Joseph said, "Of the Twelve Apostles chosen in Kirtland, and ordained under the hands of Oliver Cowdery, David Whitmer and myself, there have been but two but what have lifted their heel against me—namely Brigham Young and Heber C. Kimball," 28 May 1843, HC 5:412.

5. William Earl McLellin, Luke Johnson, John Boynton, and Lyman Johnson.

6. Oliver Cowdery, Thomas B. Marsh, Orson Hyde, and Orson Pratt.

7. HC 2:488 ftnt, from Pratt, *Autobiography of Parley P. Pratt*, 183-84.

8. HC 5:412.

9. June 1831, D&C 52:9, 36. The apostles are to write all things that are to be taught and the priesthood, declaring none other things but what the apostles have seen, heard, and believed that these prophecies may be fulfilled.

10. The Savior was with them only three days. The first day the Savior chose and called twelve and gave them power and

authority to minister baptism (3 Nephi 12:1-3). The second day they received the ordinances, Nephi first and then all the disciples. Coming out of the water, they received the Holy Ghost like the Day of Pentecost for the Judean apostles (3 Nephi 19:10-13). Next, angels administered unto the disciples, and then Jesus came into the midst and ministered unto them again (verse 15). Then, the beautiful experiences Jesus gave them with prayer (verses 17-24). While they were praying, he again blessed them, "and his countenance did smile and shine upon them" (verse 25). So sacred was the event that all that was spoken could not be written (verse 34). Jesus said of this occasion, "So great faith have I never seen among all the Jews" (verse 35).

On the third visit, he gave to them their most sacred wish and pronounced upon them the "fullness of joy . . . in the kingdom of my Father . . . ye shall be even as I am" (3 Nephi 28:10). Then, he touched nine of them with his finger (verse 12). To the three remaining, "the heavens were opened, and they were caught up into heaven, and saw and heard unspeakable things . . . that they could behold the things of God" (verses 13 and 15). They performed all the same miracles as the Judean apostles and entered into eternal marriage (4 Nephi 1:11). When they died, they "had all gone to the paradise of God" (verse 14).

11. Mark 3:14; Luke 6:12, 13.

12. John 15:16.

13. Matthew 10:1-4; Luke 6:2-16.

14. D&C 18:9.

15. D&C 18:28.

16. D&C 28:12, 13.

17. D&C 27:13.

18. D&C 107:23-24.

19. Matthew 16:19.

20. October Conference 1840. Joseph's remarks on the priesthood concerning Elijah included: "Why send Elijah? Because he holds the keys of the authority to administer in all the ordinances of the Priesthood; and without the authority is given, the ordinances could not be administered in righteousness" (TPJS, 172).

21. TPJS, 158.

22. TPJS, 337.

23. On 4 May 1842, Joseph Smith met in the upper part of the red brick store "in council with General James Adams, of Springfield, Patriarch Hyrum Smith, and Elders Heber C. Kimball and Willard Richards, (William Marks and William Law) instructing them in the principles and order of the priesthood, attending to washings, anointings, endowments and communication of keys pertaining to the Aaronic Priesthood, and so on to the highest order of the Melchizedek Priesthood, setting forth the order pertaining to the Ancient of Days, and all those plans and principles by which anyone is enabled to secure the fullness of those blessings which have been prepared for the Church of the Firstborn, and come up and abide in the presence for the Eloheim in the eternal worlds. In this council was instituted the ancient order of things for the first time in these last days" (TPJS, 237; HC 5:1).

24. Ehat, "Joseph Smith's Introduction of Temple Ordinances"; HC 5:1-2; and TPJS, 237.

25. HC 5:1-2; TPJS, 237.

26. HC 5:2-3. With this, Joseph said, "The dispensation of the fullness of the Priesthood in the last days, that all the power of earth and hell can never prevail against it" (HC 5:139-40).

27. HC 5:2-3.

28. HC 5:139-40.

29. Matthew 18:18.

30. John 13:10.

31. JST John 13:1-10.

32. John 14:1-27; D&C 88:1-5; TPJS, 150.

33. John 15:12-16.

34. Isaiah 22:22; Matthew 16:19; D&C 124 :93; Helaman 10:4-10.

35. Acts 1:4-8; 2:1-4; 1 John 2:20-27; D&C 88:1-5.

36. 2 Peter 1:19; D&C 131:5.

37. Revelation 5:10; TPJS, 369.

38. 1 John 2:20.

39. 1 John 2:25.

40. 1 John 2:25, 27.

41. See Chapter 11, Note 7.

42. May 1843, D&C 132:26. Sealing power "by him who is anointed, unto whom I have appointed this power and the keys of this priesthood." Joseph said, "Have we not learned the Priesthood after the order of Melchizedek, which includes both Prophets, Priests and Kings: see Rev. 1 Chap. 6th v., and I will advance your Prophet to a Priest, and then to a King—not to the Kingdoms of this earth, but of the Most High God, See Rev. 5 Chap., 10th v.—'Thou hast made us unto our God, Kings and Priests, and we shall reign on the earth'" (TPJS, 318).

43. HC 5:4; Joseph Smith Diary, 26 and 28 May 1843; D&C 132:26.

44. "[A]nd the holy priesthood which he administered unto us" (HC 5:4; Joseph Smith Diary, 26, 28).

45. Revelation 1:6; TPJS, 318.

46. TPJS, 322-23.

47. 2 Peter 4, 10; *Ensign*, May 1985, 10.

48. Ware, "The Holy Priesthood."

49. Ibid.

50. Smith, *Lectures on Faith*, Lecture Seven, Item 13, 65.

51. Ware, "The Holy Priesthood."

52. Letter from Orson Hyde to Ebenezer Robinson, 19 September 1844.

53. 1839, January 26: Brigham Young and the Twelve organized a committee to conduct the removal of the Saints from Missouri.

    1840, April 15: The Twelve in England started assignments.

    1841, October 24: At a site on the Mount of Olives in Jerusalem, Orson Hyde dedicated Palestine for the gathering of the Jews.

    1842: Elder Lorenzo Snow presented the Book of Mormon to Queen Victoria of England.

    1844, February 20: Joseph Smith instructed the Twelve to organize an exploratory expedition to locate a site for the Saints in California or Oregon.

1877, September 4:The Council of theTwelve, with JohnTaylor as president, publicly assumed its position as the head of the Church.

1883,August 26:The twelve authorized the Church to be taken to New Zealand.

1887, June 3: Under instructions from President John Taylor, a gathering place for Latter-day Saints in Canada was selected.

1901, August 12: Elder Grant of the Council of the Twelve dedicated Japan and opened a mission there as a first step in renewed emphasis on preaching the gospel in all the world.

1920-21: Elder David O. McKay of the Council of the Twelve traveled 55,896 miles visiting the Saints in the Pacific Islands, New Zealand,Australia, and Asia and then made stops in India, Egypt, Palestine, and Europe.

1925, December 6: Elder Melvin J. Ballard of the Council of the Twelve opened the Church's official work in South America.

1955, January-February: President David O. McKay took a trip covering more than 45,000 miles to the missions of the South Pacific, selected a site for the New ZealandTemple, and discussed plans for the building of a Church college in New Zealand.

1961, March 12: Under the Twelve's direction, the first non-English-speaking stake of the Church was organized at The Hague in The Netherlands.

1970, March 15:The first stake in Asia was organized in Tokyo, Japan.

1970, March 22: The first stake in Africa was organized in Transvaal, South Africa.

1971,August 27-29: Under theTwelve, the first area conference of the Church was held in Manchester, England.

1973, March 8:The first stake on mainland Asia was organized in Seoul, Korea.

1977, February 5: The First Presidency announced that the Council of theTwelve would oversee ecclesiastical matters and the Presiding Bishopric would have responsibility for temporal programs.

1985, August 24: The Johannesburg South Africa Temple was dedicated by President Gordon B. Hinckley. With the dedication of this building, there was now a temple on every continent except Antarctica.

1985, October 16: Elder David B. Haight created the seventeen hundredth stake in Manaus, Brazil, a city of 1.5 million in the heart of the Amazon jungle.

1989, January 28: Elders Russell M. Nelson and Dallin H. Oaks of the Council of the Twelve completed an eight-day visit to China and were assured by high-level Chinese leaders that people are free to practice religious beliefs in that country.

1990, January 21: The Twelve sustained David Hsiao HsinChen as the Church's "traveling elder" to oversee Church affairs in China.

1990, July: The Twelve opened new missions in Czechoslovakia, Hungary, and Poland.

1990, September 13: Under the Twelve, the Leningrad Branch of the Church was approved in the Soviet Union.

1992, December 7: The Central American nation of Belize, located on the Yucatan Peninsula, was dedicated by Elder Russell M. Nelson of the Council of the Twelve for the preaching of the gospel, an act that completed the dedication of all seven nations in Central America.

1993, May 11: Elder Russell M. Nelson dedicated Belarus for the preaching of the gospel.

1993, May 20: Elder M. Russell Ballard dedicated Lithuania for the preaching of the gospel.

1993, August 27: Elder James E. Faust of the Council of the Twelve broke ground for a new Brazil Area Missionary Training Center.

1993, August 28-September 5: Elder Russell M. Nelson of the Council of the Twelve represented the Church at the 1993 Parliament of the World's Religions in Chicago, Illinois.

1993, September 14: Elder Joseph B. Wirthlin of the Council of the Twelve dedicated the Mediterranean island of Cyprus for the preaching of the gospel.

1994 September 14: Elder Dallin H. Oaks of the Council of the Twelve dedicated the Republic of Cape Verde, a string of ten rugged islands and five islets located four hundred miles west of Senegal on the African coast.

54. D&C 29:12.

55. D&C 90:5.

56. D&C 35:17-18.

57. D&C 90:3-4.

58. 1 Cor. 4:1.

59. *Times and Seasons,* Vol. 5, No. 6, 15 March 1844, 474.

60. Lucile C. Tate, *Boyd K. Packer, A Watchman on the Tower,* 83.

61. Ezra Taft Benson, at Korea Area Conference, 1975, p. 52.

Chapter 12: Passing the Mantle

1. D&C 112:30.

2. Acts 5:34-38.

3. See the calling and fullness of the Twelve Apostles in the dispensation of the meridian of times and the dispensation of the fullness of times, Chapter 10.

4. D&C 107:21-38, 58-67, 77-84.

5. D&C 128:11, 18-21.

6. D&C 107:23-24.

7. Joseph Smith, Jr., Sidney Rigdon, and Hyrum Smith.

8. Heber C. Kimball's Journal, Liberty, 16 January 1839.

9. D. Michael Quinn, "The Mormon Succession Crisis of 1844," 219, for an in-depth study of the above.

10. Quinn, *The Mormon Hierarchy Origins of Power,* 61 ftnt 105.

11. *Millennial Star* 5:104.

12. HC 7:236.

13. Edward W. Tullidge, *Life of Brigham Young* (New York, 1877), 115.

14. HC 7:231-40.

15. Wilford Woodruff, *Discourses of Wilford Woodruff,* 73-74.

16. D&C 107:22-30.

17. D&C 107; 112.

18. Brigham Young: Senior Apostle, 27 June 1844; sustained President of the Church 7 April 1845; sustained President of First Presidency 27 December 1847; died 29 August 1877.

   Upon meeting Joseph the Prophet for the first time, Brigham was asked to give the invocation at a meeting that night. During the prayer, Brigham spoke in tongues. Joseph revealed that he had spoken the Adamic language. Some said to him they expected he would condemn the gift brother Brigham had, but he said, "No, it is of God, and the time will come when Brother Brigham Young will preside over this Church." *Millennial Star*, Vol. 28 (11 July 1863), 439.

19. Quinn, "The Mormon Succession Crisis of 1844," 219 ftnt 87.

20. *Deseret News*, 6 June 1877, 274 on Brigham Young.

21. D&C 107:23-24; 112:15.

Chapter 13: Prophecies

1. D&C 57:2-3.

2. D&C 84:62.

3. HC 5:85 ftnt; harmonizes with Isaiah 2:2 and Micah 4:1.

4. Roberts, *Comprehensive History of the Church*, 1:494.

5. Pratt, *Autobiography of Parley P. Pratt*, 210.

6. HC 5:305.

7. The Prophet's exact words were never recorded, but a journal notation can be found in James Jepson, "Memories and Experiences" MS, 9-10.

8. Letter to Junius F. Wells, New York, 7 February 1902, from L. M. Lawson, *Improvement Era*, Vol. 6, p. 8.

9. Letter to Junius F. Wells, Salt Lake City, Utah, 25 August 1902, from A. Saxey, *Improvement Era*, Vol. 6, p. 10.

10. *Improvement Era*, February 1962, 114-16.

11. B.H. Roberts, *Improvement Era*, July 1921, 81.

12. HC 4:461.

13. HC 5:1.

14. Jeremiah 28:9, as seen in Duane S. Crowther, *Prophecy Key to the Future*, Introduction.

15.   Deuteronomy 18:15.

Chapter 14: Conclusion

1.   Moroni 10:3-5.

2.   D&C 93:18.

3.   JD 25:183.

4.   TPJS, 231-32.

5.   *Times and Seasons,* Vol.5, No. 6, 15 March 1844, 474.

6.   JD 23:362-63.

7.   Madsen, *Joseph Smith the Prophet,* Endnote 50, Chapter 7.

8.   2 Nephi 32:7.

9.   Charles W. Penrose, *"Mormon" Doctrine Plain and Simple,* 25.

10.   Joseph F. Smith: An Address, 7 October 1883.

11.   Revelation 14:6.

12.   Habakkuk 2:14.

13.   Bruce R. McConkie, *A New Witness for the Articles of Faith,* 17.

Appendix A: Jail Calendar—128 Days

1.   Dyer, *Refiner's Fire,* 288; HC 3:257. This reference of Alexander McRae also states that George A Smith and Don Carlos Smith visited several times and brought some of the prisoners' families.

2.   HC 3:215.

3.   RLDS 2:309.

4.   Jones, *Emma's Glory and Sacrifice,* 90; Hill, *Joseph Smith The First Mormon,* 254, where the author states of only two visits and says the blessing of Joseph was on this date. She uses as her reference "Memoirs of President Joseph Smith, 1832-1914," *The Saints Herald,* 81 (6 November 1934), 1414 and Smith, *Joseph Smith III and the Restoration,* 14.

5.   RLDS 2:309.

6.   Orange L. Wight's recollections, p. 5.

7.   RLDS 2:309.

8.   Ibid.

9.   Ibid.

10. Ibid.

11. Ibid.

12. HC 3:226-33.

13. RLDS 2:309.

14. Ibid.

15. Ibid.

16. Letter written by Alexander McRae, 9 October 1854, HC 3:257.

17. RLDS 2:309.

18. Ibid.

19. Ibid.

20. HC 3:244; RLDS 2:309.

21. RLDS 2:309.

22. RLDS 2:310.

23. RLDS 2:315.

24. Ibid.

25. Ibid.

26. Ibid.

27. Ibid.

28. Ibid.

29. Ibid.

30. Ibid.

31. Ibid.

32. HC 3:246.

33. Heber C. Kimball's Journal, Liberty, 16 January 1839. With a very important N.B. "N.B. Appoint the oldest of these of the Twelve, who were first appointed, to be the president of your quorum." "JS," S.R., "H.S."

34. RLDS 2:315.

35. Ibid.

36. Ibid.

37. Ibid.

38. Ibid.

39. Smith, *Joseph Smith III and the Restoration*, 13. This, then, is used by Newell, *Mormon Enigma: Emma Hale Smith*, 77, where it seems they take great privileges in saying that the wives actually stayed in the dungeon over night on two occasions. Even if they did stay in the jail, which seems really questionable, the probability would have been that they stayed in the upper compartment.

40. RLDS 2:315-16.

41. RLDS 2:315.

42. HC 3:247; RLDS 2:311.

43. RLDS 2:315.

44. RLDS 2:316.

45. RLDS 2:315.

46. RLDS 2:315-16.

47. RLDS 2:315; Dyer, *Refiner's Fire*, 288-89. Here, the tender recount is given in Mercy Thompson's letter of 1894 where she describes this visit and states the visit was in February.

48. RLDS 2:316.

49. *The Juvenile Instructor*, 27:398-400.

50. RLDS 2:315.

51. RLDS 2:316.

52. Hill, *Joseph Smith The First Mormon*, 252; Percindia H Buell's journal.

53. HC 3:421.

54. RLDS 2:316.

55. RLDS 2:317.

56. Hyrum Smith, Letter to Mary Fielding Smith and RLDS 2:316 gave this date.

57. HC 3:257.

58. HC 3:264.

59. Ibid.

60. Smith, *The Personal Writings of Joseph Smith*, 416.

61. RLDS 2:317.

62. RLDS 2:316.

63. RLDS 2:317. Presendia H. Buell (Mrs. Bull), Letter of 15 March; HC 3:285.

64. RLDS 2:317.

65. HC 3:272-73.

66. HC 3:272, 273-74.

67. Smith, *The Personal Writings of Joseph Smith*, 388.

68. Smith, *The Personal Writings of Joseph Smith*, 389, Ref. 2.

69. Smith, *The Personal Writings of Joseph Smith*, 386.

70. HC 3:277-81.

71. HC 3:281; see page 282 where it is recorded that Caleb Baldwin, Lyman Wight, Alexander McRae, and Hyrum Smith each made a similar petition.

72. HC 3:264, 277; RLDS 2:317-22; Buell (Bull), Letter of 15 March; HC 3:285.

73. Hyrum Smith, Letter to his wife Mary, same date.

74. Hyrum Smith, Letter to his wife Mary, same date.

75. RLDS 2:323.

76. See Appendix E, this date.

77. *Ensign*, August 1992, 33; Smith, *The Personal Writings of Joseph Smith*, 388-89.

78. RLDS 2:317, 323; *Times and Seasons*, Vol. 1, No. 7, May 1840, 100.

79. Hyrum Smith, Letter to his wife Mary, same date.

80. Hyrum Smith, Letter to his wife Mary, same date.

81. HC 3:289; RLDS 2:324-25.82; *Times and Seasons*, Vol. 1, No. 9, July 1840, 133-34.

82. Smith, *History of Joseph Smith, the Prophet*, 155.

83. HC 3:288.

84. RLDS 2:324.

85. Hyrum Smith, Letters, same date.

86. Hyrum Smith, Letters, same date.

87. RLDS 2:327.

88. Schindler, *Orrin Porter Rockwell: Man of God Son of Thunder.*

89.   Hyrum Smith, Journal, same date.

90.   Hyrum Smith, Journal, same date.

91.   Hyrum Smith. Journal, same date.

92.   Hyrum Smith, Journal, same date.

93.   Smith, *History of Joseph Smith, the Prophet*, 155.

94.   For individual comments see RLDS 2:327; Hyrum Smith, Journal, same date; Dean C. Jesse, "Walls, Grates and Screeking Iron Doors: The Prison Experience of Mormon Leaders in Missouri, 1838-1839," *Missouri Historical Review*, 32, and Joseph Smith, Letter to Emma, 4 April 1839.

95.   HC 3:309.

96.   HC 3:309; RLDS 2:327.

97.   HC 3:310-11.

98.   HC 3:313-14.

99.   HC 3:314.

100. HC 3:319; RLDS 2:329.

101. HC 3:319-21; RLDS 2:329-30.

Appendix C: Former Prisoners for Christ

1.   Isaiah 61:1-2.

2.   Genesis 37-41.

3.   Genesis 37:2.

4.   Genesis 41:46.

5.   Genesis 39:20, 40:4.

6.   Genesis 41:14.

7.   Psalms 105:18.

8.   Psalms 105:19.

9.   Jeremiah 37:15-16.

10.   1 Nephi 7:14.

11.   Alma 14:20-22, 24.

12.   Alma 14:26.

Appendix D: Doctrinal Expansion 1839-44

1. TPJS, 237. Also see pages 51, 137, 163, and 325.
2. *Times and Seasons*, Vol. 1, No. 7, May 1840, 102.
3. TPJS, 145-50.
4. TPJS, 188-90.
5. *Times and Seasons*, Vol. 3, No. 9, 1 March 1842, 706-10.
6. TPJS, 198-99.
7. TPJS, 205.
8. TPJS, 242-48.
9. TPJS, 268-69.
10. TPJS, 79-280.
11. HC 5:423-27.
12. TPJS, 343-55.
13. TPJS, 242-62.
14. Smith, *The Words of Joseph Smith*, 378.
15. HC 3:289-300.
16. HC 3:382-92.
17. TPJS, 157.
18. TPJS, 159.
19. TPJS, 160.
20. TPJS, 191.
21. HC 4:608-09.
22. TPJS, 325-26.
23. TPJS, 335; HC 6:249.
24. HC 4:553-57.
25. TPJS, 354.
26. TPJS, 242-62.
27. HC 6:363-367.
28. TPJS, 373.
29. *The Contributor*, 3:91-95; JD 6:237-40.
30. HC 3:383-92.

31. TPJS, 163.

32. TPJS, 170.

33. TPJS, 169.

34. TPJS, 172.

35. TPJS, 173-80.

36. TPJS, 180.

37. TPJS, 183.

38. HC 4:414.

39. TPJS, 190.

40. *Times and Seasons*, Vol. 3, No. 9, 1 March 1842, 706-10.

41. TPJS, 204-05.

42. TPJS, 207.

43. TPJS, 219-20.

44. TPJS, 228-29.

45. HC 4:608.

46. HC 5:1.

47. HC 5:2.

48. TPJS, 248-54.

49. TPJS, 271-74.

50. TPJS, 308.

51. HC 5:554-56.

52. TPJS, 318.

53. HC 6:146.

54. TPJS, 329-30.

55. TPJS, 333; HC 6:224.

56. TPJS, 242-62.

57. TPJS, 354.

58. TPJS, 187-90.

59. TPJS, 354.

60. TPJS, 196-200.

61. HC 4:571-81; TPJS, 202-208.

62. TPJS, 217.

63. TPJS, 220.

64. TPJS, 261-62.

65. TPJS, 294.

66. TPJS, 297-99.

67. TPJS, 300-301.

68. HC 5:423-27.

69. HC 5:425-27.

70. "Kingdom of Heaven," Ms.

71. TPJS, 322-23.

72. HC 6:50-52; TPJS, 325.

73. TPJS, 342-62.

74. TPJS, 374.

75. *The Contributor*, 111:92-95.

76. TPJS, 163.

77. TPJS, 190.

78. HC 5:391.

79. HC 5:387, 401.

80. William Clayton Journal, 20 October 1843.

81. HC 6:183-85.

82. TPJS, 373.

83. TPJS, 168.

84. TPJS, 173.

85. TPJS, 173-80.

86. TPJS, 182.

87. D&C 124:39-42.

88. *Times and Seasons*, Vol. 3, No. 9, 1 March 1842, 703.

89. TPJS, 224.

90. TPJS, 230-31.

91. HC 5:1.

92. TPJS, 274.

93. D&C 131:5-6.

94. HC 5:423-427; Smith, *The Words of Joseph Smith*, 215.

95. TPJS, 309.

96. TPJS, 314; HC 5:498-500.

97. D&C 132.

98. Smith, *The Words of Joseph Smith*, 232.

99. Ibid., 233-34.

100. *The Contributor*, 4:52-55.

101. Ehat, "Joseph Smith's Introduction of Temple Ordinances."

102. TPJS, 331.

103. HC 6:183.

104. TPJS, 333.

105. HC 6:249-54.

106. HC 6:363.

107. TPJS, 338.

108. TPJS, 340.

109. TPJS, 362-63.

110. HC 6:230.

111. Ehat, List of ordinance prior to Nauvoo Temple

112. *Times and Seasons*, Vol. 3, No. 12, 15 April 1842, 759.

113. HC 5:148-153; D&C 128:18.

114. HC 5:391-92; D&C 131:4.

115. HC 5:554-56.

116. TPJS, 321.

117. HC 6:146.

118. Ehat, "Joseph Smith's Introduction of Temple Ordinances."

119. TPJS, 343-46.

120. D&C 137.

121. Church Education System, *Church History in the Fullness of Times*, 251-52.

122. TPJS, 172-73.

123. TPJS, 179-80.

124. D&C 124:27-33.

125. TPJS, 191.

126. TPJS, 193.

127. TPJS, 201.

128. TPJS, 201.

129. TPJS, 217-19.

130. HC 5:423-27.

131. TPJS, 321-22.

132. TPJS, 329.

133. TPJS, 335-37.

134. *The Contributor*, 11:290-92.

135. HC 4:358-60.

136. TPJS, 194.

137. TPJS, 255.

138. TPJS, 302.

139. TPJS, 342.

Appendix E: Secular Knowledge After 1837

1.   D&C 121:26.

2.   TPJS, 350-53.

3.   Book of Abraham, Figure 1 for Facsimile 2; D&C 84:100; 88:109-110; 93:13, 23, 28-29; 130:4-5, 7; and Alma 40:8.

4.   *Cambridge Fact Finder*, 525; and Webster's New World, *Inventions and Scientific Discoveries*, 100-102.

BIBLIOGRAPHY

Allen, James B. and Glen M. Leonard. *The Story of the Latter-day Saints*. Salt Lake City: Deseret Book Company, 1992.

Anderson, Richard L. *Joseph Smith's New England Heritage*. Salt Lake City: Deseret Book Company, 1971.

Andrus, Hyrum L. *Joseph Smith, the Man and the Seer*. Salt Lake City: Deseret Book Company, 1960.

Andrus, Hyrum L. and Helen Mae Andrus, comps. *They Knew the Prophet*. Salt Lake City: Bookcraft, 1974.

Avant, Gerry. "Collector Finds Rare Book, Autographed Statement by Prophet," *Church News*, 23 June 1985.

Bachman, Danel W. "The Authorship of the Manuscript of Doctrine and Covenants Section 132." Sidney B. Sperry Symposium. Brigham Young University, 26 January 1980.

———. "The Eternity of the Marriage Relationship," *Riches of Eternity*. Edited by John K. Challis and John G. Scott. Salt Lake City: Aspen Books, 1993.

———. "Even the Faith of Elijah," Chapter 14. *Riches of Faith*. Edited by John K. Challis and John G. Scott. Salt Lake City: Aspen Books, 1995.

———. "New Light on an Old Hypothesis: The Ohio Origins of the Revelation on Eternal Marriage." *Journal of Mormon History*. Vol. 5, 1978.

———. "A Study of the Mormon Practice of Plural Marriage Before the Death of Joseph Smith." M.A. Thesis, Department of History, Purdue University, 1975.

Beardsley, Harry M. *Joseph Smith and His Mormon Empire*. Boston: Houghton Mifflin Company, 1931.

Bennion, Lowell L. *The Religion of the Latter-Day Saints*. Provo, Utah: LDS Department of Education, Brigham Young University, 1962.

Benson, Ezra Taft. In Conference Report, Korea Area Conference, 1975.

Berrett, William Edwin. *The Restored Church*. Salt Lake City: Deseret Book Company, 1965.

Black, Rosa V. *Under Granger Skies*. Granger, UT: Granger State Relief Society, Church of Jesus Christ of Latter-day Saints, 1963.

Black, Susan Easton and Charles D. Tate Jr., eds. *Joseph Smith The Prophet, The Man*. Vol. 17, Religious Center Monograph Series, Religious Studies Center, Brigham Young University.

Britton, Rollin J. "Early Days on the Grand River and the Mormon War," 14 *Missouri Historical Review*, 1920.

Brodie, Fawn M. *No Man Knows My History*. New York: Alfred A. Knopf, 1946.

Brooks, Melvin R. *LDS Reference Encyclopedia*. Salt Lake City: Bookcraft, 1960.

Burnett, Peter H. *Recollections and Opinions of an Old Pioneer*. New York: D. Appleton & Company, 1880.

Buell, Percindia H. Journal.

Butler, John Lowe. "Autobiography of John Lowe Butler." Harold B. Lee Library, Special Collections, Brigham Young University, Provo, Utah; hereafter given as BYU Special Collections.

Cambridge Fact Finder. Cambridge University Press, 1993.

Cannon, Abraham H. Diary. Church Archives, Church of Jesus Christ of Latter-day Saints, Salt Lake City, Utah; hereafter given as Church Archives.

Cannon, George Q. *Life of Joseph Smith the Prophet.* Salt Lake City: Deseret Book Company, 1958.

Church Education System. *Church History in the Fulness of Times.* Salt Lake City: Church of Jesus Christ of Latter-day Saints, 1989.

Church Education System. *Doctrine and Covenants Student Manual.* Salt Lake City: Church of Jesus Christ of Latter-day Saints, 1981.

Clay County Census, History, Probate Records and Record Book, Clay County Archives, Liberty, Missouri.

Clayton, William. Journal. Church Archives.

Conference Reports of the Church of Jesus Christ of Latter-day Saints. Salt Lake City: Church of Jesus Christ of Latter-day Saints, October 1840, April 1977, October 1981.

Contributor. Salt Lake City, 1879-96.

Corbett, Pearson H. *Hyrum Smith—Patriarch.* Salt Lake City: Deseret Book Company, 1963.

Cottle, Thomas D. "Priesthood and Temple Chronology." Unpublished.

Crowther, Duane S. *Prophecy: Key to the Future*. Salt Lake City: Bookcraft, 1962.

———. *The Prophecies of Joseph Smith*. Salt Lake City: Bookcraft, 1963.

Daily Missouri Republican. St. Louis, 14 February 1839

The Deseret Evening News. Salt Lake City, 11 December 1906.

The Deseret News. Salt Lake City, 1867-.

Durham, G. Homer. "Joseph Smith and the Political World." Eighth Annual Joseph Smith Memorial Sermon, Logan LDS Institute of Religion, 3 December 1950.

Dyer, Alvin. *Refiner's Fire*. Salt Lake City: Deseret Book Company, 1980.

Easton, Susan Ward, comp. *Membership of the Church of Jesus Christ of Latter-Day Saints, 1830-1848*. Provo, Utah: BYU Religious Studies Center, 1987.

Ehat, Andrew F. "Joseph Smith's Introduction of Temple Ordinances and the 1844 Mormon Succession Question." M.A. Thesis, Department of History, Brigham Young University, 1981.

———. List of ordinances prior to Nauvoo Temple. In authors' possession.

Elliott, R. Kenneth. "The Rhetoric of Alexander Doniphan," *The Trail Guide*, December 1969, No. 4.

Ensign. Salt Lake City, 1971-.

Evans, John Henry. *Joseph Smith: An American Prophet*. New York: Macmillan Company, 1933.

Far West Record, 8 November 1831 Conference, Portage County, Ohio.

"The Father and Son." The First Presidency and the Twelve. 30 June 1916 Doctrinal Exposition.

Flake, Lawrence R. *Mighty Men of Zion*. Salt Lake City: Karl D. Butler, 1974.

Foster, Lawrence. *Religion and Sexuality: Three American Communal Experiments of the Nineteenth Century*. New York/Oxford: Oxford University Press, 1981.

Gilbert, Kathryn Smith et al. *Histories of Caleb Baldwin by Family Members*. A copy can be obtained at the LDS Liberty Jail Visitors' Center, Liberty, Missouri.

The Heritage of Liberty, A Commemorative History of Liberty, Missouri. Bicentennial Edition. Narrative by Don M. Jackson. Liberty Township, Clay County, Missouri, 1822-1872.

Hill, Donna. *Joseph Smith The First Mormon*. Garden City, New York: Doubleday and Company, 1977.

Historical Department Letterbooks. Church Archives.

Historical Review of Clay County Sheriffs, 1822-1986.

History of Clay and Platte Counties, Missouri. St Louis National Historical Company, 1885.

History of Daviess County. Kansas City: Birdsall and Dean, 1882.

Holzapfel, Richard Neitzel and T. Jeffery Cottle. *Old Mormon Kirtland and Missouri*. Santa Ana, California: Fieldbrook Productions, 1991.

Huntington, Oliver B. Diary. 2 vols. BYU Special Collections.

Hyde, Orson. Letter to Ebenezer Robinson, 19 September 1844. Church Archives.

Illustrated Historical Atlas of Clay County Missouri. Edward Brothers of Missouri, 1877.

Improvement Era. Salt Lake City. 1897-1970.

Irving, Gordon. "Alexander and Eunice McRae." Unpublished Endowment House Sealings, Book E.

Irving, Zina McRae. Statement of Zina McRae Irving, 15 March 1966. Copy in author's possession.

Jaques, John. "Life and Labors of Sidney Rigdon," *Improvement Era* 3, 1899-1900.

Jenson, Andrew. *Autobiography of Andrew Jenson.* Salt Lake City: Deseret News Press, 1938.

―――. *The Historical Record.* 9 vols. Salt Lake City: Andrew Jenson, 1882-90.

Jenson, Andrew and Edward Stevenson. *Infancy of the Church.* Salt Lake City, 1889.

Jepson, James. "Memories and Experiences," Ms. BYU Special Collections.

Jessee, Dean C. "Walls, Grates and Screeking Iron doors": The Prison Experience of Mormon Leaders in Missouri, 1838-1839." *The Missouri Historical Review.*

Jones, Garcia N. *Emma's Glory and Sacrifice.* Hurricane, Utah: Homestead Publishers and Distributors, 1987.

Johnson, Clark V., ed. *Mormon Redress Petitions Documents of the 1833-1838 Missouri Conflict.* Vol. 16. Provo, Utah: Religious Studies Center, Brigham Young University.

Johnston, Jerry. "Liberty Jail may not be contradiction" Oct. 10, 1990. Newspaper unknown. Copy in possession of author.

Journal of Discourses. 26 vols. London: Latter-day Saints' Book Deport, 1854-86; cited as JD.

The Juvenile Instructor. Salt Lake City, 1866-1930.

Kimball, Heber C. Journal. Church Archives.

"Kingdom of Heaven," Ms. Church Archives.

LDS Eleventh Ward Record, Salt Lake City, Utah.

Lundwall, N. B. *The Fate of the Persecutors of the Prophet Joseph Smith.* Salt Lake City: Bookcraft, 1952.

———. *Temples of the Most High.* Salt Lake City: Deseret Book Company.

———. *Joseph A. and Eunice H. McRae.*

Madsen, Truman G. *Joseph Smith the Prophet.* Salt Lake City: Bookcraft, 1989.

Matthews, Robert J. *What is the Book of Moses?*

Maynard, Gregory P. "Alexander William Doniphan, the Forgotten Man from Missouri." Master's Thesis, Brigham Young University, 1973.

Maxwell, Neal A. *But for a Small Moment.* Salt Lake City: Bookcraft, 1986.

McCloud, Susan Evans. *Joseph Smith: A Photo Biography.* Salt Lake City: Aspen Books, 1992.

McConkie, Bruce R. *Mormon Doctrine.* Salt Lake City: Bookcraft, 1966.

———. *A New Witness for the Articles of Faith.* Salt Lake City: Deseret Book Company, 1985.

———."This Final Glorious Gospel Dispensation." *Ensign*, April 1980: 23.

McConkie, Joseph F. *His Name Shall Be Joseph.* Salt Lake City: Hawkes Publishing, 1980.

McConkie, Mark L. *The Father of the Prophet: Stories and Insights from the Life of Joseph Smith, Sr.* Salt Lake City: Bookcraft, 1993.

McKiernan, F. Mark. "Sidney Rigdon's Missouri Speeches." *BYU Studies.* Vol. 11, Summer 1971, No. 4.

———. *The Voice of One Crying in the Wilderness: Sidney Rigdon, Religious Reformer 1793-1876.* Herald House, 1979.

McRae, David F. "Sketch of the Life of Alexander McRae."

McRae, Joseph A. Personal letter, 7 March 1839, see N. B. Lundwall.

McRae, Joseph A. and Eunice H. McRae. *Historical Facts Regarding the Liberty and Carthage Jails.* Salt Lake City: Utah Printing Co., 1954.

McRae, Regina. History written by Regina McRae, copy in authors' possession.

"Memoirs of President Joseph Smith, 1832-1914." *The Saints Herald.* 6 November 1934, 81.

Messenger and Advocate. Kirtland, Ohio, 1834-37.

Millennial Star. Liverpool and London, England, 1840-1970.

Millet, Robert. *Seven Letters, Found in Regional Studies in LDS Church History-Missouri.* Edited by Arnold K. Garr and Clark V. Johnson. Brigham Young University, 1994.

Nauvoo Neighbor. 19 June 1844.

Newell, Linda King and Valeen Tippetts Avery. *Mormon Enigma: Emma Hale Smith*. New York: Doubleday, 1984.

Nibley, Hugh W. *Nibley on the Timely and the Timeless*. Provo: Religious Studies Center, Brigham Young University, 1978.

Nibley, Preston. *Stalwarts of Mormonism*. Salt Lake City: Deseret Book, 1954.

Patriarchal Blessings. Church Archives.

Patton, Annaleone D. *California Mormons by Sail and Trail*. Salt Lake City: Deseret News Publishing, 1961.

Penrose, Charles W. *"Mormon" Doctrine Plain and Simple*. Independence, Missouri: Zion's Printing and Publishing Co., 1929.

Peterson, H. Donl. "Moroni: Joseph Smith's Tutor." *Ensign*. January 1992.

Petty, Evelyn. "History of Clay County." *Liberty Tribune*. 27 April 1973. Clay County Museum Association.

Porter, Larry C. and Susan Easton Black, eds. *The Prophet Joseph Smith: Essays on the Life and Mission*. Salt Lake City: Deseret Book Company.

Pratt, Orson. *The Seer*. Orem, Utah: Grandin Book Co., 1994.

Pratt, Parley P. *Autobiography of Parley P. Pratt*. Edited by Parley P. Pratt Jr. Salt Lake City: Deseret News Publishing.

Quinn, D. Michael. *The Mormon Hierarchy Origins of Power*. Salt Lake City: Signature Books in association with Smith Research Associates, 1994.

———. "The Mormon Succession Crisis of 1844." *BYU Studies*. Provo, Utah: BYU Press, 1976.

Reimann, Paul E. *Plural Marriage Limited*. Salt Lake City: Utah Printing Company, 1974.

———. *The Reorganized Church and The Civil Courts*. Salt Lake City: Utah Printing Company, 1961.

Riddle, Chauncey C. "As a Prophet Thinketh in His Heart So Is He: The Mind of Joseph Smith."

Roberts, B. H. *Comprehensive History of the Church of Jesus Christ of Latter-day Saints*. 6 vols. Salt Lake City: Deseret News Press, 1930.

———. *The Missouri Persecutions*. Salt Lake City: Bookcraft, 1965.

Schindler, Harold. *Orrin Porter Rockwell: Man of God Son of Thunder*. Salt Lake City: University of Utah Press, 1966.

Smith, Emma. Letter to Joseph Smith, March 1839, Reorganized Church of Jesus Christ of Latter-day Saints Archives; hereafter given as RLDS Archives.

Smith, George A. "Memoirs of George A. Smith." Ms.

Smith, Hyrum. Letters and Journal. Church Archives.

Smith, John. Journal. Church Archives.

Smith, Joseph. Diary 1832-36. Church Archives.

———. *The Essential Joseph Smith*. Forward by Marvin S. Hill. Salt Lake City: Signature Books, 1995.

———. *History of Joseph Smith, the Prophet*. Chattanooga, Tennessee: Southern States Mission, 1911.

———. *History of the Church of Jesus Christ of Latter-day Saints*. Edited by B.H. Roberts. 7 vols. Salt Lake City: Deseret Book Company, 1971; cited as HC.

———. *The Journal of Joseph—The personal Diary of a Modern Prophet*. Compiled by Leland R. Nelson. Provo, Utah: Council Press, 1980.

———. *Lectures on Faith*. Compiled by Nels B. Lundwall. Salt Lake City: Bookcraft.

———. Letter to Emma. Yale University, 4 April 1839.

———. *The Papers of Joseph Smith Vol. 2, Journal 1832-1842*. Edited by Dean C. Jessee. Salt Lake City: Deseret Book Company, 1992.

———. *The Personal Writings of Joseph Smith*. Compiled and edited by Dean C. Jessee. Salt Lake City: Deseret Book Company, 1984.

———. *Teachings of the Prophet Joseph Smith*. Compiled by Joseph Fielding Smith. Salt Lake City: Deseret Book Company, 1977; cited as TPJS.

———. *The Words of Joseph Smith*. Compiled by Andrew F. Ehat and Lyndon W. Cook. Provo, Utah: BYU Religious Studies Center.

Smith, Joseph III and Heman C. Smith. *History of the Church of Jesus Christ of Latter-day Saints*. Lamoni, Iowa: Board of Publication of the Reorganized Church of Jesus Christ of Latter-day Saints, 1922; cited as RLDS.

Smith, Joseph III. *Joseph Smith III and the Restoration*. Edited by Mary Audentia Smith Anderson and Bertha Audentia Anderson Hulmes. Independence, Missouri: Herald House, 1952.

Smith, Joseph F. Address given 7 October 1883.

Smith, Joseph Fielding. *Church History and Modern Revelation*. 4 vol. Salt Lake City: Council of the Twelve Apostles of the Church of Jesus Christ of Latter-day Saints, 1949.

―――. *Doctrines of Salvation*. Complied by Bruce R. McConkie, 3 vols. Salt Lake City: Deseret Book Company, 1956.

Smith, Lucy M. *History of Joseph Smith by His Mother Lucy Mack Smith*. Salt Lake City: Bookcraft, 1958.

Snow, Eliza R. *Biography and Family Records of Lorenzo Snow*.

Spease, Samuel. Reference Book, RLDS Archives.

Sperry, Sidney B. *Doctrine and Covenants Compendium*. Salt Lake City, Bookcraft, 1960.

Stevenson, Edward. *Reminiscence of Joseph, the Prophet*. Special Collections, Harold B. Lee Library, Brigham Young University.

Stewart, John J. *Joseph Smith the Mormon Prophet*. Salt Lake City: Mercury Publishing Company, 1966.

Sun Liberty Edition, 5 February 1986.

Talmage, James E. *Jesus the Christ*. Salt Lake City: Deseret Book Co, 1982.

Tate, Lucile C. *Boyd K. Packer, A Watchman on the Tower*. Salt Lake City: Bookcraft, 1995.

Thompson, Mercy Fielding. "Letter to My Posterity." Opened the Centennial Year, 6 April 1930.

Times and Seasons. Nauvoo, Illinois, 1839-46.

Tullidge, Edward W. *Life of Brigham Young*. New York, 1877.

―――. *Life of the Prophet Joseph*. Publisher and date not identifiable.

Turk , T. R. "Lyman Wight Texas Community." Unpublished manuscript, RLDS Library.

Van Wagoner, Richard S. *Sidney Rigdon: A Portrait of Religious Excess*. Salt Lake City: Signature Books, 1994.

Walker, Charles L. Diary. Church Archives.

Watt, Ronald G. "A Dialogue Between Wilford Woodruff and Lyman Wight," *BYU Studies* 17, Autumn 1976.

Ware, Richard. "The Holy Priesthood, A History and Doctrine of the Priesthood as Taught by Joseph Smith and his Successors and as Contained in Latter-Day Saint Scripture." Rosetta Research Group, 1996, in author's possession.

Webster's New World, 1st Edition, 1989, *Inventions and Scientific Discoveries*, New York Public Library Desk Reference.

Webster's II New Riverside Dictionary. New York: Berkeley Books, Houghton Mifflin Company, 1984.

Whitney, Orson F. *Life of Heber C. Kimball*. Salt Lake City: Bookcraft, 9th ed., 1979.

Widtsoe, John A. *Joseph Smith: Seeker After Truth, Prophet of God*. Salt Lake City: Deseret News Press, 1951.

Widtsoe, O. J. P. *The Utah Genealogical and Historical Magazine*, April 1911.

Wight, Jeramy Benton. *The Wild Ram of the Mountain*. Afton, Wyoming: Afton Thrifty Print, 1996.

Wight, Orange L. Recollections.

Wilcox, Pearl. "Clay County—A Haven for the Exiled." Part IV, Clay County Museum, Liberty, Missouri.

Woodruff, Wilford. *The Discourses of Wilford Woodruff.* Selected by G. Homer Durham. Salt Lake City: Bookcraft, 1946.

———. Woodruff Collection. Church Archives.

ABOUT THE AUTHORS:

Thomas D. Cottle is a graduate of Utah State University (BS) and Marquette University Dental School (DDS). He is a veteran of the Korean War, where he flew with the United States Air Force. He has served as a Bishop, Stake President and as a counselor in the presidency of the Portland Oregon Temple. He and his wife Mary Lou (now deceased) served as missionaries in the Minnesota, Minneapolis Mission. They have eight children.

Patricia C. Cottle is a graduate of Brigham Young University (BS). She has served as both a ward Young Women's and Relief Society President. She has worked in several corporate offices and was Vice President of Benjamin Franklin Academy. She is the mother of four children.

Tom and Patti were married in 1994 and spent 18 months in the Missouri, Independence Mission where they served as guides in both the Independence and Liberty Jail Visitors Centers. They recently returned from serving on a Church mission in the Kiev, Ukraine Mission.